I0953339

SAVING TALK THERAPY

SAVING
TALK
THERAPY

HOW HEALTH INSURERS, BIG PHARMA, AND SLANTED SCIENCE ARE RUINING GOOD MENTAL HEALTH CARE

ENRICO GNAULATI, PhD

BEACON PRESS, BOSTON

BEACON PRESS
Boston, Massachusetts
www.beacon.org

Beacon Press books
are published under the auspices of
the Unitarian Universalist Association of Congregations.

21 20 19 18   8 7 6 5 4 3 2 1

This book is printed on acid-free paper that meets the uncoated paper
ANSI/NISO specifications for permanence as revised in 1992.

Text design and composition by Kim Arney

Library of Congress Cataloging-in-Publication Data

Names: Gnaulati, Enrico, author.
Title: Saving talk therapy : how health insurers, big pharma, and slanted
    science are ruining good mental health care / Enrico Gnaulati.
Description: Boston : Beacon Press, [2017] | Includes bibliographical
    references and index.
Identifiers: LCCN 2017016613 (print) | LCCN 2017018734 (ebook) |
    ISBN 9780807093412 (e-book) | ISBN 9780807093405 (hardback : alk. paper)
Subjects: | MESH: Psychotherapy—trends | Psychotherapy—economics | Mental
    Health Services—trends | Mental Health Services—economics | Drug
    Industry | Professional-Patient Relations | Quality of Health Care
Classification: LCC RA790.6 (ebook) | LCC RA790.6 (print) | NLM WM 420 |
    DDC 362.19689/14—dc23
LC record available at https://lccn.loc.gov/2017016613

To Tom,
a perpetual source
of clinical inspiration

CONTENTS

INTRODUCTION

THE PRIMARY AIM of this book is to evocatively document and help preserve the practice of traditional talk therapy at a time when its availability is in decline. No less important is my attempt to unpack the reasons for that decline—the questionable arrangement of economic incentives promoted by the health insurance and pharmaceutical industries, as well as biased academic research that leads to the overvaluing of medications and quick-fix therapies in our culture. One motive for writing it is personal. Coming of age in the early 1980s, I was a forlorn, shame-prone, desperate-to-be-loved young man with an enfeebled sense of self. Therapy was psychological oxygen for me. It enabled me to chip away at the shame, lessen the desperation, feel lovable, and begin to acquire a solid sense of self. Therapy was not set up as a quasi-medical endeavor aimed at lessening my symptoms of anxiety and depression—as is mostly the case these days. I experienced it in psychological-qua-spiritual terms as vital to liberating my capacity to live more intentionally and act more lovingly. Before long, I desired not only to pursue therapy but also to offer its wonders to others. I changed my career plans accordingly.

Back then, troubled souls like me could find an abundance of books written by humanistically oriented psychoanalysts. Classics like Rollo May's *Love and Will*, Erich Fromm's *Escape from Freedom*, Karen Horney's *Are You Considering Psychoanalysis?*, and Alice Miller's

Drama of the Gifted Child were written in accessible language, spoke directly to my angst, and reinforced all that I was learning about myself in therapy. Nowadays, leading figures in psychoanalytic and existential-humanistic psychology (the schools of therapy I associate with traditional talk therapy) mainly write books using dense clinical jargon for fellow professionals. On reading such texts, someone seeking insight into his or her own human predicament would need a glossary of terms to decipher the specialized clinical terminology. The act of reading would turn into a form of puzzle solving rather than something emotionally inspiring. I shudder to think how I would have turned out if I had had no access to books like those mentioned or to quality talk therapy.

People who entertain the idea of going into therapy often conjure up an image of a distressed person talking freely and openly to a skilled and devoted listener. They probably assume a therapist will want to hear what ails them in ordinary human terms: how they are trapped in a loveless marriage; how they feel empty and adrift in life; how they are completely emotionally drained by parental chores and have precious little time for themselves; how they are counting down the days to retirement, ten years out; how marital disagreements always lead to days of stalemate; how they prematurely committed to a career to please their parents. They probably expect some exploration of painful childhood events. They might guess that therapy will take time since it's hard to untangle life problems that are decades in the making or to undo unpleasant personality traits that cannot just be willed away.

These images encapsulate the most humanistic aspects of Freud's original therapy model. In this model, the analyst embodies a serene and open-minded presence (evenly hovering attention) as the patient earnestly strives for honest self-disclosure (free association). So, there's a legacy I hope to continue. I want this book to be highly readable and offer up usable personal insights. I also aim to thoroughly acquaint you with the history and practice of talk therapy. In this way, I hope to sharpen your appreciation for talk therapy's unsurpassed benefits as a cultural medium to maximize peoples' ability to live more intentionally and act more lovingly. In the first two chapters, I step back in time to illustrate how Freud actually conducted psychoanalysis, as distinct from how he recommended that it should be conducted. We'll look through the eyes of several patients who went on record about their experience. Remarkably, talk therapy had to be rescued from none other than Freud himself because of his frequent refusal to take patients' painful disclosures at face value; instead, he badgered them into admitting to esoteric sexual fantasies.

The person who rescued talk therapy from Freud was a little-known Hungarian psychoanalyst named Sándor Ferenczi. It was Ferenczi's brand of psychoanalysis—showing genuine regard for patients and consensually validating their real sources of upset—that influenced a whole generation of American psychoanalysts during and after World War II. Indeed, the widespread availability of talk therapy to military personnel pre- and postwar was responsible for its increased popularity. Movie depictions of psychoanalysis and celebrities writing and talking about their time on the couch furthered the popularity of talk therapy. The practice seemed cemented as a treasured cultural resource.

All this was before Prozac, managed care, and the privileging of short-term therapy that focused on solutions and reducing symptoms. These days, what legions of people experience when they pursue therapy is starkly different. The psychotherapy office is less of the cultural sanctum it once was, less a place that gives people permission and ample time to step back from life to explore, verbally process, understand, and master dark emotions. Most people enter therapy expecting talk therapy, only to encounter a therapist poised to offer so-called evidence-based cognitive behavioral therapy (CBT) techniques, whose job is to shunt the discussion in the direction of eliminating symptoms and addressing thinking errors. A sizable part of the therapy takes place outside the office in the form of homework geared toward a client's jotting down and changing dysfunctional thought patterns. There's also an increasing use of smartphone apps and web-based programs to help clients monitor their negative thinking and track behavior goals.

A client recently told me of her former therapist's use of such a practice. The therapist called it *cubbyholing* and framed it as a "scientifically validated procedure to help people develop a more balanced mind." The client was advised by her therapist to carve out time between therapy sessions and use worksheets on a website to type out thoughts that were causing her to make poor life decisions. My client confessed to me that she found the whole procedure artificial. She felt that cubbyholing satisfied the therapist's need for a cheat sheet with which to conduct therapy, as opposed to just listening to my client discuss issues that mattered to her as they arose naturally. Practiced like this, in the least sophisticated way, CBT treats the mind as a sort of computer in need of reprogramming. Therapy becomes like a software update, where kinks in thinking are corrected. It is not uncommon for therapy sessions to be spaced weeks apart and for a full course of treatment to entail a dozen sessions or fewer.

Nowadays, people don't "go into therapy" (with all the soul-searching this implies); they "receive mental health interventions." And medications have long since become the dominant mental health intervention. The entire enterprise of seeing a shrink has been shrunk. In chapters 3 through 6, I'll be picking apart and documenting the factors that led to this state of affairs. I argue that they have neither improved mental health care nor realized true cost savings.

As we'll see, since the advent of Prozac in the late 1980s, pill therapy has steadily surpassed talk therapy as the treatment of choice for mental health conditions. Although 90 percent of people claim they would rather meet with a therapist to talk about their problems than take medications, somehow they get shunted into believing that the use of mental health drugs is the superior option.[1] The latest data reveals that almost 58 percent of emotionally troubled people take medications only, with no psychotherapy (up from 44 percent in 1998).[2] About 10 percent of such people attend psychotherapy only and opt out of medication usage (down from 16 percent in 1998).

Many readers will be familiar with the usual reasons cited for the popularity of psychotropic medications. The pharmaceutical industry has long been flexing its marketing muscles, promoting poorly substantiated claims that its drugs are uniquely designed to correct the chemical imbalances ascribed to psychological problems. Moreover, direct-to-consumer advertising has driven up the demand for medicinal solutions to everyday emotional difficulties. But the single most important reason that medications eclipse psychotherapy as a treatment option is that primary care physicians perceive themselves as fully equipped to treat the average person's mental health issues. In the old days, the typical physician encountering a distraught patient would refer the person to a therapist for psychotherapy or to a psychiatrist for psychotherapy and medications. Nowadays, the majority of primary care physicians classify the source of a patient's emotional distress as quasi-medical and hence treatable from within their specialty with medications. In fact, alarmingly, the vast majority of psychotropic medications (drugs prescribed for emotional troubles) in the United States are prescribed by nonpsychiatrist physicians.

At odds with the skyrocketing use of mental health drugs is a burgeoning scientific literature calling into question their safety and effectiveness. Such drugs can be instrumental in improving the mood and everyday functioning of people with true psychiatric illnesses. But rarely are they magic bullets wiping away all pain and suffering. Unwelcome side effects often accompany the use of these drugs. Throughout the book, I will share stories from my own practice highlighting the best and the worst of what these drugs have to offer.

Managed-care health insurance personnel are not fond of therapists like me. When a client crosses the threshold into my office, I usually settle in and want to hear his or her life story in all its complexity. I assume that the length of therapy will be open-ended, depending on the pace at which thorny life problems can be addressed. Over the years, I've witnessed a handful of clients take the bull by the horns in therapy and immediately set about making substantive changes in their lives. These are outlier cases. For most clients, real and lasting change is hard-won and takes time. Unless a client insists on it, or unless everyday functioning is impaired, I hold off on any referral for medication until therapy is given a chance. I view symptoms of anxiety and depression as signifying underlying psychological concerns such as repressed traumas, thwarted grief, unawareness and poor expressive mastery of primal emotions (e.g., envy, lust, pride, shame, rage) frozen-over dreams and aspirations, an extreme reluctance to live life proactively, or myriad other covert psychological phenomena. Since my effectiveness as a therapist is rooted in my depth and wisdom as a person, I assume an ethical obligation to engage in lifelong learning and self-understanding. The cornerstone of my professional development has been my own personal therapy and my never-ending odyssey of reading texts in psychology, philosophy, anthropology, history, and English literature—anything that broadens my knowledge of the human condition.

I pride myself on being a dedicated therapist who strives to make solid connections with clients, so it may come as no surprise to the reader that my therapy dropout rate is, accordingly, extremely low. On a bad year, about 95 percent of my clients who enter therapy stay for twenty or more sessions. And because of the emotional and psychological investment required of a dedicated therapist, hour in and hour out, as I reside in my clients' painful life narratives—with the compassion fatigue and vicarious trauma that doing so can cause—I like to be paid a good fee, with annual increases.

While the public may endorse reasonably well-paid ongoing psychotherapy focused on substantive psychological change provided by wise, dedicated therapists, this attitude is far from the reality under managed-care health insurance plans. Average reimbursement rates for psychotherapy sessions have slipped precipitously over the past twenty years. During this same period, the annual number of psychotherapy visits people attend has declined by 20 percent. Psychotherapy dropout rates are at an all-time high. About 50 percent of clients who initiate therapy drop out within the first few visits. A mere 9 percent attend more than twenty visits.[3] And make no mistake, the scaling back of psychotherapy visits hardly reflects a lesser need, that is, a large-scale improvement in the mental health of our citizens. Rates of anxiety, depression, and suicide are on the rise, not the decline. In the following pages, I will dig into the myriad causes of the underutilization of psychotherapy—everything from the red-tape, onerous preauthorization requirements of health insurers to the overly scientific training of mental health professionals, which can impede rapport building with therapy clients.

Not a year goes by without some public outcry over yet another increase in insurance premiums. But as I'll show, this revenue isn't allocated to making more generous amounts of therapy available or to raising psychotherapy reimbursement rates to mental health professionals. Rather, the added revenue goes toward administrative costs and executive pay. Whenever mental health services receive more money, the increase is due to the spiraling costs of psychotropic medications. Although the financial incentives seem to favor psycho-therapy—the less expensive treatment option—it remains a stepchild of the medical field, perceived as a nonmedical treatment or somehow less medically valuable than drugs. In short, health insurance plans underfund psychotherapy and overfund medications.

The system is set up to favor less experienced clinicians working for lower fees. Forces work against the time-honored and scientifically backed ingredients of effective psychotherapy: empathy, genuine regard, acquired clinical wisdom, patience, and attentiveness. Instead, under managed care, an in-and-out, crisis-management, symptom-reduction, solution-focused model of psychotherapy rules the day.

Sadly, one of the most prominent endorsers of this scaled-back, medicalized model of psychotherapy is Kaiser Permanente. With more than ten million subscribers receiving services in eight states and the District of Columbia, Kaiser is the largest managed health-care plan in the United States.[4] I say "sadly" because I am a huge fan of Kaiser's health-care program. My immediate family and I have been Kaiser members for more than twenty years. My son was born at Kaiser's flagship Hollywood, California, medical complex. I had partial knee-replacement surgery there (and went on to win a local tennis tournament five months later). The quality of the medical care we have received has been remarkable. The same cannot be said of the quality of Kaiser's mental health care. In the pages ahead, I draw on interviews with current and former Kaiser mental health professionals to document the substandard amount and quality of psychotherapy provided by Kaiser. This shortfall should give us pause, since Kaiser Permanente is often heralded by federal officials as an exemplary health insurance plan worthy of replication by other entities.

Another reason for the erosion of psychotherapy across the nation is that most graduate schools preparing the next generation of therapists place an undue focus on scientific education, to the detriment of more humanistic ideas and methods for understanding and helping people. I spell out how aspects of my own educational pathway as a clinical psychologist—courses on research methods, experimental design, and the like—seemed irrelevant to the human enterprise of sitting in the presence of, and being helpful to, suffering persons. That was thirty years ago. In the halls of academia today, the requirement of tethering one's clinical training strictly to scientifically supported forms of psychotherapy is even more far-reaching. Immersion in evidence-based treatments is the new educational protocol for the current generation of practitioners. The belief is that psychotherapists, like medical doctors, should only familiarize themselves with scientifically backed treatment methods that are supposedly uniquely tailored to remedy specific symptoms and diagnoses. Gone are the days when conducting research and interpreting studies fell far behind one's own intensive therapy, knowledge of psychological theories, and immersion in supervision as the best preparation to become a psychotherapist.

Cognitive behavior therapy is considered the standout evidenced-based treatment. I will show that CBT approaches have gained dominance in graduate schools because they are research friendly. Academics are under constant pressure to conduct studies that can be completed and published quickly, to remain competitive in their field and to maximize their chances of obtaining tenure. Since CBT approaches typically focus on the short term, tend to measure progress in terms of symptom reduction, and zero in on standardized techniques that can be uniformly adopted by therapists, they are eminently researchable. So we have a peculiar situation: CBT is the predominant school of therapy taught in graduate programs around the country because it is considered the most scientifically valid. Meanwhile, scant attention is paid to how its popularity within academia might reflect how well suited CBT is to the speedy, streamlined research that favors the career prospects of academics.

But as I'll outline, mounting evidence suggests that many of the positive findings associated with CBT in clinical studies do not extend to real clients in the real world. The research hits the target but misses the point. Often, such studies are conducted on simple, clear-cut cases of mental conditions—say, someone who meets the criteria for generalized anxiety disorder but shows no signs of difficult personality traits or a troubled marriage. Yet most clients who enter the consulting room manifest a complex blend of symptoms and life difficulties that cannot be shoehorned into a distinct diagnosis. Most people seeking therapy speak of existential agonies—loving a daughter, but not liking her as a person; feeling trapped in a bad marriage; fearing one chose the wrong career; worrying that a divorce will irreparably harm the children; being tired of lying about one's homosexuality—and don't complain of symptoms. And most anxious and depressed clients don't self-measure progress in terms of fewer hopeless and catastrophic thoughts or reduced rumination on personal failures. A sustained global feeling of self-confidence, less defensiveness, an active sex life, a renewed capacity to show and receive love, and a better job that taps into true talents are some of the common personal criteria they use to measure progress.

Thankfully, there's a small but growing body of academics who do underscore the importance of measuring client progress more in terms of enhanced personal well-being than symptom reduction. They are also adding to the scientific literature some findings that practitioners like me have long believed are the key ingredients of effective psy-chotherapy: therapist empathy, genuine regard, rapport building, and competence at using naturally occurring interactions in the therapy relationship to help clients build greater self-understanding and inter-personal awareness. Solid data is starting to emerge substantiating the benefits of long-term humanistic and psychoanalytic psychotherapy. That said, this research is still dry and statistical, lacking rich descrip-tions and elaborate case-study material that psychotherapists in train-ing might use to bolster their therapeutic know-how.

In the spirit of Freud and those who challenged and built upon his ideas—such luminaries as Ferenczi, Horney, Fromm, and May—I use my personality and authoritative voice, as well as self-disclosure and humor, to catalyze client change. Publicly, Freud exhorted psychoana-lysts to be abstinent, to neutralize their personalities, and to assume an emotionally reserved way of working. But privately (according to the historical record), Freud acted more like a wise uncle than a neutral party with his patients. He dabbled with the roles of confidant, con-fessor, humorist, and advice giver. As I'll demonstrate, there's a ther-apeutic value to being in the moment with clients without the safety of a script or a set of readily identifiable techniques. But as I'll also show, a therapist needs to understand the level of self-discipline, tact, and interpersonal sophistication required in saying the right thing, in the right way, at the right time to leave clients feeling understood and treated as unique beings. Capable therapists skillfully use emotion to treat emotion. There is a performative element to being an effective therapist. Knowing when and how to prolong or foreshorten a response, use a loud or quiet voice, extend or avert eye contact, be gesturally animated or sedate—all in the service of emotionally drawing clients out—is a veritable labor of love. After you read this book, I hope you will know exactly what I mean by this effort.

You the readers will probably identify closely with some of the client problems I try to evocatively describe. You'll probably wonder what transpired in therapy to remedy such problems. Through my descriptions, I aim to demystify the psychotherapy process for aspiring therapists, would-be clients, or those who are already in therapy but who are disenchanted with its quality and want a more transformative experience.

In all the case vignettes and clinical examples I've included, I have altered names and disguised some facts to ensure client confidentiality. But essential themes, meanings, and outcomes remain intact. At no time do I use fictional material. In the final chapter, my goal is a lofty one. I take the position that humanistic psychotherapy and therapeutic values are vital for a healthy democracy and the social good. First, I assert that an empathy deficit in our culture works against the basic interpersonal tenets of democracy. Citizens must feel their way into the lives of those different from themselves if they are to respect the rights of others. Because the type of psychotherapy I espouse in this book engenders empathy in its adherents, it represents a valuable cultural corrective. Second, I argue that psychotherapy is a precious cultural space for people to acquire an authentic self—the psychological prerequisite for truly feeling, thinking, and acting like an individual. Strong democracies need large pockets of citizens with enough self-assurance to think with and against tradition; to accept what is good and bad within themselves and others; and to see the good and bad in their nation's history, social arrangements, and revered ideologies. Finally, I show that psychotherapies wedded to the psychoanalytic and existential-humanistic tradition are uniquely suited to address the self-esteem regulation problems that often underlie people's obsessions with fame and fortune. Contemporary obsessions like these undermine the pursuit of genuine happiness obtained from prioritizing close, loving personal relationships and wholesome everyday activities.

One last point: since the passage of the Mental Health Parity Act in 1996 and its updated 2010 version embedded in the Patient Protection and Affordable Care Act (colloquially, Obamacare), strides have been made to ensure that those in need of mental health services have greater access. The legislation has forced health insurers to cover mental health care the same way that medical care is covered. Mental health parity remains such a valued policy agenda across political camps that it is unlikely to be undone by the push by President Donald Trump and the Republican-led Congress to repeal and replace Obamacare. However, this book is a testament to how improved access to mental health care alone is insufficient. In the halls of government, academia, and medicine, debate on the quality of mental health services currently available nationwide needs to be ignited. In particular, we must address the erosion and necessary restoration of time-honored and scientifically backed, in-depth, humanistically oriented talk therapy. If this book in some small way contributes to igniting such a necessary debate, I will have not labored in vain.

CHAPTER ONE

In the Beginning, There Was Freud

HAD TWENTY-ONE-YEAR-OLD Anna O. lived two centuries ear-lier, she would most certainly have been singled out as demon pos-sessed. The patient credited with inspiring Freud's psychoanalytic talk therapy exhibited a host of symptoms that, even to our hardened twenty-first-century eyes, appear both freakish and exotic. She had visions of black snakes; refused to drink water and restricted her diet to only fruit for six months; shrieked randomly for no apparent rea-son; engaged in rhythmic coughing; complained of deafness; devel-oped double vision and a squint; became paralyzed down one side; and insisted on speaking English, claiming to have forgotten how to speak her native German. In the minds of Josef Breuer, the popular Viennese physician who treated her, and his thirty-something protégé, Sigmund Freud, Anna O. was a clear-cut case of hysteria, if not an unrelenting one.[1]

From December 1880 until June 1882, Breuer put aside two hours of his busy practice almost every day to treat his patient, often going to her home in the evenings.[2] It is estimated that Breuer allocated upward of a thousand hours of patient care to this young woman, whom he fondly characterized as "bubbling over with intellectual vitality" and thwarted by "an extremely monotonous existence in her puritanically-minded family."[3] Together they hit on a procedure from which Anna O. seemed to obtain great relief. If allowed to enter a trance, whether hypnotically induced by Breuer or self-induced, and speak honestly and freely about disturbing memories and events in her life, she subsequently "became perfectly calm, and next day she would be agreeable, easy to manage, industrious, and even cheerful."[4] Sometimes there was a direct link between a given symptom and the precise nature of a memory. For instance, Anna O.'s refusal to drink water was traced to a memory of an English lady-companion permitting her dog to drink out of a glass placed on the floor. By talking uninhibitedly about her disgust over witnessing this act and of her residual anger at this person, Anna O. was able to subsequently ask for a glass of water, never swearing off water again. Her deafness cleared up when she recounted troubling memories of the noise of a coughing fit her fatally ill father once had experienced, and her brother's attacking her for putting her ear up to the door of her father's bedroom. During a lucid moment, Anna O. referred to this procedure as a "talking cure." She also wisecracked that it was a type of "chimney sweeping."

By the time Freud had opened his medical practice in the spring of 1886, he was already disenchanted with the methods at his disposal to treat patients with hysteria.[5] The main treatments were cold and warm baths and the use of electrical devices and magnets to stimulate nerves. Struggling to establish himself as a physician and needing to convince his fiancée of his marriageability, Freud was primed to entertain new ideas and techniques that had some promise of success. He was captivated by Breuer's notion that symptoms with no ostensible physical cause, like limb paralysis, insomnia, muscle spasms, and fainting spells, could be alleviated through remembering and talking out traumatic life experiences, all the while purging oneself of pent-up emotions. It was Freud, not Breuer, who took this idea and ran with it. He went far beyond both the theory that "hysterics suffer mainly from reminiscences" and a bare-bones cathartic psychotherapy to develop an approach to, and a treatment for, disturbed mental states. And despite fierce opposition to this approach over the decades, it still informs the practice of many psychotherapists today.

Much of what remains therapeutically beneficial about the practice of Freudian psychoanalysis is not appreciated today. It has fallen into disfavor because of the very real flaws in Freud's methods and ideas. Freud has been roundly denounced, understandably, for assuming that repressed, dark, lurid, sexual, and aggressive wishes universally explain the mental health symptoms people complain of. As we will discover, Freud was prone to pin on his patients sexual motives derived from his intricate theories, with little anchoring to the content of patients' immediate experiences and self-beliefs.

From the beginning of his career, Freud saw symbolic meaning in everything patients did, and, in ways that defied common sense, he presumed that repressed memories alone caused confusing symptoms. Long after Anna O.'s real identity, Bertha Pappenheim, was uncovered, the historian Henri Ellenberger looked into what had become of her.[6] He uncovered some embarrassing information. Just one month after the end of her treatment with Breuer, she was admitted to the Bellevue Sanatorium at Kreuzlingen, Switzerland, where she continued to demonstrate signs of marked instability. Records showed that Pappenheim had become addicted to morphine, which Breuer had been administering to ease her pain from unsuccessful jaw surgery. Breuer had also been giving Pappenheim chloral, a drug with sedative and hypnotic effects, to help her sleep. It certainly leaves one wondering whether all along, Pappenheim's unstable behavior might have been caused or aggravated by the effects of powerful narcotics, more so than by hidden motives and repressed memories.

Equally problematic was Freud's lesser-known tendency to view psychoanalysis as an intellectual endeavor with which to gain self-knowledge, rather than a therapeutic one to reduce human suffering. When a former patient once asked him to comment on his abilities as an analyst, Freud replied, "I'm glad you ask because, frankly, I have no great interest in therapeutic problems."[7] Similarly, Freud confessed to the pioneering American speech pathologist Smiley Blanton, "The chief aim of psychoanalysis is to contribute to the science of psychology and to the world of literature and life in general."[8] By temperament and ideology, then, Freud probably preferred that his patients not emote much and instead indulge him in his dry, intellectualized insights into their behavior.

Nonetheless, we should not dismiss Freud entirely. Many core elements of psychoanalytic practice are as invaluable now as they were in Freud's day. For example, psychotherapists will give clients ample time and opportunity to speak freely about whatever is on their mind, no matter how seemingly irrelevant, illogical, or troubling it may seem. Therapists also insist on emotional honesty that is unburdened by feared consequences. And by having their clients consciously remember the childhood roots of destructive life habits, psychotherapists help people avoid repeating these habits. Other valuable Freudian practices that psychotherapists employ today include the encouragement of emotionally cathartic experiences related to childhood traumas and an emphasis on how expected reactions from a therapist can offer a window into emotional wounds suffered at the hands of caregivers (*transference*). Finally, psychotherapists can encourage ownership of primitive feelings, wishes, and fantasies that clients are strongly inclined to disown.

Despite his statements to the contrary, Freud's psychoanalytic psychotherapy, as we will discover, had immense therapeutic potential. This potential was baked into the method itself and honed by many of his colleagues and followers, who were more invested in its being a form of treatment to reduce the suffering of the emotionally troubled than was the great man himself.

THE FREUDIAN METHOD

Freud was a self-admitted failure at hypnotizing patients.[9] Moreover, he quickly realized that not everyone who crossed the threshold into his office was hypnotizable. In time, he discovered that he could evoke troubling memories, ideas, and feelings from patients by simply instructing them to say the first thing that came to mind after he had stopped cupping their heads in his hands or rubbing their temples: "Now it will come to you under the pressure of my hand. At that moment when I remove the pressure something will appear to you or suddenly come to mind, and you will pick up on it. It will be what we're looking for. Now what have you seen, or what has come to mind?"[10] Hypnosis could be discarded as a therapeutic tool because, for Freud, the average patient did not need to be in an unconscious state of mind to actively remember forgotten experiences.

After being rebuked by one of his early patients, Elisabeth von R., for interrupting her flow of thoughts with his overbearing prodding, Freud took heed and espoused a more nondirective style of allowing patients to speak free-flowingly about their inner life.[11] Freud named this technique *free association* and underscored it as a fundamental rule of his approach: "We instruct the patient to put himself into a state of quiet, unreflecting self-observation, and to report to us whatever internal observations he is able to make [being careful not to] exclude any of them, whether on the ground that it is too *disagreeable* or too *indiscreet* to say, or that it is too *unimportant* or *irrelevant*, or that it is *nonsensical* and need not be said."[12]

Lying back on the couch, in a state of reflective repose, and encouraged to speak aloud without due regard to rationality or decorum, patients encountered the ideal conditions to give voice to their darkest thoughts and feelings. For Freud, the hidden cause of the patient's symptoms was, all too commonly, sexual. Up until the late 1890s, he held firm to his seduction hypothesis, believing that hysterical symptoms belied memories of uncomfortable sexual situations or actual sexual assaults patients had suffered. Because it was too emotionally overwhelming to consciously acknowledge or remember, patients might unconsciously convert these psychic events into physical ones, complaining of medically inexplicable pain. Freud's treatment of Elisabeth von R. adheres to this model.[13] She complained of leg pains and walked unsteadily for two years before seeing Freud. When she was pressed to share her associations, Freud discovered that her distress was psychic, not physical. It stemmed from the distressing awareness that she was in love with her brother-in-law, which was morally offensive to her: "She screamed aloud when, summarizing the matter dryly, I said, 'You have been in love with your brother-in-law for a long time, then.' She complained of the most dreadful pains at this moment and made one more desperate effort to reject the explanation—it wasn't true, I had talked her into it, it was impossible, she was incapable of such wickedness. . . . I told her that one was not responsible for one's feelings and that her behavior, falling ill on those occasions, was proof enough of her moral nature—it was a long time before either made an impression on her."[14]

The seeds of what Freud later called *resistance* were embodied in Elisabeth von R.'s reactions, in her denial of what she knew within to be true. Freud maintained that resistance to consciously acknowledging uncomfortable thoughts and feelings can manifest itself in peculiar ways. A patient might habitually arrive late for sessions, engage in small talk, complain that the noise in the next room was distracting, or suddenly ask to use the bathroom. Freud perceived these seemingly innocuous gestures as indicators that the patient was probably avoiding sharing a troubling thought or feeling. Often patients were unconscious of not only the content they were fending off but also their resistance in the first place. This lack of awareness is what made psychoanalytic therapy long and arduous. Since symptoms were overdetermined, or caused by numerous repressed memories, each of which had to be ferreted out, and because each memory, as well as the very process of remembering, would be actively resisted by the patient, therapy was destined to be a drawn-out affair. Freud, given to efficiency by temperament, was slow to accept the lengthy, intractable nature of his method. In 1900, when he treated Dora, the therapy was conducted six days a week (Freud worked on Saturdays) for a total of eleven weeks. Hourly sessions, six days a week—even taking certain patients with him on vacation—were a staple for Freud.[15] By 1913, Freud told his followers, "Psychoanalysis is always a matter of long periods of time, of six months or a year, or more—a longer time than the patient expects."[16]

By the early 1900s, Freud was no longer convinced that repressed memories of actual uncomfortable sexual situations or sexual traumas were the main cause of hysterical symptoms.[17] He shifted his focus to the disruptive effects of repressed sexual and aggressive wishes and fantasies during childhood and beyond. With deeper exploration and analysis, patient disclosures about present-day events—say, an argument with a coworker over who gets the corner office—could be traced back to unresolved childhood conflicts with a sibling or rivalry with a same-sex parent for the affection of an opposite-sex parent. The latter conflict, the archetypical Oedipus complex, was a favorite theme of Freud's. In the ancient Greek myth, Oedipus meets a stranger on the road to Thebes and kills him in a quarrel. He then marries the queen of Thebes, having won her hand through another brave deed. Ignorant of the identity of his real parents because he had been abandoned at birth, he later learns, tragically, that the stranger and the queen were actually his birth parents. Freud perceived universal relevance in the Oedipus myth. He believed that a course of psychoanalysis was not complete until a patient had delved deeply into the unconscious Oedipal origins of any emotional troubles. This might take the form of fessing up to the sensual pleasure you felt as a child being cared for by your mother or father or admitting you wished you could have possessed a parent all to yourself. Or you might come clean that during infancy, you were bent on competing with and outdoing a parent, even wishing he or she had died off.

These carnal and unruly passions often appeared in dreams in disguised ways. Freud was never more in his element than when analyzing the content of a patient's dreams to decode the latent or rightful meaning behind the obvious or "manifest" images they contained. He was notorious for emphasizing the sexual symbolism of dreams images: assuming rooms with their entrances and exits to signify the female body with its vaginal, anal, and oral openings; sharp weapons and neckties to represent the male phallus; or staircases to denote sexual intercourse. But Freud was also sensitive to the nonsexual representational aspects of dream images. For instance, in the summer of 1898, his prized patient, the Rat Man, told him of a dream in which he was awestruck by the intricacies of a large machine full of wheels. Freud interpreted this as reflecting how impressed the Rat Man was by the complexity of a girlfriend.[18]

In his 1923 publication, *The Ego and the Id*, Freud outlined his overarching model of the workings of the mind. Peter Gay, a distinguished Yale historian, called this text "the decisive work of Freud's late years."[19] In it, Freud maps out his tripartite model of the mind, which continues to be compelling and practically useful to psychoanalytically informed therapists down to today. Freud divides the mind into three functions: the id, the ego, and the superego. The id (in German, *das Es*, "the it") is our animal self or the instinctual part of us that is given to raw emotion and impulsive action. It operates according to the pleasure principle. This part of us wants what we want when we want it, no delay, no waiting. We are largely unconscious of primal id urges even though they influence our outward behavior. For example, compulsive handwashing may be a desperate way to control unconscious urges to use your hands to masturbate or throttle your obnoxious neighbor.

The ego (in German, *das Ich*, "the I") is our rational self. It is the part of us that is attuned to outside reality. Our ego propels us to strive, plan, prepare, and do the cost-benefit mental work associated with acting on our immediate feelings, as opposed to curbing them. Our ego also serves a protective function, keeping us from getting flooded with anxiety. An array of what Freud's daughter Anna later defined as *defense mechanisms* do precisely that.

Repression is the ego's global way of keeping painful memories and feelings out of conscious awareness. We are unconsciously motivated to selectively remember and forget life experiences, depending on how much our core sense of self can emotionally handle. Whatever we are emotionally capable of remembering, we remember. Whatever is dangerous to remember, we forget; we even forget that we are forgetting.

Denial comes into play when a person appears oblivious to, and unconcerned about, profoundly unpleasant ways they are behaving. For example, an alcoholic might seem completely unaware of the effects of his or her drinking and deny its severity to keep from feeling the unconscious shame connected with a messy life and hurting others.

Projection is a way to attribute unlikable feelings and traits to someone else, when they really exist in you. The anxiety aroused by admitting to being an angry person, for example, is controlled by becoming preoccupied with how much your mother-in-law is an angry person.

Displacement occurs when a person finds a substitute target on whom to vent his or her frustrations. Often, that substitute is an unsuspecting, safer person to direct frustration at—as when a teenager, reeling from an interaction with an authoritarian school principal, comes home and lashes out at a warm-hearted mother.

When people use logical arguments to explain away their, or someone else's, questionable behavior, they are engaging in *rationalization*. For example, a worker whose boss expects the employees to be on time every morning at the office pigeonholes the overseer as very uptight. The unconscious reason for the rationalization would be the worker's fear and anxiety about being criticized for not being punctual.

Regression applies when a person strives to relive and cling to a habit that was adaptive in early childhood, but is maladaptive in adulthood. A husband might expect his laundry to be done, his meals served, and his sexual needs promptly serviced, as if his wife, like his mother, should function as a life-support system for him.

Sublimation is the self's way of finding constructive outlets for primal sexual and aggressive urges. Sports are classic ways that people can channel aggression in socially appropriate ways. Dance, music, and art are other mature ways to satisfy our basic eroticism.

The final part of Freud's tripartite model of the mind is the superego (*das Uber-Ich*, the "over-I"). The superego is essentially our conscience. It comprises all the morals, values, and prohibitions we have internalized throughout our upbringing. It's the voice in our head telling us when some thought, feeling, or desired course of action is wrong, unacceptable, or punishable. If our superego is too harsh—which was the case with most of Freud's Victorian-era patients—we can be ruthlessly self-critical and self-denying. Casting aside normal pleasures, we feel lifeless and robotic. On the other hand, if our superego is too relaxed, life can be chaotic and unruly, leaving us at the mercy of our pleasurable cravings. Our only hope is the strength of our ego, the rational inner voice that talks back to both our judgmental self and our hungry self, giving each self half an ear.

The Freudian mind is in perpetual conflict. We always want more than we can have, and we are hard on ourselves for wanting these things in the first place. Psychoanalytic psychotherapy serves as an expressive outlet for our id. Lustful, vengeful, ugly, and illogical inclinations can be talked through and talked out so they can be more rationally managed. This is what Freud meant by his pithy phrase "where Id was, there Ego shall be." This notion remains a stalwart element of effective talk therapy, namely, that the more clients verbally acknowledge forbidden, primitive thoughts and emotions, the more they feel in control of them, rather than controlled by them.

HOW FREUD ACTUALLY PRACTICED

In October 1934, at the age of twenty-eight, Joseph Wortis, an American psychiatrist pursuing a training fellowship in Vienna, embarked on a four-month-long analysis with Freud, who was then seventy-six years old. After each session, Wortis dashed off to a nearby coffee-house to jot down his meeting notes on cards he carried with him. In 1954, he published the results in his *Fragments of an Analysis with Freud*—a book that is a veritable treasure trove of information on Freud's therapeutic style.[20] Wortis's firsthand descriptions, along with interviews conducted by Paul Roazen on former patients of Freud's who were still alive in the 1960s, give us an intimate portrait of Freud at work.[21]

The overriding impression one gets from Wortis is that Freud put forthrightness front and center in psychotherapy. He embodied an earnestness to demystify, to do away with pretense, to cut to the chase. Freud emphasized from the outset that "psychoanalysis demands a degree of honesty which is unusual, and even impossible in bourgeois society." Midway through the treatment, he reminds Wortis, "Politeness doesn't enter into analysis." And not just on the part of the patient. Once, when Wortis confessed to being the sort of person who was uninterested in a great deal of self-examination, Freud bluntly replied, "You have made everything you said up to now so clear it has not interested me either." On another occasion, when Wortis confronted Freud for implying that he, Wortis, was not suited to the profession of psychiatry, Freud answered, "I didn't say you were not suited to it. I had simply said 'no extraordinary talent.'"

Freud tended to interpret Wortis's disclosures with conviction, as if the younger man were issuing objectively true statements about his inner life. Freud was disinclined to appreciate how Wortis might feel judged or criticized in the process. Absorbing the content of his interpretations was what mattered to Freud, not the interpersonal realm, where this very action might engender bad feelings. From time to time, Freud's interpretations involved loose inferences and logical leaps as if he had special access to Wortis's deep unconscious motives. Sometimes these inferences and leaps took on a sexual coloration. Six weeks into analysis, Wortis presented a dream in which he attended the theater to watch a play about a soldier performing tricks with a sword and then, in the dream, Wortis suffered an attack of vertigo looking down into the orchestra pit. Freud proposed that the dream meant Wortis was "watching coitus, was identifying with the female part and was disturbed by the feminine elements in myself." Wortis was probably not exposing his naïveté by claiming the dream instead captured his anxiety about the rampant militarism and danger of future war he had been reading about in the newspaper. After all, the place and time was Vienna in the winter of 1934.

Although Freud could be far-fetched and heavy-handed in his interpretations, he clearly tolerated honest, plucky rebuttal. During a session in which Freud appeared cheerful, Wortis casually mentioned that he himself felt under the weather. He remembered that Freud said Wortis's condition was due to "the conflict with my unconscious he had aroused." Wortis shot back that his gloominess was brought on by "more immediate troubles, with my work, and with my still uncertain future." Freud was capable of leniency even when Wortis rejected his more plausible formulations. During a rather heated session, Freud dealt head-on with Wortis's obvious tendency to speak in abstractions or to intellectualize: "But when I said you had a tendency to ruminate you didn't like the idea and rejected it right away. . . . It doesn't matter what I say, you always disagree." Wortis shot back, "I don't disagree. I simply examine everything you say critically."

There is spunk in their exchanges. After a prolonged pause during a session, Wortis said that he was reticent because he feared that Freud would again point out his habitual intellectualizing.

Freud retorted, "But you see that this is only a kind of resistance." He then invited Wortis to be open with his feelings about him. "You can say anything you like about me too."

Wortis boldly replied, "I don't know. I don't know which of us is the most sensitive."

Freud quips back, "You know very well which of us is. It is you."

"Anyway," Wortis said, "I don't usually like to fight."

Freud was known to be quite headstrong in his approach, believing that the psychoanalyst should hold firm to his or her understanding of the patient whether or not it jibed with the patient's own
self-understanding. He might expect and allow pushback from patients,
but their protestations rarely seemed to change his ideas about them.
In an early publication, he asserted: "It is of course of great importance
for the progress of the analysis that one should always turn out to be
right vis-à-vis the patient, otherwise one would always be dependent
on what he chose to tell one."[22] This observation reflects Freud's core
belief that patients were poised to resist, to throw up smoke screens,
to dance around the truth. The psychoanalyst, like a self-assured detective interrogating a shifty suspect, should not back down from the
facts of the case as he or she had arranged them. The strength of the
patient's resistance had to be matched, even outmatched, by the psychoanalyst's steadfast adherence to his or her formulations. Conveying
confidence and certitude was also crucial to bolster the credibility of
the psychoanalyst. Freud once quizzed a patient of his: "Suppose I
were to admit a mistake, what would you think?" The patient replied,
"That you might make more of them." Freud then countered that this
was precisely why he should not admit to mistakes.

This raises the question of how do we know when the psychoanalyst is wrong? Wortis put this very question to Freud, whose answer
was revealing: "From the reaction of the patient. He usually says nothing, because it doesn't concern him." For Freud, impassioned reactions on the part of patients to his interpretations were proof that his
ideas were right. If they were wrong, the patient would be nonplussed.
There seemed to be little room in Freud's therapy for patients to
change his mind about themselves, to get his confirmation about their
own self-understanding, if this was at odds with his own. To disagree
with Freud was to burnish the great master's perception that you were
resisting. But then again, he did seem to tolerate much disagreement
without judgmental counterattack.

Nevertheless, psychoanalysis with Freud was not a never-ending
cat-and-mouse affair, with him making far-fetched interpretations and
patients agreeing out of intimidation or disagreeing out of revulsion.
Mostly he was a serene, quiet, pensive presence sitting behind the

couch on which his patients lay, providing them with ample time and opportunity to open up. Freud's piercing eyes were known to many. Fritz Wittels, who was part of Freud's circle of colleagues—and the poet E. E. Cummings's first psychoanalyst—recalled that Freud's eyes were "brown and lustrous" with a "scrutinizing expression."[23] He seemed to personify the "evenly hovering attention" he instructed psychoanalysts to utilize. That is, sit back, rid one's mind of any agendas, and listen caringly and carefully to what patients have to say. Albert Hirst, who emigrated from Vienna to the United States and became a tax lawyer in New York, remembered that Freud allowed him to "run the show" when he was in analysis with the doctor at age twenty-three in 1909–1910. Hirst was adamant that "Freud did not decide the issues that were to be discussed."[24]

Of course, Freud ultimately had his agendas and biases. His interpretations with patients tended to pivot around his favorite theories as they evolved. But in his consulting room, these ideas were like signposts spaced well apart on a long country road. Patients mostly talked, and he mostly listened. For Hirst, whose parents were strict Puritans, the great freedom to talk at length about his inner troubles was invaluable. When Hirst was interviewed for the Freud Archives, he was emphatic that "the mere fact that he was talking to Freud had more of a therapeutic effect than anything that Freud had said to him."[25] Similarly, Sergei Pankejeff, the man behind Freud's famous Wolf Man case, went on record to say, "I never thought much of dream interpretation. . . . Freud traces everything back to the primal scene. . . . It's terribly far-fetched." He concluded that any benefit he got from analysis was due to Freud's being a like a "new father," someone on whom Pankejeff could rely and who had "a great deal of personal understanding for me, as he often told me during the treatment, which naturally strengthened my attachment to him."[26]

Other patients also felt the benefit of who Freud was rather than what he did. The American poet Hilda Doolittle, who entered analysis with Freud in the early 1930s, affectionately referred to him as "Papa" and concluded that it was her "connection with a person of such stature," "the strength of Freud's personality . . . his interest and involvement," not his "interpreting her unconscious conflicts," that helped

her.[27] Freud may have dismissed the curative elements of the relationship—his dedicated and attentive listening presence in the room—
but, apparently, some of his patients did not. For those who improved,
it was often not because of, but despite, his abstruse interpretations.

In 1912, in one of his few publications about psychoanalytic technique, Freud wrote that the analyst "should be opaque to his patients
and, like a mirror, should show them nothing but what is shown to
him."[28] The quintessential psychoanalyst neutralizes his or her personality, keeping his or her own personal life and subjective reactions
in check. No self-disclosure. No advice giving. No niceties. The hour
is all about the patient. That way, whatever dramas the patient lures
the analyst into—reacting as if the analyst is like an overbearing father or a neglectful mother—can be viewed as of the patient's own
making. Being as neutral as possible is what makes an analyst a potent
transference figure, someone on whom a patient can project unresolved
childhood conflicts.

According to patient accounts, Freud did not always practice what
he preached about analytic neutrality. His personality frequently shone
through in his work. Late in life, after numerous jaw surgeries and the
regular use of a prosthetic device in his mouth, he spoke with difficulty
and was hard of hearing. Instead of admitting his hearing difficulty to
Wortis, he got on the younger man, rather cantankerously, for not
speaking clearly and loudly enough: "You're always mumbling (and
he gave a mumbling imitation) like the Americans do. I believe it is
an expression of the general American laxity in social intercourse, and
it is sometimes used as resistance." At the same time, Freud could be
reassuring in his own edgy way. Wortis recalled how Freud felt at liberty to be tough on him because the old man had faith in Wortis's self-
confidence. "There is no need to show *you* any consideration," Freud
said. "You have a degree of self-confidence that fortifies you against
criticism. It is really enviable."

Freud was not immune to giving advice. Once, when Wortis mentioned that he and his wife were undecided about whether and when
to have children, Freud butted in: "But your wife, who is twenty-eight,
ought to have her children now while she is young." During another
session, in response to Wortis's admission that he was shy and not

easily predisposed to meet with strangers, Freud cautioned, "You should break yourself of that." Pankejeff also portrayed Freud as "not hesitating to give him direct advice when he thought it appropriate."[29] Sometimes Freud's advice was didactic and focused on strengthening the patient's ego or resolve to better control impulses, as when he remarked to Wortis, "You cannot give your impulses free hand. You have to keep them in control, not repress them; keeping oneself in control does not lead to neurosis, at worst merely to discontent."

At other times, Freud simply came right out and prescribed a beneficial course of action. When Bruno Walter, the conductor of the Vienna orchestra, consulted with him in 1910 over a cramp in his right arm that threatened to ruin his career, Freud instructed him to vacation in Italy for a few weeks and ignore his arm problem. When the analysis resumed, according to Walter, Freud entreated him to start conducting again. They then had the following exchange:

WALTER: "But I can't move my arm"
FREUD: "Try it at any rate"
WALTER: "And what if I should have to stop?"
FREUD: "You won't have to stop"
WALTER: "Can I take upon myself the responsibility of possibly upsetting a performance?"
FREUD: "I'll take the responsibility."[30]

Freud was also famous for using humor and his aphoristic wit to get a point across with patients or just to share a spontaneous moment. Hirst agonized with Freud over whether to pursue poetry writing as a career. In response to this indecision, Freud mused, "The sand in almost every river contains gold, the question is whether there is enough gold to make it worth exploiting."[31] Freud frequently poked fun at America and Americans and once wryly told Hirst that he should not emigrate there but should go to South America instead. Hirst reminded Freud that he knew no Spanish, to which Freud retorted, "Oh, hell, it takes three weeks to get there," implying he could learn Spanish on the journey over. Hirst also remembered Freud telling him a joke about a high-society lady who visits with her physician to get advice about effective contraceptives. The physician proffered that the best method was a glass of cold water. The lady asks, "Before, or after?" The physician replies, "Oh, instead."[32] And in response to a dream Wortis had about making love to a girlfriend of his brother's, Freud asked, "Was your brother present?" Wortis responded, "Fortunately, no," to which Freud had a good laugh. Wortis also caught Freud snickering to himself behind the couch, seemingly revealing that he did not always take himself and his ideas too seriously.

But Freud took his ideas seriously enough. In his psychoanalytic role, he all too often functioned as an omniscient, if not beneficent, narrator. A kindly authority figure, more focused on helping patients acquire self-knowledge than helping alleviate their emotional suffering. Remarkably, with patients like Pankejeff, who had been a victim of childhood sexual abuse and whose sister and father had committed suicide, Freud overlooked such traumas to fixate on arcane sexual minutiae.[33] Freud's sexual theorizing blinded him to commonsense causes for patients' problems. In Pankejeff's case, Freud presumed his chronic intestinal discomfort was due to an unconscious desire to be penetrated by his father and thus take the feminine position he had observed his mother take during sexual intercourse with his father. It turns out the real reason Pankejeff was experiencing intestinal discomfort was his use of calomel, a strong laxative commonly prescribed for horses, not humans. None other than Freud's closest friend and respected colleague would call him to task for these errors. In some respects, the first person who needed to be saved from talk therapy was Freud himself.

FERENCZI'S HUMANISTIC CHALLENGE

Sándor Ferenczi was seventeen years Freud's junior, though a prominent Hungarian psychiatrist and the author of more than sixty scientific papers, when he and Freud first met in February 1908.[34] By all accounts, Ferenczi was an endearing and warm person, with a refreshing playfulness and naïveté about him. He struck people as somewhat deferential and ingratiating, traits that Freud found off-putting, as he secretly acknowledged in a letter to Carl Jung, another of Freud's protégées, a few years later: "a dear fellow, but dreamy in a disturbing kind of way, and his attitude towards me is infantile. He never stops admiring me, which I don't like, and is probably sharply critical of me in his unconscious when I'm taking it easy."[35] Even so, since Freud expected a good deal of submissiveness and loyalty in those he inducted into his close circle of associates, it is likely that the very traits that Freud found vexing in Ferenczi actually enabled an enduring professional bond between the men.

Ferenczi quickly rose in stature in Freud's eyes, and within a year of their first encounter, he was one of two people (the other being Jung) given the honor of accompanying Freud to America, where he lectured in 1909 at Clark University in Massachusetts. In the fall of 1914, Ferenczi himself undertook a seven-week analysis with Freud, notwithstanding that by then they had established a friendship and were tight-knit colleagues.[36] Freud even entertained the idea of exchanging the favor and entering analysis with his junior colleague. The older man considered Ferenczi a brilliant clinician, a "master of analysts."[37] During World War I, Ferenczi kept Freud's practice alive by sending a steady stream of Hungarian referrals to him.[38] By 1925, Freud was positioning Ferenczi to assume the presidency of the International Psychoanalytic Society.

That same year, Ferenczi's coauthored short text *The Development of Psychoanalysis* was published. In it, he bemoaned the field's lack of emphasis on innovations in therapy techniques and practices: "The rapid growth of the psycho-analytic theory, the technical and therapeutic factor which was originally the heart of the matter and the actual stimulus to every important advance in the theory has been strikingly neglected, in the literature, as well as in practice."[39] Ferenczi was onto something.

Freud had published few papers on psychoanalytic technique, preferring instead to devote his time and energy to building a grand theory of the human mind. At best, he was a reluctant therapist. "We do analysis for two reasons," he once explained, "to understand the unconscious and to make a living."[40] Elsewhere he noted, "The chief aim of psychoanalysis is to contribute to the science of psychology and to the world of literature and life in general."[41] Freud was also peculiarly unsympathetic to any mention of psychoanalysis as a method to heal human suffering. He preferred to see it as a sort of scientific method through which to gain self-knowledge. Strangely, he could be quite contemptuous of his neurotic patients, letting it slip to Ferenczi that he considered them "rabble who only serve to provide us with a livelihood and material to learn from. We certainly cannot help them."[42] In a letter to a colleague, Freud confessed he experienced work with neurotic patients repetitive and was worn out by them: "In the first place I get tired of people. Secondly, I'm not basically interested in therapy, and I usually find that I'm engaged—in any particular case— with the theoretical problems with which I happen to be interested at the time. . . . I am also too patriarchal to be a good analyst."[43] When he discovered that Joseph Wortis wanted to be in analysis with him more as a student curious about the process than as a person with neurotic difficulties, Freud made a "disparaging gesture," gave out a hearty laugh, and announced, "I prefer a student ten times more than a neurotic."[44]

Furthermore, Freud lashed out at Ferenczi for having a *furor sanandi*, or a passion to cure, as if this were a liability and not an asset to a psychoanalyst. Ferenczi, for his part, shot back that he was an unrepentant empiricist "whose ideas would be rejected or confirmed by the progress of his patients."[45] Toward the goal of truly improving patients' emotional lives, the Hungarian set about innovating with psychoanalytic techniques far away from Vienna, in Budapest.

Ferenczi was a more active practitioner than his contemporaries, not content to passively sit back, pondering the patient's free associations and awaiting to be struck by some insightful idea to alert the patient's attention to.[46] Early in his psychoanalytic career, he believed he needed to frustrate his patients more effectively as a catalyst for breaking down their defenses and thereby helping them access underlying feelings and conflicts. To realize this goal, he did things like cut patients off midstream and redirect them back to a more relevant topic, insist they forgo sexual activity so that damned-up sexual energy might motivate them to be more expressive, and limit the length of therapy to add pressure to the whole enterprise. Over time, Ferenczi realized he was harming more than helping his patients with this frustration approach: "I started to listen to my patients when, in their attacks, they called me insensitive, cold, even hard and cruel, when they reproached me with being selfish, heartless, conceited."[47]

By the mid- to late 1920s, Ferenczi had swung in the other direction with his so-called relaxation technique, taking a more indulgent approach with patients.[48] He was now of the mind-set that patients needed to feel safe and cared for if they were to expose their innermost fears, sorrows, and aggravations. The good therapist, like the good mother, should be warm, inviting, tactful, and understanding. A wholesome therapeutic attitude enabled the vulnerable child to come out in the patient. It allowed patients to rediscover and outwardly express childlike parts of themselves that had been stifled through harsh parenting. When the American psychoanalyst Clara Thompson saw him for analysis beginning in the summer months of 1928, Ferenczi regularly let her kiss him. It is highly unlikely Ferenczi viewed this action as a permissive way for her to satisfy some erotic impulse. Rather, his style of working would suggest that he believed open expressions of tenderness would undo the effects of being raised by a stern, unapproachable mother and would better enable Thompson to feel and show affection.[49] We know from the historical record that Thompson's mother was devoutly religious, and when the psychoanalyst abandoned the Baptist church as a young woman, mother and daughter became estranged for more than twenty years.[50]

Therapy with Ferenczi could be lively and convivial. One of his patients was a Croatian musician whose self-consciousness was debilitating. Convinced she had foul-smelling breath, she bounced from dentist to dentist in search of a remedy, but to no avail. She also imagined that her breasts were unusually large and the object of ridicule by passersby on the street. Worst of all, she had stage fright—a crippling symptom for a musician. During one session, Ferenczi encouraged her to sing a song in front of him that was a favorite of her older sister. Two hours in, she was singing with zest. Ferenczi then invited her to engage in any other activities she feared. She played piano pieces for him and imitated orchestra instruments with mouth noises. Ferenczi watched on and took great delight in her antics.[51]

For Ferenczi, Freud's psychoanalytic therapy had become a stale, intellectualized game whereby the insights that patients walked away with did little to transform them as people. He wrote that Freud "still remains attached to analysis intellectually, but not emotionally. His therapeutic method, like his theory, is becoming more and more influenced by his interest in order."[52] In a seminal paper, he asserted, "I may remind you that patients do not react to theatrical phrases, but only to real sincere sympathy."[53] He was clearly targeting Freud's favorite interpretations involving people's supposed unconscious homosexuality, unresolved Oedipal conflicts, and the like. Ferenczi wanted to return to the early years of psychoanalysis, the Breuer years, when emotional release, or catharsis, was considered a key component of the process. If the method was to be of real benefit to patients, their emotions had to be evoked, then affirmed.

Ferenczi also wanted to revisit the role that sexual abuse played in causing neurosis. In his defense, Freud still considered that some of his patients' neuroses could be caused by true sexual abuse. In practice, however, his overriding concern was with the contribution of repressed primal childhood sexual fantasies. Rightly, Ferenczi perceived Freud's attitude as "professional hypocrisy" and potentially retraumatizing to treat a patient's sexual abuse disclosures as if they were the product of an overactive sexual imagination.[54]

Instead, when there is evidence of sexual abuse, patients need the therapist's extreme sensitivity and confirmation if they are to come to terms with the reality of what happened. On this score, Ferenczi was eminently clear: "Patients cannot believe that an event really took place, or cannot fully believe it, if the analyst, as the sole witness of the events, persists in this cool, unemotional, and, as patients are fond of stating, purely intellectual attitude, while the events are of a kind that must evoke, in anyone present, emotions of revulsion, anxiety, terror, vengeance, grief, and the urge to render immediate help."[55]

Ferenczi went one step further. He proposed there was deception and abuse of power embedded in the very way traditional psychoanalytic practice was set up. The revered stance taken by psychoanalysts—detached, enigmatic, making conviction-filled comments, refusing to admit mistakes, emphasizing punctuality—might simply reproduce for certain patients the conditions of their childhood with a rigid, unapproachable, uncaring parent. When patients then recoil, he said, feeling rejected, judged, or unheard, it is "professional hypocrisy" for the analyst to smugly refer to this as transference and to guide them to their past.[56] Categorizing their reactions as transference, or only relevant to some historical figure or situation in the patients' past, is essentially telling them their perceptions of the analyst in the room are delusional. An ethical analyst would engage in honest self-appraisal and confirm the patient's perceptions if there is accuracy to them. As we will see, this approach was also an essential part of Ferenczi's cure through love.

On September 1, 1932, the inevitable showdown between Freud and Ferenczi occurred at the Twelfth International Psycho-Analytical Congress in Wiesbaden, Germany. Ferenczi had hammered out all his criticisms of traditional psychoanalytic techniques into a manifesto he titled "Confusion of Tongues." Freud grasped the paper's drift ahead of time and tried to prohibit its presentation. In defiance, Ferenczi read it anyway and afterward extended his hand to Freud. The patriarch of the psychoanalytic movement declined a handshake and departed the room in silence.[57]

CURE THROUGH LOVE

"Psychoanalysis is in essence a cure through love," Freud wrote in a letter to Jung in 1906.[58] Some thirty years later, in *Analysis Terminable and Interminable*, we get some clarification of what he was hinting at: "We must not forget that the relationship between analyst and patient is based on love of truth, that is, on the acknowledgment of reality, and that it precludes any kind of sham or deception."[59]

From Freud's writing, as well as firsthand accounts of how he practiced, we can glean that he believed patients needed to be frustrated into acknowledging unpleasant truths about themselves. Encouraging free-associative expression without judgment is a form of love. So too is hanging in there when the inevitable resistances are thrown up to the analyst's truthful interpretations of those free associations. Nobody likes being told they are in denial, projecting, and confusing someone in their life for a person in their past. So-called transference insights can be useful. When a patient learns he or she is unconsciously stuck seeing the analyst as a cold, withholding person, like one of the patient's parents, and if this patient is extra sensitive to viewing most authority figures that way, then this insight can help the individual take some ownership of how he or she reacts to such figures. Typically, the insight is at first dismissed, only to be embraced after multiple examples of it arise over time in therapy. Showing forbearance and being a bit of a nag in persistently instilling such insights is what Freud meant by psychoanalytic love.

Ferenczi, on the other hand, thought that transference had to be *acted out*, not just *pointed out*, if the patient was to really improve. This idea is at the heart of what he thought constituted psychoanalytic love. It's a complicated idea that needs some explaining. He agreed with Freud that patients unconsciously place expectations on the analyst in line with what they were used to from parents growing up, but unlike Freud, he was in favor of letting these expectations play themselves out in the office. In the above example, if a patient finds the analyst to be cold and withholding, Ferenczi thought the analyst should give the patient free license to express whatever reactions he or she felt in the here-and-now about this. He assumed that there was some legitimacy to the patient's perceptions and reactions, and he worked with them. He did not categorically assume the perceptions had no basis in the reality of how the analyst was actually behaving in the room. The analyst might acknowledge how painful this perception must be, given what the patient was used to, growing up with this parent. The analyst might admit that he or she indeed was feeling detached for some reason. Optimally, the patient would relive the original upsetting parent-child dynamic in the room with the analyst in an emotionally charged way. There would be anger. There would be tears. The interaction would be a vast improvement on how such a dynamic historically played itself out with the parent. Any insight the patient derived about a sensitivity to perceive authority figures as cold and withholding would be decisive. Ferenczi called this type of emotionally charged insight "conviction."

Ferenczi parted ways with Freud on the overall stance the analyst should take with patients. He used terms like "unshakable good will" and "real sincere sympathy" to characterize his approach. If patients were to improve, they needed to feel the analyst's genuine regard for them. Unlike Freud, Ferenczi saw the psychoanalytic endeavor as an emotionally charged one in which the psychoanalyst's real attunement to and affection for his patients had salutatory effects. In his *Clinical Diary*, Ferenczi was forthright on these matters: "Should it ever occur, and it does occasionally to me, that experiencing another's and my own suffering brings a tear to my eye (and one should not conceal this emotion from the patient), then the tears of doctor and of patient mingle in a sublimated communion. . . . And this is the healing agent, which, like a kind of glue, binds together permanently the intellectually assembled fragments, surrounding even the personality thus repaired with a new aura of vitality and optimism.[60] He also put it more succinctly: "Psychoanalytic 'cure' is in direct proportion to the cherishing love given by the psychoanalyst to the patient."[61]

Session by session, week by week, patients absorb the analyst's caring attention, which has direct reparative effects. The analyst must give this attention to address deficits in love and recognition with which patients are afflicted, such as those stemming from parental and societal neglect and ill treatment. In Ferenczi's eyes, the analyst should also exemplify honesty, transparency, and sincerity, thereby undoing the confusion many patients experienced from parental hypocrisy. (By *hypocrisy*, he meant parents seeing themselves as infallible, hiding behind their own authority, and making excuses for their own insensitivity and cruelty.)

Ferenczi's more humanistic model of psychoanalysis made its way to the United States in the years leading up to World War II primarily through his patient Clara Thompson. She was in analysis with Ferenczi off and on for five years until his untimely 1933 death from pernicious anemia.[62] As director and cofounder of the William Alanson White Institute, in New York City, Thompson had great influence over a whole generation of trainee analysts. She was closely aligned with psychoanalysts like Erich Fromm and Karen Horney, whose books were mass-marketed and shaped the average American's views of talk therapy in the years before and after World War II.

Freud would not live long enough to witness the popularization of psychoanalysis in America. When the Nazis annexed Austria in 1938, it took aggressive negotiations by foreign dignitaries stepping in on

Freud's behalf to secure his and his family's release to England. Given that he was Jewish and presumed to have bountiful hard currency, his life was in danger. Freud's wit was there to the end. When required by the Nazis to write a statement verifying that he had not been mistreated by them, he wrote, "I can most highly recommend the Gestapo to everyone." Freud escaped the ravages of another world war, dying by a lethal dose of morphine he requested his personal physician to administer on September 23, 1939. Pain from his jaw cancer had become unbearable. A rational choice, by a rational man.[63]

Max Eastman, an American writer and a prominent political activist, badgered Freud about his espoused hatred of America during Freud's 1909 visit to Clark University. Retorted Freud: "Hate America? I don't hate America. . . . I regret it. I regret Columbus ever discovered it."[64] Freud did not live long enough to witness how foresight on the part of top brass in the American military to provide psychoanalytic interventions to traumatized troops was largely responsible for his therapy's popularization. And because Europe was decimated after the war, America would become psychoanalysis's new seat of power.

CHAPTER TWO

Before Prozac

Psychotherapy Comes of Age in America

DEMAND FOR PSYCHOTHERAPY among Americans from all walks of life mushroomed during the postwar decades. Veterans who had directly benefited from professional help or heard of its appeal while on active duty sought it out after the war to help them adjust to civilian life. Public policy advocates and lawmakers pushed for widespread access to mental health care to help stabilize the war-torn nation. The federal government assumed immense responsibility for the psychological well-being of returning troops and the US population as a whole by quickly passing laws to ensure that sufficient numbers of mental health professionals were educated and trained to meet the large demand for psychotherapy. The burgeoning supply of psychiatrists, psychologists, clinical social workers, and marriage and family therapists reflected the growing sentiment that a person didn't need to be mentally disturbed to benefit from mental health care. Psychotherapy rapidly became a popular, socially sanctioned medium for ordinary people to overcome normal human struggles.

Hollywood movies of the day captured the lure and mystique of psychotherapy, underscoring the public's fascination with it. Movie depictions of psychotherapy changed with the times and, in a sense, informed the public about what type of therapy was current and preferable. Celebrities went on record providing favorable testimonials about their therapy experiences, further normalizing—if not endorsing—psychotherapy as unequaled in its capacity to help people know themselves more deeply, feel more emotionally vital, live more authentically, and strive for greater meaning and purpose in life.

With few parallels today, leading theorists and practitioners penned scores of best-selling books that simplified complex ideas in psychoanalysis, existential psychology, and psychotherapy practice. Lay readers in large numbers seemed to have an insatiable appetite for psychological concepts to better understand their own and others' behavior and to learn about what to expect in therapy.

By the 1980s, talk therapy's status as the mental health intervention of choice was secure in American society. However, as will become apparent, this view radically changed with the advent of new generations of medications such as Prozac, the underfunding of psychotherapy by health insurers, and the rise of quick-fix therapies that academics favored as scientifically valid.

PSYCHOTHERAPY AND WAR TRAUMA

If you were an American in psychotherapy before 1941, there's every chance you'd be a high-society woman sauntering into a high-rise building in New York City. By 1943, after Roosevelt's fateful decision to plunge the country into war, an American in psychotherapy would most likely be a common citizen, a man—a battle-weary serviceman, that is—somewhere behind the front lines around the globe. Psychotherapy's public acceptance in America originated in its use with legions of traumatized troops during the latter stages of World War II and its aggressive postwar promotion by leading military psychiatrists, who considered psychotherapy essential to helping returning servicemen adjust to civilian life. Easy access to psychotherapy was also seen as the remedy for the nation's collective war trauma.

These were heady days for mental health professionals. The prominent psychiatrist Carl Binger was quoted in the *New York Times*, comparing the healing effects of psychotherapy on the military to that of "penicillin, sulfa drugs . . . and life-saving transfusions with blood plasma."[1] From our contemporary vantage point, this august comparison seems more than a tad grandiose. Yet psychotherapy interventions conducted at "exhaustion centers" close to combat situations had an important role in restoring the mental health of traumatized combatants. And there were plenty of personnel needing the help. An estimated 30 to 40 percent of all military casualties were due to some form of psychoneurosis.[2] Indeed, by 1943 the US Army was discharging more than ten thousand soldiers a month for psychiatric reasons.[3] It was generally recognized that even the hardiest fighter had a breaking point, or as the famed psychiatrist William Menninger put it: "It became obvious that the question was not *who* would break down, but *when*."[4] It might be a bent-over infantryman complaining of back pain with no ostensible medical cause. Or a decorated officer might be found miles from his men, lost while wandering around a small town, not knowing his name or how he got there. Or perhaps a jittery sergeant is given to hitting the ground and curling up into the fetal position at the slightest unexpected noise. There was a great need for places of psychotherapeutic respite where traumatized men could be assessed, treated, and either restored to the point of being able to return to combat or taken to a military hospital, where they could receive more intensive care.

Upwards of 60 percent of emotionally wounded military members returned to combat after either a short rest period of a few days or nearly a week of rest and short-term therapy.[5] Hundreds of thousands of ordinary people experienced psychotherapy for the first time. As depicted in the postwar US Army training film *Shades of Gray*, they encountered a discerning psychiatrist or psychologist who emotionally drew them out with questions like "What's your trouble? Go ahead and tell me"; "Where did you see people killed?"; "What happened up there?"; and "How did you feel about leaving your buddies behind?"[6] This last question was aimed at uncovering survival guilt, relieving the person of the self-blame and self-destructive tendencies that accompanied surviving while your army unit or buddy was wounded or perished. Often aided by injections of disinhibiting drugs like sodium pentothal, patients were actively encouraged to relive

traumatic experiences to acknowledge and express the full range of
fear, terror, guilt, shame, and rage unconsciously swirling around in
the dark recesses of their minds. The doctors confidently expected
that once repression was lifted and all the memories and feelings were
uncovered, the "sound personality" of the battle-fatigued combatant
would return.[7]

Word of these compelling battlefront interventions made its way
to the popular press, awakening the public's interest in psychotherapy. In a September 1944 magazine article titled "Repairing War-
Cracked Minds," journalist-turned-novelist Kyle Crichton described
the benefits of psychotherapy clearly: "Any doubts about the efficacy
of psychiatric treatments have been dissipated in the heat of war.
Thousands of men have been returned to normal life and even to
combat life by uses of the new therapy."[8] At the end of the war, mul-
titudes of Americans were beguiled by psychotherapy and primed to
perceive it as a usable service that was no longer stigmatized. Part of
the destigmatization resulted from frequent on-air commercial radio
messages observing that "most people have some degree of mental
illness at some time" just as "most of us have some physical illness
some of the time."[9]

A shocking discovery during the war was the phenomenally high
number of men rejected for military service for psychiatric reasons.
From January 1942 until December 1945, approximately 1.9 million
men were deemed mentally unfit for active duty. That amounted to
12 percent of all inductees.[10] It was estimated that throughout the war,
the total number of people disqualified from military service for mental health reasons was close to 2.5 million.[11] These numbers were so
striking that politicians began wondering whether large swaths of the
American public were mentally unstable and a threat to the postwar
effort to build a stable, productive workforce. This concern, combined
with the objective of assisting veterans to adjust to everyday life, led
the federal government to make an unprecedented investment in the
psychological well-being of all Americans with the passage of the National Mental Health Act of 1946.

Senator Claude Pepper, the Florida Democrat who crafted the
legislation, fervently articulated the urgency of the situation: "The

enormous pressures of the times, the catastrophic world war which ended in victory a few months ago, and the difficult period of reorientation and reconstruction, in which we have as yet achieved no victory, have resulted in an alarming increase in the incidence of mental disease and neuropsychiatric maladjustment among our people."[12] The lofty goal at the heart of the National Mental Health Act when President Truman signed it into law on July 3, 1946, was the "improvement of the mental health of the people of the United States."[13] The National Institute of Mental Health (NIMH) was formed with an initial budget of $18 million, an amount that mushroomed to $315 million by 1967.[14] A whopping 70 percent of that original budget was allocated for the education and training of mental health professionals.[15] The NIMH focused on training for a very good reason. While the demand for psychotherapy after the war was at an all-time high, there was a drastic scarcity of mental health professionals qualified to provide it. In 1946, the American Psychiatric Association had fewer than 4,300 members.[16] During the war, the army had requisitioned the services of 350 psychologists. By the war's end, only 250 of these positions had been filled.[17] A monumental push was under way to supply the nation with the skilled mental health professionals it sorely needed.

THE POSTWAR BOOM IN
THE MENTAL HEALTH PROFESSIONS

Before World War II, psychiatry was still a fledgling profession. Its practitioners perpetually struggled to define effective methods that would give them credibility in the larger field of medicine. Most psychiatrists found employment in the state mental hospitals dotting the country. The methods used to treat the emotionally disturbed under their charge were often experimental and were scrutinized and disapproved of both within and outside the medical establishment. The hospital treatments included psychosurgery, or lobotomy, to remove brain tissue supposedly causing mental disturbance; insulin shock therapy to induce comas; and barbiturate-induced sleep therapy. The latter two techniques were thought to help patients regain their sanity. Psychoanalytic psychotherapy emerged as a more humane alternative treatment that psychiatrists could use to address both severe and nonsevere mental health problems, in either a hospital or a private practice setting, thus increasing the profession's social acceptance and respectability within the field of medicine.

Because psychoanalysts, the vast majority of whom were psychiatrists, had stepped into leadership positions during the war, the policies and procedures they put in place had a decidedly psychoanalytic flavor. William Menninger, a founder of the famed Menninger Clinic in Topeka, Kansas, was appointed chief psychiatrist for the US Army and became an untiring promoter of psychiatry and psychoanalytic ideas. After the war, the Menninger Clinic became the largest psychiatric training site in the world and the jumping-off point for many of the European psychoanalysts who had fled Nazi Germany to set up practice in the United States. In fact, World War II all but decimated the practice of psychoanalysis in Europe while America became its home base. In 1931, about 22 percent of members of the International Psychoanalytic Association lived in the United States, but nineteen years later, the figure had risen to 64 percent.[18] In 1948, the Menninger Clinic trained 15 percent of all psychiatrics residents in the country.[19] Menninger was president of the American Psychiatric Association that year, as well as chair of the Group for the Advancement of Psychiatry, a 150-strong group of brash psychiatrists referred to in the profession as the "Young Turks" because of their zeal in promoting psychiatry among lawmakers and the public.[20]

Menninger had a knack for making dense psychoanalytic ideas accessible to the average person. In a *Time* magazine piece devoted to him, he gave the following nifty definition of how the unconscious mind can interfere with the workings of the conscious, rational mind: "The mind is something like a clown act featuring a two-man fake horse. The man up front (the Conscious part of the mind) tries to set the direction and make the whole animal behave; but he can never be sure what the man at the rear end of the horse (the Unconscious) is going to do next. If both ends of the horse are going in the same direction, your mental health is all right. If they aren't pulling together, there's likely to be trouble."[21]

The American public ate up these accessible ways of analyzing the mind. In *Shrink: A Cultural History of Psychoanalysis in America*, Lawrence Samuel captures the spirit of the times: "The once rather radical prospect of seeing a shrink had become nothing short of an all-American activity."[22]

Psychiatry fast became an attractive, lucrative profession. With the NIMH heavily subsidizing the education and training of psychiatrists after the war, the number of psychiatrists increased sixfold, from 4,700 to 27,000, between 1948 and 1976.[23] No longer was psychiatry a profession confined to mental hospitals. As early as 1947, the majority of psychiatrists were in private practice or working in outpatient clinics.[24] Private practice and psychoanalysis practically went hand in hand. The allure of the profession was not the use of a surgical instrument or medicinal cocktail, but a couch—and, of course, the use of devoted attention and cleverness to encourage patients to let down their guards and share repressed secrets, fantasies, and desires and open up emotionally. Leading psychiatrists of the day, like Menninger, took great pains to characterize their craft as a scientific endeavor: "Through evolution and refinement [psychoanalysis] has become a scientific therapy—a process of clearing away, stratum by stratum, diseased psychological material."[25]

The high point for psychoanalytically oriented psychiatrists was the 1970s. In 1973, about half of all psychiatrists labeled themselves as psychoanalysts.[26] However, in subsequent decades, with the introduction of effective medications like imipramine (approved by the US Food and Drug administration [FDA] for depression in 1959), Valium (FDA approved for anxiety 1963), Xanax (FDA approved for anxiety 1981), and then the blockbuster Prozac (FDA approved for anxiety and depression 1987), psychiatry took a sharp turn into the realm of biochemistry. Of the approximately forty-nine thousand psychiatrists in the United States, the overwhelming majority exclusively prescribe medications, and fewer than 11 percent now provide talk therapy to their patients.[27]

In the years leading up to World War II, clinical psychology was a relatively neglected and marginalized field. It held this second-class status partly because it was considered a female profession; clinical psychology was made up mainly of women with master's degrees serving children and families in child guidance clinics in large metropolitan areas. Moreover, psychology departments in universities were notoriously resistant to endorsing clinical psychology as a legitimate area of study, considering it a soft, unscientific endeavor.

This anemic state of affairs changed when generous grants were awarded by the US Department of Veterans Affairs (VA) and the NIMH to universities agreeing to provide PhD-level clinical training in clinical psychology. As early as the academic year 1946–1947, grants were distributed to twenty-two universities across the country to fund the education and training of two hundred graduate students.[28] Within three years, this financial support extended to fifty universities and involved more than fifteen hundred students.[29]

The VA also contracted with more than four hundred universities and colleges to establish campus-based counseling centers to provide counseling and vocational training to veterans who either attended their institution or lived in the surrounding community.[30] These counseling centers became training sites for a whole generation of counseling psychologists (a person can become a licensed psychologist by obtaining a PhD in either clinical or counseling psychology). One of these sites was the Chicago Counseling Center, which the preeminent psychologist Carl R. Rogers had founded at the University of Chicago in 1945. Rogers's counseling center saw five hundred to eight hundred clients per year over its first eight years in operation.[31] Like its spin-off university counseling centers nationwide, the Chicago Counseling Center embodied a humanistic helping agenda, determined to address both the educational and the psychic needs of students by "optimizing their educational and vocational choices, and increasing their life satisfaction."[32] By 1960, the number of practicing psychologists had edged above seven thousand, and ten years later, that figure had risen to twenty-four thousand.[33]

Up until the 1970s, psychologists still practiced under the aegis of psychiatrists and billed clients through them. The economic base for psychologists to practice independently from psychiatrists was largely nonexistent. With the advent of employer-offered health insurance in the 1970s, leaders in the psychology profession realized that if their practitioners were to survive, they would have to be considered autonomous providers by insurance companies. A cadre of militant psychologists, mischievously named the Dirty Dozen, set about ensuring that psychologists would be eligible to bill insurance companies directly for their psychotherapy services. They devised a strategy that one of their ranks, Jack Wiggins, called "freedom-of-choice legislation." The idea was that every patient had a solemn right to select what type of mental health provider he or she preferred. The Dirty Dozen systematically lobbied state legislators across the nation to add three words—"which includes psychologists"—after "physician" in their insurance codes. The strategy worked perfectly. After various legal countermeasures, the insurance industry eventually yielded and allowed psychologists to bill for services as autonomous providers in all fifty states. The insurers had decided that it was too costly and cumbersome to separate out and process claims from different types of providers according to whether the state recognized the independent practice of psychology.[34]

Eligibility to bill Medicare, the federal program that reimburses health-care providers for services to people over sixty-five and to people who are disabled, further secured the economic base for psychologists to practice as independent mental health professionals. The Dirty Dozen had singled out Medicare reimbursement by psychologists as a top advocacy priority as early as 1965. By then, all the legislative support was in place and the measure had a good shot for approval by federal authorities. Ironically, the change did not to come to fruition, because a secretary at the American Psychological Association's headquarters failed to file paperwork—which was already completed—on time. Twenty-five years were to pass before psychologists were recognized as Medicare providers.[35]

As the economic base for the independent practice of psychology was secured, the number of psychologists flourished. By 1980, the figure reached thirty thousand, climbing to fifty-eight thousand by 1990.[36] The number reached eighty-five thousand by the year 2000 and stood at ninety-three thousand by 2011.[37] The Center for Workforce Studies at the American Psychological Association estimates that four to five thousand doctoral-level psychologists graduate each year.[38] The profession is alive and well, considering that the army could not fill 350 positions by the end of World War II, in 1945.

Even though it was possible to obtain clinical social work training as early as 1904 through the New York School of Philanthropy—later renamed the Columbia University School of Social Work—clinical social work did not truly thrive as a mental health profession until after the 1970s, as its practitioners entered private practice and community mental health centers in droves to offer psychotherapy.[39] In the 1950s and 1960s, the general impression was that social work was ill defined as a profession. There was a conscientious disinclination to train social workers to perform psychotherapy, since such a practice was considered an abandonment of the central mission of practical service to, and advocacy for, the poor and oppressed of society. One leader in the field, Marion Sanders, described this new role of social work rather cynically: "The day after the bomb fell the doctor was out binding up radiation burns. The minister prayed and set up a soup kitchen in the ruined chapel. The policeman herded the stray children to the rubble heap where the teacher had improvised a classroom. And the social worker wrote a report; since two had survived, they held a conference on Interpersonal Relations in a Time of Intensified Anxiety States."[40]

In the 1970s, there were approximately 4,000 clinical social workers in the United States.[41] By the 1990s, that figure had blossomed to 81,500, with more than a third having established themselves in private practice.[42] Within a generation, the field of clinical social work had embraced the provision of psychotherapy as a core professional service its practitioners could offer. Paul Saxton, a prominent California-based clinical social worker, emphatically underscored the type of psychotherapy his cohorts should provide at that time: "It's not about problem solving and coping. It is, rather, a grindingly painful struggle for transformation and birth of the self. . . . [It is] about confrontations with the demons within and without."[43] It is estimated that just upwards of two hundred thousand clinical social workers now provide direct mental health services to clients.[44] Today, there is a far greater chance that when a person visits a therapist's office to bear his or her soul, the therapist will be a clinical social worker instead of a psychiatrist or a psychologist.

The last remaining mental health profession, marriage and family therapy, emerged in response to the rising divorce rates in the 1970s to offer specialized training in couples and family therapy. In 1986, only eleven states regulated the practice of marriage and family therapy. By 2009, every state in the union had some level of certification or licensure for these therapists, whose number in North America now stands at around forty-eight thousand.[45]

In the decades after World War II, the supply of psychotherapists—be they psychiatrists, psychologists, clinical social workers, or marriage and family therapists—kept pace with the public's seemingly insatiable demand for psychotherapy. In the late 1950s, about 14 percent of Americans had visited a psychotherapist of some sort at some point in their lives.[46] That number roughly doubled, to 26 percent, by the 1970s and then nearly doubled again, to 50 percent, by 2010.[47] As psychotherapy made its way into American culture, it was portrayed with greater frequency in movies and television by those in the roles of doctors and therapists seeming to possess uncanny powers of persuasion and healing. These portrayals in turn demonstrated the promise of therapy to the culture at large, teaching Americans about what to expect in therapy and how to think more psychologically about their feelings, motives, and true desires.

CHANGING DEPICTIONS OF PSYCHOTHERAPY IN POPULAR CULTURE

The 1945 Alfred Hitchcock movie *Spellbound*, with its convoluted plot, confused identities, and symbolic dream sequence, is an excellent representation of psychoanalysis as practiced in midcentury America.[48] In a tagline at the beginning of the movie, the essence of the psychoanalytic experience is laid out: "Once the complexes that have been disturbing the patient are uncovered and interpreted, the illness and confusion disappear . . . and the devils of unreason are driven from the human soul." Alex Brulov, played by Michael Chekhov, is the main psychoanalyst in the movie. He is supremely confident in his ministrations: "My dear child, do you think that old Alex Brulov, one of the biggest brain squeezes in psychiatry, is unable to make two and two come out four?" Part sage, part all-knowing scientist—but mostly master detective—he is out to determine why a man, played by Gregory Peck, is posing as Anthony Edwardes, another psychoanalyst. Peck's character knows that the real Edwardes has been murdered, but he doesn't know who he himself is. In the end, the imposter recovers an emotionally charged, repressed memory involving him sliding down a wall and kicking his brother onto an exposed railing, causing his accidental death. Through some unconscious mental gymnastics, the imposter had falsely assumed the identity of the real Edwardes to protect himself against his unconscious guilt over believing he had murdered his brother. The psychic mystery and the gateway to discovering the identity of the murderer of Edwardes are solved as the Peck character tearfully announces in analysis, "I didn't kill my brother. It was an accident." Brulov, much like a detective triumphant over just having solved a crime, gleefully responds, "That's what haunted you all your life. That was the memory you were afraid of."

It is a classic psychological suspense tale: the puzzle is solved, the patient cured. Freud himself was a big fan of detective novels and, like a shrewd crime buster in his practice of psychoanalysis, often fixated on the possible meaning in seemingly trivial details or scrutinized a patient's speech for signs of oddities. He prided himself on guessing early into his reading of a detective novel who the murderer was, and he could become quite irate if he was wrong. Albert Hirst, a patient of Freud's as a young man, remembered Freud's *Spellbound*-like focus on weaving together images in patients' dreams and oddly worded disclosures to get at long-forgotten fantasies and traumatic events.[49] Traditional psychoanalysis, as it was practiced in the 1940s and 1950s, and still is in some circles, has continued to cast the analyst as all-knowing detective, taking clues from the client's disclosures to solve the mystery of repressed childhood traumas or fantasies.

Lucy Freeman's 1951 *Fight Against Fears* offers a comprehensive popular account of midcentury psychoanalysis. One of the first women to be hired as a reporter for the *New York Times*, Freeman turned to psychoanalysis because of painful shyness. Of her experience, she wrote: "Some know what they feel. I did not dare know. Analysis for me was a continuous discovery. I felt like the intended victim in a murder, with the analyst as hero-detective trying to rescue me from a life of inner terror."[50] As a girl, Freeman kept meticulous records on the New York Giants' batting averages. Her analyst smartly inferred a connection: "It's interesting that you chose a team with the name Giants. A little girl afraid of many things might cling to a team of Giants."[51] In one passage, Freeman remembers that her parents laughed after she had thrown up an egg they had just served her. The analyst interprets the memory: "Your parents never really tried to kill you, but in your unhappiness it seemed to you as though they wanted to. Intellectually you know they did not, but in your inner, unrealistic world you felt at times they wished you dead."[52]

With the social and political changes of the 1960s, popular depictions of therapy began to focus less on solving psychological puzzles and more on emotional honesty, being real and alive, and just feeling what needed to be felt. In the 1969 film *Bob & Carol & Ted & Alice*, Bob (played by Robert Culp) returns from an encounter group experience and announces, "The truth is always beautiful."[53] In *An Unmarried Woman*, a movie released nine years later, Jill Clayburgh's character, Erica, meets with a psychiatrist who warmly reassures her: "It's certainly OK to feel lonely when you get divorced. You're supposed to in a situation like this. . . . Don't feel ashamed of your feelings; they have no IQ, no morality. They're your feelings. Just feel them."[54]

The culture was changing, and so was Freudian therapy. Into the 1970s and 1980s, the film that best represents the shift from the distant, intellectualized Freudian to the approachable, authentically engaged ideal embodied by a new wave of practitioners—the humanistic Freudians—is *Ordinary People*, released in 1980.[55] Both a box-office success and winner of an Academy Award for Best Picture, the movie reflected the popular interest in psychotherapy—talk therapy in particular, with its more caring, emotionally evocative approach.

In the film, psychotherapist Tyrone C. Berger (Judd Hirsch) agrees to meet with Conrad (Timothy Hutton) twice weekly for therapy to deal with the traumatic effects of his brother's drowning death in a boating accident, which Conrad himself survived. He has just been released from the hospital after a suicide attempt, in a classic case of survivor's guilt. Their therapy is full of exchanges in which Berger is authentic, even punchy. After Conrad reveals he wants help to be more in control, Berger rolls his eyes and says, "I'll tell you something. I'll be straight with you. I'm not big on control, but it's your money, so to speak." During a quiet moment, he gently asks Conrad, "What are you thinking?" When Conrad openly admits, "I jack off a lot," Dr. Berger refreshingly answers, "So what else is new?!" In a later session, Conrad agonizingly discloses, "I can't do this. I can't make myself mad. It takes too much energy." Dr. Berger lovingly admonishes him, "You know how much energy it takes to hold it back!" and tauntingly sings, "I beg your pardon, I didn't mean to promise you a rose garden."

Conrad angrily swears at him, to which Dr. Berger retorts, "A little advice about feelings, kiddo; don't expect it to always tickle."

In movies like *Ordinary People*, psychotherapists were portrayed as wise souls with years of clinical experience, intermingling with life experience, etched into their faces. They were devoted to their clients' emotional well-being. They were warm, approachable, and authentic, while remaining eminently professional. They treated their clients as real people, with real feelings, who were suffering and desperately in need of relief. The themes were existential: openness, realness, honesty, living in the now, assuming responsibility for one's own life course. There was emotional synchrony in the room during therapy sessions, where doctors' feelings engender clients' feelings of their own. Gone were the earlier movie therapists' tendencies to treat clients as human puzzle pieces serving up an intellectual challenge. Gone were the images of doctors being one step ahead of the clients, knowing the truth before it's revealed, almost smug when clients told them what they as doctors knew all along. In short, Freudian therapy had taken on a new face. It was a face provided by the humanistically oriented Freudians, and it was a decidedly American one.

FROM COUCH TO CHAIR:
THE HUMANISTIC FREUDIANS

It has been said of psychoanalysis that the European cure was one of *self-domination*, whereas the American cure was one of *self-liberation*.[56]

Freud was quite clear that his therapy method allowed patients to access instinctual urges or dangerously dark feelings and fantasies so that the feelings could be more rationally controlled and creatively channeled. American psychoanalysts, such as Karen Horney, Erich Fromm, and Rollo May, in contrast, saw therapy as a process of putting the client in touch with emotions so that the person could feel vital and fortified in the unavoidable, never-ending pursuit of personal meaning and purpose in life. They were apt to help clients perceive and recognize their inner goodness as much as their inner badness. Hope and aspiration were as much a part of therapy as despair and regret. Reliving the past in therapy had its place, but so too did anticipating and forging a future. Authentic self-expression was at the heart of effective treatment because therein lay the client's hope for facing the dehumanizing and alienating effects of living in mass societies. Empathy, or feeling your way into the client's shared life experiences, was the crucial medium of therapy. And to do that, you needed to see the client's face as the person is speaking, which you can't do sitting behind someone who's lying on a couch.

Karen Horney was one of the first high-ranking women in the German psychoanalytic community. She was among scores of émigré analysts who relocated to the United States in the 1930s to escape the rise of Nazism. Horney was associated with a variety of US psychoanalytic institutes, none of which she remained at for long. She tended to operate outside the psychoanalytic establishment, focusing on writing psychology books for the public. These books sold extremely well; her *Neurosis and Human Growth*, *Our Inner Conflicts*, and *Are You Considering Psychoanalysis?* are still in print.

Horney proposed that neurosis stems from the overshadowing of the client's "real self" as he or she dully accommodates the unreasonable demands of parents.[57] It might be that overly controlling parents bent on obedience and compliance lead to children who then feel "compelled to adopt their standard for the sake of peace." Or it could be overly ambitious parents who need their child to be a high achiever and exceptionally attractive and accomplished to puff up their own self-importance. That child may then grow into an adult who fluctuates between grandiosity and self-loathing, depending on whether his or her unreasonably high standards are met. To undo the neurosis, psychotherapy aims to put the client in touch with his or her spontaneous individual self, or real self—"what I really feel, what I really want, what I really believe, what I really decide." The client emerges from the tyranny of *should*s: what he or she should feel, want, believe, and decide.

A former patient sent Horney a letter in which she recapped the therapy between them: "The first thing she tackled was that which was readiest at hand: my cast-iron 'should-system.' My complete armor of 'shoulds': duty, ideals, pride, and guilt. This rigid and compulsive perfectionism was all that held me up; outside it and all around lay chaos. . . . I began to mention spontaneity—to dare to think of it, and at last to realize how I longed for it—I who had always deliberately fought it."[58]

Free association was still the method Horney relied on in therapy to cultivate a client's real self in therapy, and she took great pains to distinguish it from idle chatter: "Free association means revealing oneself with utter frankness. It is telling what one is thinking and feeling, without selecting, preparing, figuring out, or holding back. . . . [I]t is not the same as rambling, which also involves saying whatever comes into one's mind but in a way that's superficial rather than connected to one's inner depths."[59] Horney was saying that associations are *made free* by clients in therapy, by their repeated risking of spontaneity.

Horney frowned on the psychoanalytic practice of the day: the making of interpretations, in a conviction-filled, gotcha way, about what the client's thoughts and feelings really mean. Her advice to psychotherapists when they offer deeper understanding about clients' thoughts and feelings was quite postmodern: "They should regard all interpretations as more or less tentative and should be truthful about the degree of certainty they feel."[60] In fact, the process of floating possible explanations of the client's difficulties for him or her to wonder about was part of the therapy. It respected the client's autonomy and choice-making capacities.

Wholeheartedness was the attitude Horney strove for in her helping role. She tried to marshal an amalgam of all her clinical and life experiences to be of service to her clients: "Wholeheartedness involves observing with all our capacities and faculties. We listen, we see, and feel with our intuition, undivided interest, reason, curiosity, and specialized knowledge."[61] She believed that therapists have a solemn duty to grow and develop as persons and to take good care of themselves if they are to be of maximum benefit to their clients: "The mind is our analytic tool, as is our total personality, and we have an obligation to keep this tool in good shape if we are to do such concentrated work with it."[62]

Erich Fromm was a colleague of Horney's at the Berlin Psychoanalytic Institute. A sociologist by education, he became a trained psychoanalyst in Germany in the 1920s and immigrated to the United States two years after Horney did, in 1934. In 1946, Fromm cofounded the William Alanson White Institute in New York City, which produced multiple generations of humanistically oriented psychoanalysts and even today remains a think tank of cutting-edge ideas and practices in the world of psychoanalytic psychotherapy. Fromm and Horney were lovers throughout much of the 1930s, and at one point, he was the long-term psychotherapist of Horney's daughter. Fromm and Horney greatly influenced each other's thinking; some scholars maintain that she learned sociology from him, while he learned psychoanalysis from her.[63]

Fromm's ideas about psychology and psychotherapy not only influenced those training to be therapists in the decades after World War II, but also shaped the mind-set of millions of ordinary citizens both in America and abroad. His revelatory book *Escape from Freedom*, published in 1941, is still a classic. It has sold more than five million copies worldwide and has been translated into twenty-eight languages.[64] In the book, he maps out the danger inherent in individuals' giving over power to authority figures, becoming dependent on their approval, and vicariously living through them to feel strong. This sort of dependency is what repressive communities and totalitarian states thrive on. The solution, as outlined by his biographer, Lawrence Friedman, was for the individual to "summon the energy and courage to make spontaneous, productive, reasoned, and life-affirming use of his autonomy."[65] One route to acquiring such a vital sense of autonomy, of course, was psychotherapy.

Like the other neo-Freudians, Fromm probably abandoned the use of the couch in favor of sitting face-to-face or side by side, in comfortable chairs, for a more democratic arrangement. The iconic image of the analyst, notepad in hand, sitting behind the couch on which the client is lying, was an authoritarian setup that Fromm would reject. Detached, looking down on the client, waiting to be misperceived as a parent figure, all the while being cool and intellectual, were not therapeutic methods to which he aspired. He set his mind and heart on what he called "central relatedness." He once told a friend, "To see a person, means to penetrate him or her in a timeless manner and be 'in' the person."[66] He elsewhere wrote: "I have to be related to the patient, not interested in him as a scientific object. . . . [O]ne can only understand it if one has had an experience of the difference between liking somebody, being interested in somebody and feeling fully the central relatedness to a person: 'This is you.'"[67]

His definition of an empathic way of conducting psychotherapy is a timeless, desirable template for any therapist: "If we really understand the patient, then we experience in ourselves everything the patient tells us, his fantasies, whether psychotic, criminal, or childish. We understand only if they strike that chord within ourselves. This is why we can talk with authority to the patient, because we are not talking about him anymore, we are talking about our own experience which has been made manifest through his telling us what he experiences."[68]

Clients and those he supervised often found Fromm to be quite direct. He saw little place for small talk in therapy and went after "big talk"; a client's deep concerns and other feelings were ripe for discussion. He frowned on telling half-truths or dancing around issues, likening this to the effects of a phone not ringing because not enough digits were punched in. He once suggested to a supervisee whose client was routinely late for sessions that if it were his client, he'd say something like, "Now look here, we're not playing a game. If you continue to come late I won't see you. We're not playing cat and mouse. Twenty minutes late and that's it."[69] The supervisee did not consider such directness an assault on a patient but "an expression of hope and faith that speaking honestly and clearly to the healthy, striving adult in the patient would foster awareness and ultimately the freedom to fulfill unexplored potentialities."[70] One of Fromm's favorite expressions to evoke spontaneous feelings in clients was, "Tell me what is in your mind right now."[71] Time was precious and not to be wasted during sessions. He pushed for real emotional encounters where raw feelings would arise and be recognized. The one criterion Fromm listed for determining a session's success was that it be "interesting."[72]

Rollo May, a onetime Fromm student, cofounded the Saybrook Institute in San Francisco in 1971. Saybrook is now one of a handful of US universities preparing psychotherapists to specialize in existential-humanistic psychology. May's life crises formed a crucible for the existential themes permeating his work.[73] His parents were divorced during his childhood, and he was often left to care for his sister, who had schizophrenia. He underwent an emotional breakdown while teaching English in Greece in his early twenties and barely survived tuberculosis in midlife. Not surprisingly, in his prolific career as a psychotherapist and writer, he delved into the role of anxiety, loneliness, choice, and responsibility in human growth and development. Books he penned were best sellers in the 1960s and 1970s. His most noteworthy publication, *Love and Will*, sold in excess of 135,000 copies within the first year and a half of its 1969 release, prompting a *New York Times* reporter to claim that it was "fast becoming the source book for post-Freudian man."[74]

May parted ways with Freud by asserting that anxiety and depression do not stem from repressing sexual and aggressive urges but from living an unlived life, or avoiding taking ownership for pursuing a preferred life. In a 1958 *Time* magazine article devoted entirely to him and his ideas, he thus clarifies how these negative emotions arise: "The trouble lies in dammed-up potentialities rather than repressed instincts."[75] Late in life, during a thought-provoking interview, May insisted that anxiety was not a symptom to be eliminated or medicated but rather a sign that "the world is knocking at your door saying you need to create, you need to make something, you need to do something. . . . It's a stimulus toward creativity, toward courage. It's what makes us human."[76] For May, clients needed to realize that low-grade anxiety is a constant feature of the life of any freedom-welcoming person who senses that, whatever choices he or she makes, life will have its ups and downs. Despair and hopelessness are emotional states that May thought had the same awakening functions, telling us that drastic changes were necessary to make our lives worth living.

For May, the realization and acceptance of one's mortality, one's short time on earth, was not a morbid thought but a necessary life stance to galvanize the individual into meaningful action. It was what motivated people to muster the courage to be creative and see meaningful life commitments through to completion. Borrowing from the Danish philosopher Søren Kierkegaard, May contended that there is no ultimate source of meaning and identity in life to rely on. By facing this angst, people can start making true choices and forging ahead with commitments that bring real meaning and purpose in life. In his work with clients, May valued the philosopher Pascal's dictum "Here rather than there, now rather than then." He encouraged them to honestly and directly communicate whatever they were presently feeling and thinking in the moment with him.[77]

Building on the great Swiss psychoanalyst Carl Jung's idea of the shadow self, May proposed that the "daimonic" exits in all of us. There are parts of us that we assume are shameful or evil but which still need to be acknowledged, expressed, and included into our view of ourselves. Taking it one step further, he thought that in therapy, clients could rediscover feelings of love for their partners by expressing anger and dissatisfaction. When anger is suppressed, he proposed, alienation and distance sets in, weakening the love felt. With clients, May advanced the notion that "to experience and live out capacities for tender love requires the confronting of the daimonic."[78] Candor about legitimate anger, May believed, could deepen love in relationships. By the same token, clients risked hurting their intimate relationships by holding back from communicating the degree of love they actually felt. Anxiety, for May, could stem not from the Freudian sense of sucking up one's anger or lust, but from being stingy with expressing the love that one inwardly felt for a partner.

There is still currency to May's notion that people busy themselves for the sake of keeping busy, not so much to put a cork on intense anger or lust but to avoid asking potentially ground-swelling questions about the direction their lives are taking and entertaining the gut-wrenching choices necessary for a better existence. May differentiated between pleasure and joy, seeing the latter as "the zest that you get out of using your talents, your understanding, the totality of your being for great aims."[79] The pursuit of pleasure, the greedy accumulation of wealth, or the base satisfaction of sexual urges was to May an avoidance of creating true sources of personal fulfillment in life. This point of view may have been influenced by his thirty-year-long friendship with Paul Tillich, the world-renowned theologian, and May's understanding of the Christian aphorism "What does it profit a man to gain the whole world and forfeit his soul?" May considered psychotherapy an arena to acquire archetypal human virtues such as a desire for truth, beauty, courage, joy, wisdom, and understanding. Psychotherapy was not a service used to make symptoms go away.

Books by Horney, Fromm, and May had staying power into the 1960s and 1970s. With their broad appeal, the books described, if not prescribed, to a generation of American therapists and laypeople alike the personal transformation that could occur with good talk therapy.

There were, of course, important innovations in psychoanalytic talk therapy that arose in the 1980s, with the leading luminaries being Stephen Mitchell and Heinz Kohut. Mitchell was a pivotal figure in what's called *relational psychoanalysis*. Like Fromm and May before him, Mitchell was a product of the William Alanson White Institute in New York City. Also like them, Mitchell placed importance on benevolent here-and-now interactions with clients to help undo their negative expectations of relationships. In his 1993 book *Hope and Dread in Psychoanalysis* (a title that would spark May's interest), Mitchell writes eloquently about how clients act out with therapists, secretly expecting and dreading that the therapist will react to them the same way their parents did. Underlying clients' fear is the hope that perhaps this time they will be heard and acknowledged, rather than ignored and judged. Mitchell described the value of therapists' authenticity with clients, of bringing subjectivity into the room in ways that might energize the therapy. Taking a page from Horney, he believed that a therapist's interpretation of the deeper meaning of a client's struggle was just a hypothesis, not a "God's eye viewpoint" laden with objective truth about the client's inner psyche.[80]

Heinz Kohut—and the self-psychology model he outlined—was also hugely influential to talk therapists in the 1970s and 1980s. Like Horney before him, Kohut was associated with the Chicago Psychoanalytic Institute. Also like Horney, he concerned himself with the "real self" (which he, more clinically, labeled the "nuclear self") and therapy for clients who suffer from fluctuations in self-esteem, vacillating between displays of narcissism and states of self-loathing. Client empathy was the centerpiece of Kohut's mode of therapy, just as it was for the earlier humanistic Freudians.[81]

Despite their prominence in the field, Mitchell and Kohut penned books that were readable only to clinicians who were well versed in clinical jargon and who already had a sophisticated knowledge of psychotherapy. Part of the reason for the waning availability and attraction of psychoanalytically oriented talk therapy heading into the 1980s and 1990s might have been the inability of most of its adherents to write accessibly about it for a lay audience. Regardless, the causes for the decline in talk therapy during this era were myriad and had swift effects.

TALK THERAPY UNDER SIEGE

It's highly probable that if, sometime in the mid-1980s, you had conducted a poll probing people on the street about their image of talk psychotherapy, their collective rendering would most likely resemble the experience that the character Conrad had with his therapist, Tyrone Berger, in *Ordinary People*. Most people would describe therapy as a place to have an open-ended discussion about feelings, to emotionally unburden themselves, to sit back and do an honest inventory of their lives, and to recollect and vent about their childhoods past. They also would probably concoct a collective image of the ideal therapist as a benevolent, discerning, careful, patient listener. Yet academic surveys at the time suggested that what the public presumably wanted was a far cry from how therapists were actually being educated and trained to perform therapy.

Only about 13 percent of therapists in a 1982 study listed themselves as either psychoanalytic or existential, the educational background most apt to turn you into a Berger-like therapist. More than

40 percent defined themselves as "eclectic." The authors of the study worried that this characterization "encourages an indiscriminate selection of bits and pieces from diverse sources that result in a hodgepodge of inconsistent concepts and techniques."[82]

That same year, a Texas A&M University study looked at the projections of experts in the field and predicted a rapid rise in the following therapeutic interventions: cognitive restructuring, problem-solving techniques, homework assignments, communication skills, and self-control procedures.[83] This prediction reflected the emerging dominance of cognitive behavioral therapy (CBT) in psychotherapy. CBT, an approach pioneered by Aaron Beck in the early 1960s, is a practical and goal-oriented form of therapy. It emphasizes actively challenging clients' distorted thinking about themselves and others. During and in between their sessions, clients are assigned homework in which they are coached to document and self-monitor the overgeneralizing, exaggerating, and catastrophizing of their thoughts. CBT is also a brief form of therapy, commonly lasting less than twenty sessions, with visits spaced every two or three weeks. Not surprisingly, the Texas A&M study also predicted a substantial decline in long-term therapy in the coming decade. Jonathan Engel chronicles the briefer-is-better mind-set regarding therapy in his fascinating book, *American Therapy: The Rise of Psychotherapy in the United States*. He maintains that toward the end of the twentieth century, the typical therapy experience lasted eight hundred minutes, whereas a quarter-century earlier, the standard course of psychoanalytic treatment had lasted about eight hundred hours.[84]

As we will discover in upcoming chapters, therapy approaches like CBT, which are briefer, practical, and goal directed and whose techniques can be isolated and studied, lend themselves to clear-cut research. You can define variables and measure their correlation with one another. You can define anxiety in terms of the number of catastrophic thoughts, measure the number of times a client charts these thoughts and assesses their validity, crunch some numbers, and zero in on a possible correlation. If the treatment lasts two to three months, a study of the treatment is logistically and financially manageable with a modest grant.

On the other hand, scientific evidence for core psychotherapy methods and processes can be quite elusive. Therapeutic attitudes like authenticity, Horney's wholeheartedness, and Fromm's central relatedness, as essential to good psychotherapy as they might be, are difficult to define and assess. Plus, a two-year, twice-weekly course of psychotherapy, say, for a hundred research subjects not only breaks the bank but shatters it. The types of therapy taught to legions of graduate students thus rapidly became those that were eminently researchable and thereby ensured faculty tenure. The question remains whether such briefer, tailored CBT interventions have deep human relevance and can be generalized to the emotional suffering of real people in the real world.

The plethora of studies generated by academics in the 1980s and beyond substantiating the benefits of time-limited, solution-focused CBT was music to the ears of managed-care administrators, who were eager to cut back on the increasing cost of mental health treatment. Preapproval for, and caps on, the number of psychotherapy visits clients were eligible to receive became commonplace. The incomes of shrinks shrunk, as did the length and quality of the shrinking they provided.

By far the greatest blow to talk therapy was the release of Prozac in 1987 (not to mention the various so-called serotonin reuptake inhibitors and new classes of mood-stabilizing medications that followed). Within five years of Prozac's release, eight million people—more than half of them Americans—had taken the drug.[85] Psychiatric researcher Jonathan Cole capsulized the ease with which people embraced Prozac: "One pill a day forever." Adam Gopnik reflected back on the cultural impact of the drug in a *New Yorker* essay: "Talking is out, taking is in." He wryly added, "The routine taking of drugs had become the preferred treatment not just for anxiety and depression, but for everything from hair loss to erectile dysfunction."[86]

CHAPTER THREE

Pills for All Ills

IN HER CONFESSIONAL BOOK, *Prozac Diary*, Lauren Slater captured the lure of Prozac for her generation: "Prozac may make you high. . . . [I]t will make you high by returning you to a world you've forgotten or never quite managed to be a part of, but a world, nevertheless, that you at first fit into with the precision of a key to a lock or a neurotransmitter to its receptor."[1]

Slater's alluring description is a testament to how firmly the chemical-imbalance theory of depression had taken hold in 1990s America. Prozac—and its medicinal cousins, Zoloft, Paxil, and Celexa—recalibrated the amount of the neurotransmitter serotonin a person's brain needed, curing his or her depression. At least that's how these selective serotonin reuptake inhibitors (SSRIs) were marketed. Slater's description also suggests that Prozac not only undoes a person's depression, but also redoes the personality. Peter Kramer, author of the blockbuster hit *Listening to Prozac*, was the main proponent of the notion that Prozac made its consumers "better than well": "Prozac seemed to give social confidence to the habitually timid, to make the sensitive brash, to lend the introvert the social skills of a salesman."[2]

Prozac ushered in an era in which large swaths of the American public were primed to believe that psychiatric medications were designed to correct chemical imbalances in the brain—imbalances that caused psychological problems—and could even bring about desired personality changes. Pill therapy began to edge out talk therapy. In 2010, approximately 40 percent of Americans seeking mental health treatment receive psychotherapy, down from 71 percent before the advent of Prozac.[3] Attitudes toward using psychiatric drugs have become quite relaxed, reflecting in part the marketing muscle of the pharmaceutical industry.

All classes of psychiatric drugs are now big business. In 1986, the year before Prozac was released, an NIMH survey revealed that a mere 12 percent of American adults would take a pill to remedy their depression.[4] At that time, combined sales of all antidepressants hovered around $500 million.[5] Currently, more than 40 percent of Americans have used an antidepressant at least once in their lifetime, and annual sales top $11 billion.[6] Rates of antidepressant usage in the past thirty years have risen by more than 400 percent.[7]

In the 1970s and early 1980s, benzodiazepines like Xanax, Valium, and Ativan, which were used to treat anxiety and sleep problems, were publically denounced for their addictive potential. In 1978, the media were abuzz with reports that former first lady Betty Ford had checked herself into a hospital for alcohol and Valium addiction. A year later, Senator Ted Kennedy convened a congressional hearing on the dangers of benzodiazepines, declaring that they "produced a nightmare of dependence and addiction, both very difficult to treat and recover from."[8] Today, benzodiazepines have made a silent comeback. Alarmingly, they are prescribed to one in twenty American adults.[9]

Attention-deficit/hyperactivity disorder (ADHD), once strictly considered a childhood disorder, is now thought to affect 4 percent of adults.[10] Since 2010, sales of psychostimulant medications used to treat ADHD, like Ritalin and Adderall, have grown by 8 percent annually.[11] Demand for psychostimulants was so high in 2011, there was a nationwide shortage. In 2015 alone, sales had been projected to rise by 13 percent, grossing $12.9 billion.[12]

Arguably the most bewildering statistics pertain to the skyrocketing increase in prescriptions of the so-called atypical antipsychotics. The most common of these drugs are Abilify, Risperdal, Seroquel, Zyprexa, and Geodon. This class of medications was originally designed to treat psychosis and bipolar agitation—rare psychiatric conditions. Yet the atypical antipsychotics are among the most prescribed drugs in America, earning their manufacturers stratospheric profits. From 2001 to 2010, the use of these medications among adults aged twenty to sixty-four climbed 350 percent.[13] About thirty out of a thousand seniors were taking one or more of these drugs during this same time period.[14] In 2008, sixteen million prescriptions for atypical antipsychotic drugs were written in the United States. Abilify, Seroquel, and Zyprexa were among the top-selling drugs of 2010, producing $4.5, $4.2, and $3 billion in sales, respectively.[15] In 2013, Abilify was the top-selling drug in America, generating $7.2 billion in sales for Otsuka Pharmaceutical Company.[16] A year later, it slipped to number two, earning $7.8 billion.[17]

Oddly, Americans are relying more on psychiatric drugs at a time when scientific findings and investigative news reports are calling into question their safety and effectiveness. As will be shown in the pages that follow, SSRI antidepressants have not lived up to their promise. Studies show that they are no more effective in treating depression than the older, cheaper antidepressants; that they dampen sexual functioning; and that they are linked to a risk for suicidality and violence. More damagingly, large-scale studies, or meta-analyses, have even revealed that SSRI antidepressants are no more effective than placebos, or sugar pills, in the treatment of depression.

Benzodiazepine usage has been associated with addiction, cognitive impairment, and accident-proneness because of its sedative effects. Well-known potential side effects of psychostimulant usage are sleep and appetite irregularities, mood swings, and failures in cardiac functioning in people with underlying heart problems. Weight gain, adverse metabolic functioning, breast growth in boys and men, and onset of irreversible muscle spasms are all well-documented potential side effects of the atypical antipsychotics.

Several of the atypical antipsychotics, such as Abilify, Zyprexa, and Seroquel, are FDA approved for treatment-resistant depression or for use alongside a regular antidepressant that has been minimally effective. Touted by the pharmaceutical companies as "augmentation therapy," expensive atypical antipsychotics are now regularly prescribed by physicians for people whose antidepressants need backup. The average monthly cost of these drugs can reach $1,000.[18] Yet a comprehensive 2011 *Consumer Reports* study concluded: "The available evidence indicates that antipsychotics aren't very effective as augmentation therapy for treating 'resistant' depression and aren't the best choice for this use for most people."[19]

Even the widely cited chemical-imbalance theory of depression has been roundly dismissed as more of a marketing ploy than a scientific actuality. Harvard University psychiatrist Joseph Glenmullen succinctly sums this up: "There is no established biochemical imbalance for depression. There is no established gene for depression. Prescription antidepressants should not be promoted as though these hypothetical models were established."[20] Several years ago, Ronald Pies commented in *Psychiatric Times*: "My impression is that most psychiatrists who use this expression ["chemical imbalance"] feel uncomfortable and a little embarrassed when they do so. It's a kind of bumper-sticker phrase that saves time and allows the physician to write out that prescription while feeling that the patient has been 'educated.'"[21]

Reforms implemented during the Obama presidency could be rolled back by the Trump administration, which tends to oppose government regulation of the health insurance industry. Scores of lawsuits were brought against pharmaceutical companies for giving leading psychiatrists incentives to promote medications for unapproved FDA uses. The Affordable Care Act mandated that pharmaceutical companies report any promotional payments or gifts worth more than ten dollars to physicians.[22] Fading fast are the freewheeling days of the 1990s and 2000s, when drug companies paid thousands of dollars to key opinion leaders in the field of psychiatry to publish and promote favorable findings and uses of drugs to legions of fellow professionals. The FDA now requires that direct-to-consumer advertising of psychiatric drugs make only scientifically backed claims about their benefits and list all the major side effects.[23]

The public, as well as the average mental health professional, should feel confused about which psychiatric drugs have real scientific backing for what psychological conditions. Yet prescription trends suggest there's less confusion than there should be. Despite frequent news blasts about pharmaceutical companies' use of deceptive tactics to overpromote and oversell psychiatric drugs, and despite the drugs' questionable effectiveness, most laypeople and practitioners seem to lack an understanding of the historical events that led to our overreliance on pills. As we will see, although psychiatric drugs can be lifesaving for patients with disabling psychiatric problems, the medications are massively overprescribed and reports of their safety and effectiveness have been overstated.

THE PROZAC MARKETING JUGGERNAUT AND ITS AFTERMATH

In 1999, *Fortune* magazine added Prozac to its Products of the Century list, putting it in the company of penicillin, the Band-Aid, radio, television, and the World Wide Web.[24] Gary Tollefson, then president of neuroscience products for Eli Lilly, which discovered and developed Prozac, announced: "The recognition by *Fortune* underscores the critical role that Prozac has played in elevating awareness of major depression as a disorder of the brain, the importance of seeking medical evaluation and the existence of safe and effective treatment."[25] The reputation of Prozac as a safe, chemically elegant way of targeting depression by treating faulty brain chemistry appeared sealed. Prozac's name recognition had "attained the familiarity of Kleenex and the social status of spring water," according to an oft-quoted *Newsweek* piece.[26] In 2001, when its patent expired, Prozac had forty million users worldwide and generated annual sales of $2.7 billion.[27]

The marketing success of Prozac was so spectacular that the drug's marketing approach became standard operating procedure for subsequent psychiatric drug campaigns. As chronicled in a 2005 Stanford University Graduate School of Business article, Interbrand, a world leader in product branding (responsible for coming up with such recognizable names as Sony, Microsoft, Nikon, and Nintendo) was hired to find a zesty, communicable name for the blandly titled chemical compound fluoxetine hydrochloride.[28] Prozac was chosen because *pro* connoted positivity and professionalism, and *zac*, action. In the months preceding the January 1988 release of Prozac, Ken Cohen, a marketing manager at Eli Lilly, convened a series of educational meetings involving 150 of the company's leading psychiatrists and senior executives. This marketing move kicked off what was to become the standard practice of grooming key opinion leaders as prominent spokespersons when a company was launching a new drug to bolster its acceptability within the larger medical community.

Teams of drug reps were hired and meticulously prepared to familiarize doctors with the therapeutic benefits of Prozac. Cohen knew that if drug reps were to be persuasive in changing physicians' prescribing habits, the reps would have to be more than just informed— they would have to fervently believe in the product. He told Eli Lilly executives: "Personal relations with physicians are key and the reps have to believe in the drug or they will not be effective. So, for such a novel drug, the sales reps are the first customer—you have to convince them first."[29] Key opinion leaders and drug reps began disseminating identical information about the wonders of Prozac.

Prozac was considered a clean drug, targeting serotonin levels in the brain, in contrast to the so-called dirty effects of tricyclic antidepressants, or TCAs (e.g., imipramine, desipramine, and amitriptyline), the prevailing medications on the market. These older agents required that blood levels be drawn and dosages carefully monitored to gauge therapeutic effects. A 1990 *Newsweek* article picked up this theme and quoted one psychiatrist: "Instead of using a shotgun you're using a bullet."[30]

There was no presumed lethality to taking Prozac. Evidence indicated you could swallow up to three hundred capsules and only develop a stomachache. By comparison, you could swallow fewer than ten capsules of TCAs and end up dead.[31] At therapeutic levels, TCAs left many patients with headaches and blurred vision, as well as feeling bloated, sluggish, and constipated. Those taking Prozac were more likely to lose weight and feel energized.[32]

The once-a-day dosage increased treatment compliance. This fact, combined with research findings supplied by Eli Lilly showing that between 75 and 80 percent of depressed patients responded well to Prozac, positioned the drug to be widely prescribed.[33] And if it were to be widely prescribed, primary care physicians (PCPs)—that is, doctors in family practice, pediatrics, or internal medicine—not just psychiatrists, would have to develop a comfort level with the drug. Transferring the treatment of depression to PCPs, the gatekeepers of medicine, had the potential to drive the volume of drug prescriptions upward. Eli Lilly executives were well aware of this situation and capitalized on it.[34] Company-funded key opinion leaders were sent out to large PCP conferences and other medical meetings to share their expert knowledge of Prozac. Drug reps fanned out to PCP offices to make sales calls.

Before Prozac, the pharmacological treatment of depression was almost exclusively in the hands of psychiatrists. A decade after it was released, with multiple Prozac-like drugs on the market (e.g., Zoloft, Paxil, and Celexa), the pharmacological treatment of depression was now almost exclusively in the hands of nonpsychiatrist physicians. In 2001, the psychiatrist Jay Pomerantz and a team of researchers from the Massachusetts Institute of Technology analyzed data on a hundred thousand enrollees in a health maintenance organization (HMO) to obtain information on what types of doctors were prescribing antidepressant medications and why.[35] The researchers discovered that 70 percent of all antidepressants prescriptions were written by PCPs. Another 15 percent were issued by specialists, such as ob-gyns, rheumatologists, and cardiologists. The remaining 15 percent of new antidepressant prescriptions were handed out to patients by psychiatrists, the only medical specialists trained in mental health. Curiously, only 50 percent of the PCPs' antidepressant prescriptions were written to actually treat depression. The other 50 percent were written for a smorgasbord of medical ailments: fibromyalgia, migraines and other headaches, chronic pain disorder, anorexia, bulimia, gastrointestinal disorders, sleep irregularities, bladder dysfunction, smoking cessation, nocturia (frequent awaking at night to urinate), premenstrual syndrome, and premature ejaculation. Not that SSRI antidepressants are only FDA approved to treat depression. They are also considered first-line pharmaceutical agents for anxiety disorders such as obsessive-compulsive disorder, panic disorder, posttraumatic stress disorder, and social phobia.

Allen Frances, respected Duke University professor emeritus and a leading voice in the overdiagnosing of mental disorders in the United States, zeros in on PCPs' liberal prescribing habits as a central cause of mushrooming antidepressant usage. In his book *Saving Normal*, he makes this clear: "Harried PCPs are underpaid and overworked, and have minimal training in psychiatry. Convenience sometimes trumps good care, and the quickest way for them to speed the patient out of the office is to reach for prescription pad or free sample."[36] Nowadays, PCPs not only prescribe the bulk of antidepressants, but also step in to prescribe 90 percent of antianxiety drugs, 65 percent of stimulants, and 50 percent of antipsychotics.[37] PCPs are far more likely to view depression and other mental health problems as quasi-medical and treatable within their purview with medications than they are to refer a patient out for psychotherapy. According to a 2007 University of California Davis study, PCPs only refer roughly a third of their distressed patients to psychotherapists.[38]

During the Prozac era and beyond, doctors were subjected to, and enticed by, pitches from drug reps either to switch their prescribing habits over to the latest, usually more expensive, drugs on the market or to expand the treatable conditions for which a promoted drug might be used. The latter procedure is known in medicine as the *off-label* use of a drug. Even though a drug may not be FDA approved for a certain health problem, if it is judged by doctors to have medical benefits for a patient, a script can be written. In 1996, the pharmaceuticals sales force in the United States was about 45,000 strong.[39] By 2007, the figure peaked at 102,000. Today, the number of drug reps is approximately 75,000, a decline largely brought about by the medical community's greater scrutiny of abuses in the doctor-to-drug-rep relationship and the scarcity of new psychiatric drugs being released onto the market.[40]

The party line is that drug reps' sole purpose is to educate doctors. However, these reps are often hired for their good looks and charm. The agenda is more persuasion and pushing product than education. Writing for the *Atlantic*, Carl Elliott, a medical ethics commentator, once observed: "Drug reps today are often young, well groomed, and strikingly good-looking. Many are women. They are usually affable and sometimes very smart. Many give off a kind of glow, as if they had just emerged from a spa or salon."[41] Nicknamed "pharma babes" by doctors, they are often recruited from college cheerleading squads. The average annual salary of a drug rep is about $90,000, and yearly bonuses can match and even exceed an annual salary if sales goals are met.[42] In a recent YouTube interview, Gwen Olsen, a former drug-industry salesperson with fifteen years in the business and author of *Confessions of an Rx Drug Pusher*, came clean: "I was told my job was a job of education, but my job in fact was a job that was disseminating marketing information, helping to pigeonhole providers into writing prescriptions for products that would make my portfolio grow."[43]

High-prescribing doctors have special appeal for drug reps. A rep's success at altering these doctors' favorite medicines can shunt sales and profits to the rep's pharmaceutical company. Some research even shows that high-prescribing doctors rely on drug reps' expertise to gain knowledge of new drugs. A 2003 survey conducted on Blue Cross Blue Shield doctors revealed that more than half of high-prescribing doctors singled out drug reps as their main source of information about new medications.[44] Olsen confessed that she once sent a singing waiter with a bottle of champagne to deliver a dinner invitation to the office of a high-prescribing doctor. The meal cost her company $2,000, but the dividends in getting the doctor to switch over to her medication were enormous.[45] Sales tactics frequently involve discrediting a competitor's drug to which a high-prescribing doctor has taken a liking. For a spell, while touting an atypical antipsychotic medication that rivaled Zyprexa (whose weight-gain side effects were notorious), Olsen showed up at sales calls carrying a ten-pound bag of animal fat purchased from a butcher—to pull out at an opportune moment. But her tactics more often included the usual enticements: she had lavish lunches catered for doctors, bought them golf equipment, and provided tickets for sporting events.[46]

Of course, doctors' knowledge about which drugs to prescribe for what reasons is expanded and influenced by other sources besides sales reps. Publications by leading experts in the field and attendance at professional conferences rank higher as informational sources. Ironically, over the past few decades, these supposedly more objective sources of data on new psychiatric drugs have also been awash with drug-industry money. Half the top doctors earning speaker's fees of $500,000 or more from drug companies are key opinion leaders in the field of psychiatry.[47] One such opinion leader, Charles Nemeroff, the former chair of the psychiatry department at Emory University School of Medicine, is said to have earned close to $2.8 million as a speaker and consultant for a variety of pharmaceutical companies. GlaxoSmithKline reportedly paid him $960,000 to promote the antidepressants Paxil and Wellbutrin. Through his coauthorship of the American Psychiatric Association's *Textbook of Psychopharmacology*, his scholarship has influenced a generation of new psychiatrists. Any doubt about compromises to the objectivity of his scholarship because of his drug-industry financial ties was dispelled when he was forced to resign as chair of Emory's psychiatry department in December 2008 for failing to disclose his drug-industry paychecks to the university.[48]

More insidiously, hundreds of psychiatry research articles appearing in leading professional journals have been found to be the handiwork of ghostwriters hired by pharmaceutical companies to write up empirical findings favorable to their chemical products. The eminent British psychiatrist David Healy was one of the first practitioners to pull back the curtains and expose this dirty secret. In *Let Them Eat Prozac*, he describes how Pfizer retained the services of Current Medical Directions (CMD), a New York company specializing in the strategic delivery of scientific information, to coordinate the authorship of eighty-seven journal articles on the SSRI Zoloft. Healy maintains that of the fifty-five articles that were eventually accepted for publication in 2001 (in prestigious journals like the *New England Journal of Medicine, Journal of the American Medical Association,* and *American Journal of Psychiatry*), few were legitimately written by the listed authors. Common data sets and phraseology, and names of authors with ambiguous affiliations, implicated CMD staff as the likely authors. Healy suspects that as many as 50 percent of research articles in the field of psychiatry are ghostwritten in some shape or form, penned by outsiders and published under the names of prominent academics, all of whom draw paychecks from pharmaceutical companies.[49]

Beginning in 1997, patients themselves became a driving force in shaping doctors' decisions about whether to medicate and what to prescribe. That year, patients began to be primed by direct-to-consumer advertising approved by the FDA when drug companies quickly realized that key opinion leaders and drug reps were simply intermediaries and that the companies could go straight to the consumer. "Ask your doctor if *X* is right for you" became a catchphrase that emboldened patients not only to inquire about a drug, but also to directly request it. By 2007, Americans were being exposed to as many as sixteen hours of prescription drug television advertisements annually, according to a study spearheaded by Dominick Frosch in the Department of Medicine at UCLA.[50] This exposure created a demand for new drugs—a demand that doctors were inclined to satisfy. It's estimated that the average number of prescriptions for new drugs marketed through direct-to-consumer ads is nine times greater than those for the same drugs not marketed that way.[51]

In recent years, the FDA has largely ignored the cautionary statements from public interest groups like the National Academy of Medicine regarding how media ads for drugs can harm public health. The ads overstate the drugs' benefits, promoting them before long-term data is available on safety profiles. Advertising also creates a demand for newer, more expensive drugs over older, equally effective, cheaper drugs. And by medicalizing normal human unhappiness, anxiety, and distractibility, direct-to-consumer advertising drives up society's overuse of prescription medications.[52]

Instead, the FDA is poised to roll back the consumer gains made when it required pharmaceutical companies to follow broadcast ads with a detailed disclosure of all significant side effects. In early 2014, the FDA issued a request for public consent to reduce to the "serious and actionable" the list of side effects a drug manufacturer was required to insert and to allow the manufacturers simply to add this tepid disclaimer: "There are other product risks not included in the ad."[53]

DANGERS UNTOLD AND FAILED EXPECTATIONS

Prozac was heavily marketed as a safe drug. By October 1993, however, 28,623 complaints of adverse reactions had been registered with the FDA, including 1,885 suicide attempts and 1,349 deaths. This figure dwarfed the 7,000 complaints filed with the FDA by users of Valium—the most prescribed drug in America from about 1972 to 1982—over a twenty-two-year period after its release in 1963. This, despite Valium's being roundly excoriated by the medical establishment and the press alike for being extremely addictive and causing horrible withdrawal symptoms.[54]

News reports of violent acts perpetrated by individuals started on Prozac began surfacing. One such individual was Joseph Wesbecker, a worker at a Louisville printing plant. Wesbecker had a history of marital problems and work grievances. On September 14, 1989, one month after being put on Prozac, he showed up at work with an AK-47, shot eight people dead, and severely wounded twelve before killing himself. A lawsuit was brought against Eli Lilly by the victims' families, who claimed that Prozac played a role in these horrific events.[55] By 1990, fifty-four legal cases were pending, implicating Prozac in a variety of suicidal and homicidal events. Scores of similar lawsuits were brought against Eli Lilly and other manufacturers of SSRIs in the years to follow.[56]

While it is difficult, if not impossible, to ascertain the degree to which SSRIs cause relatively rare tragedies like suicide and homicidal violence, research over the years clearly shows that a sizable percentage of SSRI-medicated patients develop what has been called an *activation profile*, or *akathisia*. Trustworthy estimates suggest that anywhere between 9.7 and 25 percent of SSRI recipients develop akathisic reactions.[57] Typically, akathisia involves a general feeling of motor restlessness, agitation, jitteriness, and irritability, not dissimilar to the effects of overconsumption of caffeine. In a January 1998 feature article for the *New Yorker*, "Anatomy of Melancholy," Andrew Solomon compares the effects of Zoloft to those of drinking fifty-five cups of black coffee, and of Paxil to those of eleven cups.[58]

One line of reasoning is that SSRIs can activate patients in ways that make them feel and act out of control and thus be prone to behave self-destructively. This highly plausible point of view has been expounded by Peter Breggin—perhaps America's most vocal critique of biological psychiatry—in his myriad publications and expert legal testimony against large pharmaceutical companies. He and a band of conscientious scientists have dug deeply into Eli Lilly's unpublished data on Prozac's premarket clinical trials—data they obtained through the Freedom of Information Act. They discovered that Eli Lilly had suppressed findings indicating that approximately 38 percent of Prozac patients had developed activation symptoms. Prozac users were also six times more likely to make a suicide attempt than were placebo subjects or those placed on an older TCA antidepressant like imipramine or doxepin.[59]

The increased potential for agitation and self-harm in a person taking an SSRI, especially during the first few months that it is being used, has been officially recognized. In 2005, the FDA mandated that a black box warning (a prominent warning enclosed in a highly visible black outline on the package insert of the drug) be placed on all SSRIs, alerting the public to the increased risk for suicide associated with their usage. Below the heading "WARNINGS—Clinical Worsening and Suicide Risk" was a comprehensive list of symptoms validating potential SSRI activation effects—agitation, insomnia, irritability, aggressiveness, impulsivity, and akathisia, to name but a few. However, the black box warning pertained to SSRI usage only among children and adolescents.[60] In 2007, the FDA warning label was extended to eighteen- to twenty-four-year-olds. However, the fine print on drug brochures and media ads could now specify that there was no increased suicide risk for adults older than twenty-four and that people aged sixty-five or older had a reduced risk.[61] In reality, the verdict is still out on agitation and self-harm risks across all ages. David Healy estimates "a doubling or tripling of the risk on SSRI's compared to placebo or non-treatment."[62]

If there were such a category as a gray box warning to attach to SSRI prescription bottles, or a required notification for reduced quality-of-life side effects, sexual dysfunction should be on it. The dysfunction runs the gamut from dampened desire and weak arousal to pain during intercourse and an inability to achieve orgasm. Premarket SSRI drug trials typically report sexual difficulties in fewer than 2 to 16 percent of patients.[63] However, these rates often rely on patients' self-reporting; the people were not directly asked about sexual dysfunction. In studies where SSRI patients are directly asked about sexual matters, the rates of sexual dysfunction reach as high as 70 to 80 percent.[64] Doctors frequently advise SSRI patients to wait and see, believing that there will be a spontaneous remission of sexual problems. But recent studies show that only 8 to 10 percent of patients who develop SSI-related sexual problems regain baseline sexual functioning while remaining on the drug.[65]

Several years ago, Rebecca Stinson, a University of Iowa PhD candidate, extensively interviewed nine men and women of different ages, sexual orientation, and relationship status, asking about their experiences on an SSRI. The stories contained in her reports, sadly, are not uncommon:[66]

We were making love and all the [sic] sudden I started feeling excited. And it was really weird because I had felt nothing and I had been numb and then all the sudden I was in the moment and I was like "Wow I felt it." And then it went away. . . . It was almost like when you're trying to light a lighter and it won't come on. [from Sugar, married thirty-four-year-old heterosexual female]

There'd be times back in college, people would be trying to give me oral sex and I'd be like "If that's good for you, keep going, but I don't even care." . . . Whereas typically a guy my age would kill for any opportunity for a blow job, I'm kinda like "Well, okay. Or pizza?" [from Tom, thirty-three-year-old partnered gay male]

One woman's experience, which was written up in the *Guardian* in 2007, captures the trade-off many people relying on an SSRI face between relative emotional stability and sexual flatness. The thirty-six-year-old woman, taking Prozac for panic attacks, disclosed how it affected her: "It has cured me and calmed me, but I haven't had an orgasm since the day I started. I still want to cuddle, but beyond that, I feel no physical arousal at all. Nothing. It's a trade-off. My partner can't decide which me he prefers. The neurotic, weeping basketcase who still enjoyed sex a few times a week or the calm and collected one that's completely frigid."[67]

Helen Fisher, a Rutgers University anthropologist, even proposes that SSRIs "sap the craving for a mate—perhaps even the brain's very ability to fall in love." Together with J. Anderson Thomson, a psychiatrist at the University of Virginia, Fisher theorizes that SSRIs meddle with the brain's proper passageways to the cocktail of dopamine, norepinephrine, and serotonin that produce the feelings of elation and ecstasy surrounding falling in love. SSRIs are also known to lessen obsessive thinking, the very state of mind that allows us to be captivated by a love interest.[68] A 2002 article in the *International Journal of Neuropsychopharmacology* points to high rates of emotional blunting in SSRI-induced sexual dysfunction subjects.[69] A recent investigation substantiates the notion that SSRI usage impedes the capacity to cry over normal sad events.[70] One prominent psychiatrist with an abundance of experience treating SSRI patients describes the induced effect as "sanitizing flatness": "The emotional highs and lows are excised from experience, and one exists in a slightly foggy middle ground."[71] In *Prozac Diary*, Slater went from giddily writing, "I fell in love one day, only it was not with a person; it was with my pill," to bemoaning, "Prozac is not my lover any longer but over the very long haul has become a close friend, a slightly anemic, well-meaning buddy whose presence can considerably ease pain but cannot erase it."[72]

It's not far-fetched to extrapolate from SSRI's emotional and sexual side-effect profile that some people's capacity to feel and fall in love may be compromised. However, it's a theory that's yet to be strongly verified empirically. To date, only one study exists to back it up. In a 2004 Canadian investigation of "courtship blunting" on women taking antidepressants, researchers found that subjects taking SSRIs rated the faces of attractive men more negatively than did subjects taking no medication, and the SSRI group rushed through their viewing of the photos.[73]

The list of SSRI side effects that do have sufficient empirical validation (besides those previously mentioned) is long: nausea, dizziness, diarrhea, headaches, anxiety, insomnia, weight gain, fatigue, and lethargy.[74] Older women on SSRIs have been shown to have double the risk of bone-density loss than do their untreated peers.[75] At a 2011 American College of Cardiology meeting in New Orleans, data was presented linking SSRI antidepressant use to thicker arteries and hence to greater susceptibility for heart disease and stroke.[76] A 2012 press release by Adam Urato, chairman of obstetrics and gynecology at MetroWest Medical Center, a division of Tufts Medical Center, cited "clear and concerning evidence" that SSRI use is associated with problematic pregnancy outcomes—elevated risk of miscarriage, preterm birth, neonatal health complications, and neurobehavioral abnormalities.[77] These significant side effects might account for the high numbers (more than one-third in a 2004 study) of patients who fail to renew their initial prescriptions.[78] Sudden discontinuance of SSRI usage is itself a risk factor. There is a well-documented literature on SSRI discontinuation syndrome showing how, without steady titration off the drug, up to 20 percent of people develop flulike symptoms, strange sensory-motor experiences, and other bizarre perceptions.[79]

Bad press for the SSRIs got worse with the 2010 release of psychologist Irving Kirsch's *The Emperor's New Drugs: Exploding the Antidepressant Myth*. He collected and analyzed data from thirty-eight studies on six SSRIs (Prozac, Zoloft, Paxil, Celexa, Effexor, and Serzone). Using the Freedom of Information Act to access data on all the clinical trials submitted to the FDA by drug companies, not just those yielding positive results, Kirsch and his research team discovered that more than half of the trials showed no therapeutic benefit of an SSRI over a placebo. Their meta-analysis of the complete data pool revealed that SSRI subjects averaged a 9.6-point improvement score on the Hamilton Depression Rating Scale. Shockingly, placebo-taking subjects averaged a very close 7.8-point improvement score. The Hamilton Depression Rating Scale involves a doctor conducting a brief interview with a patient and then filling out a form rating the person on the degree of depressed mood, guilt feelings, insomnia, suicidal thoughts, and various other aspects of depression. A good or bad night's sleep can produce a 2.0-point difference. For a drug to be released on the market, the British government requires a study to produce a minimum 3.0-point difference between drug and placebo. Kirsch's meta-analysis produced a negligible 1.8 difference. However, when he and his team separated out the data on patients with severe depression, they found a clinically significant difference between drug and placebo. They concluded: "There seems little evidence to support the prescription of antidepressant medication to any but the most severely depressed patients."[80]

The reputation of antidepressant medications was further humbled by the long-awaited results from the Sequenced Treatment Alternatives to Relieve Depression (STAR*D) study. Funded by the NIMH at a cost of $35 million, the study included 4,041 outpatients with depression at forty-one clinics and hospitals across America.[81] The study was unique in that it followed real-life patients for a year; the patients had coexisting drug and alcohol problems, marital difficulties, difficult personality traits, and so forth. In that regard, STAR*D was what academics call an *effectiveness study*, as opposed to the typical efficacy study that drug companies utilize. The latter usually lasts six to eight weeks and selects ideal subjects who meet strict diagnostic guidelines.

During phase 1 of STAR*D, patients were prescribed the SSRI Celexa for three months. The original results demonstrated that only 28 percent of patients experienced full remission of their depression. The remaining 62 percent were given a different SSRI or a combination of SSRIs. By six months, if they showed little improvement, their SSRI was switched again, and lithium or a thyroid hormone was added. Those continuing to be affected by depression at the ninth-month mark were prescribed Parnate or a combination of Remeron and Effexor.

Although STAR*D investigators reported remission rates of 67 percent at the twelve-month mark, 30 to 50 percent of these patients had gotten worse when followed up a year later. The researchers had liberally estimated that 40 percent of the patients entering the trial had benefited from one or more antidepressants over a twelve-month treatment period and beyond. The data set was reanalyzed in 2009 by Allan M. Leventhal, of the Department of Psychology at American University, and several colleagues. Accounting for what they deduced was a 60 percent dropout rate, the researchers concluded that about 37.6 percent of participants got better after up to four trials of antidepressant medications. Of this cohort of 1,518, only 108, or 7.1 percent, showed sustained full remission of their depression when tracked over time in the study's free continuing care program.[82]

Exactly thirty years after the *Newsweek* cover page depicted an effervescent Prozac capsule and announced "Prozac: A Breakthrough Drug for Depression," the February 10, 2010, issue of this weekly news magazine had a cover page of a different sort. If the cover is oriented right side up, a bold white caption reads "Antidepressants Don't Work" and the center image looks like two fingers holding a pill with a crying frowny face. If the cover is turned upside down, a gray caption reads "Antidepressants Do Work," and the center image now looks like two fingers holding a pill with a smiley face. In the halls of academia and in popular media, there's growing awareness that our society has been oversold on the benefits of antidepressants. Conscientious researchers and practitioners see these drugs as having a crucial role in the treatment of severe depression but only with proper psychotherapy and social support.

Drug companies, on the other hand, seem to be operating on a different plane. The focus is not on capitulating to mounting evidence on the limited usefulness of antidepressants. It's not on restricting research and prescribing patterns to subpopulations of patients who might respond well. The new agenda is to convince all depressed patients to add an atypical antipsychotic when their SSRI fails to help. *Augmentation therapy* is the latest catchphrase.

From August 2010 to August 2011, Otsuka Pharmaceutical and Bristol-Myers Squibb spent $174 million to promote the atypical antipsychotic Abilify. The outlay by AstraZeneca to promote Seroquel was $156 million. These two atypicals accounted for 72 percent of the more than $453 million antipsychotic market promotional spending during that period.[83] The pharmaceutical industry had seized on the bad press that antidepressants were receiving and offered antipsychotics as the solution. Abilify and Seroquel were FDA approved to treat so-called treatment-resistant depression. However, the torrent of TV, Internet, and print ads for Abilify and Seroquel portrayed glum-looking, tired-eyed, otherwise sharply dressed people—think garden-variety depression. The central message was that all forms of depression should be cured with an antidepressant within weeks, and if they weren't, an antipsychotic should be tried. One Abilify ad that saturated the market depicted, in cartoon form, a fatigued-looking professional woman heading out to the office, eerily followed by a ghostlike blue robe with sad eyes. The caption read, "After 6 weeks on an antidepressant, I still couldn't shake my depression." Inscribed below was the solution: "Ask your doctor about the option of adding Abilify."[84]

The bulk of emerging research asks whether exercising that option, or adding any other atypical antipsychotic, is of much benefit for most types of depression. A 2013 *PLOS Medicine* publication by Glen Spielmans and his colleagues substantiates that conclusion. He and his research team pooled the data from fourteen studies on the treatment of depression with antipsychotic medication. Although adding an atypical antipsychotic reduced the subject's depressed mood slightly, there were no benefits over placebo in improving the person's quality of life or everyday functioning. And there were worrisome adverse side effects: substantial weight gain, sleepiness, akathisia, abnormal cholesterol levels, and impairments in metabolic functioning. Spielmans summed up his team's results: "There is little evidence of substantial benefit in overall well-being and abundant evidence of potential treatment-related harm."[85] This analysis mirrors the findings of health experts at the Oregon Health and Science University Evidence-Based Practice Center as part of the Drug Effectiveness Review Project.[86] The project is made up of experts drawn from universities and the private sector across the country to thoroughly review the evidence on drugs to inform public policy.

The lion's share of the boom in atypical antipsychotic prescriptions isn't accounted for by its governmental approval as an add-on medication for stubborn depression. The majority of scripts are written for off-label purposes. Antipsychotic treatment of anxiety disorders in adults and teenagers has doubled in recent years. The use of such medications to treat ADHD and explosive or disruptive behavior in young children and teenagers accounts for about 38 percent of all sales.[87] The US Government Accountability Office calculates that 61 percent of older dementia patients in nursing homes whose agitation levels are considered dangerous by staff are put on an atypical antipsychotic drug.[88]

In this class, the drug that is used most commonly for off-label purposes is Seroquel. Iain McGregor, a psychopharmacologist at the University of Sydney, Australia, cheekily refers to it as "the Swiss Army knife drug."[89] In 2009, AstraZeneca's legal bill topped $1.1 billion as the company defended itself against claims that its sales reps routinely pressured doctors to prescribe Seroquel for non-FDA-approved, off-label purposes.[90] In essence, marketing efforts led to a widespread tendency among doctors to start prescribing Seroquel for anxiety, agitation, and sleep problems, primarily among children, teenagers, and adults over sixty-five.

Seroquel has another distinction. It's the only atypical antipsychotic to have a street value, according to a recent publication in the prestigious journal *Psychiatry*.[91] Snorted or used intravenously on the streets, it commonly goes by the following nicknames: Quell, Susie-Q, Baby Heroin, and Q-ball. The last moniker refers to mixing Seroquel with either heroin or cocaine. Seroquel is popular among inmates; its widespread abuse in the Los Angeles County Jail has been well documented.

Casual and questionable off-label uses of atypical antipsychotics come with a hefty risk of side effects. The main risk is weight gain. Up to 70 percent of recipients gain weight, on average about twelve pounds within the first three months.[92] Atypicals have been associated with a higher risk for developing diabetes or aggravating a preexisting diabetic condition, as well as heart disease and a host of metabolic irregularities.[93]

This group of drugs was designed to reduce the extrapyramidal side effects of the older generation of antipsychotics. These are the Parkinson's-like tremors, repetitive lip smacking and facial grimacing, and wobbly gait that those of us who worked with people who had chronic mental illness used to see among those who used Haldol and

Thorazine over a long period in the 1980s. Whether the newer generation of antipsychotics measurably lessens the risk for extrapyramidal side effects is still uncertain. A 2009 Brown University School of Medicine study claims that 5.4 percent of patients on older agents will develop these side effects, compared with 0.8 percent of people put on newer agents.[94] However, some newer findings show equal risk for developing these side effects across newer and older antipsychotics.[95]

Purveyors of old-line antianxiety medications, the benzodiazepines (Valium, Xanax, and Ativan), are trying to win back the patient population that has anxiety disorders and that was inundated with SSRIs. Giovanni Andrea Fava, clinical professor of psychiatry at the State University of New York at Buffalo and an expert on this matter, recently weighed in: "There is no evidence to suggest that antidepressant drugs are more effective than benzodiazepines in anxiety disorders." Paradoxically, he added, "Certainly, benzodiazepines have fewer side effects."[96] I say "paradoxically" because thirty years ago, the SSRIs caught on because marketers capitalized on the horrible side-effect profile of the benzodiazepines: agitation, motor coordination problems, confusion, other cognitive impairments, and the drugs' notorious addiction potential. Granted, what Fava and other like-minded experts are proposing is that benzodiazepines are safe and effective when used sparingly and intermittently to help users rapidly recover from anxiety and panic.

Psychostimulants like Ritalin and Adderall are a hot new product aimed at the burgeoning population of adults thought to be afflicted with ADHD. The overprescribing of ADHD medications in children is old news. Roughly 6 percent of Americans aged seven to seventeen are on an ADHD medication.[97] The spike in prescriptions of ADHD medication for adults is fresh news. In 2012, almost 16 million ADHD drug prescriptions were issued for adults aged twenty to thirty-nine. That's almost triple the 5.6 million figure arrived at in 2007.[98] Studies show that at any given time, 4 to 14 percent of college students engage in nonprescribed psychostimulant use, typically as a "study drug" to boost concentration or as a diet pill to lose weight.[99]

All the hyped and unimpressive messages about psychiatric medications swirling around in our culture should leave any distressed person, or any treating professional, in a quandary about which medications work, for what purposes. Now more than ever, mental health consumers should question any loose definition of a psychiatric condition and casual use of medication. A smart, empowered consumer should select a physician who allots ample time and attention to explore and experiment with medication options with full disclosure about risks, benefits, and side effects.

OPINIONS AND STORIES FROM THE TRENCHES

On matters related to medications, I consider myself an uncompromising pragmatist. Philosophically speaking, I would define my pragmatism as follows: The human brain is designed to maneuver in ancient hunter-gatherer environments, to psychosocially adapt to tribes of people about 150 strong, in which everybody knows one another. This situation is a far cry from our fast-paced, technology-driven, overstimulating, globalized world. Further, we humans were not meant to live so long—perhaps until forty but certainly not ninety. Therefore, any scientifically investigated substance we can use to alter our mood, quell our anxiety, sharpen our thinking, or inhibit a potential for dangerous action is worth exploring. But a cost-benefit analysis always need to be done. Is the substance helping more than it's hurting? Does it really improve my happiness and quality of life? Does it make me more loving and lovable to those I love? Does it enhance or detract from my productivity at my chosen profession or line of work? The more mired I am in anxiety, depression, or mental confusion, the greater my need to accept the adverse side effects that all drugs have. But we should never, ever, take or keep taking a drug that makes us feel and act worse than the very condition it was meant to remedy.

My medication-related experience with clients currently in my practice is a pretty good representation of what I've encountered in my thirty years of clinical work. I'll start with SSRI success stories.

Cameron is a twenty-three-year-old man who stopped attending art school classes and began to hole up in his apartment. His parents had to fly to New York to rescue him because he refused to answer their calls and texts. They feared him dead. Cameron is an extremely talented artist. But, of late, he denigrates his work. He avoids painting and drawing because he only knows how to do it obsessively. The inferno of energy and the all-consuming commitment it takes are a setup for avoidance. With art, he's either all in or all out. One on one, in the safe confines of my office, Cameron is angst-ridden, though earnestly chatty and insightful. Outside of my office, he is mostly just angst-ridden, believing that people can see through him and into him. Cameron is afflicted with a debilitating case of social anxiety disorder and is moderately depressed on top of that. Before being placed on Celexa, he spent most of his time hidden in his bedroom at his parents' house, scouring the Internet for tidbits of information on art, music, science, and history. Cameron is a true intellectual, but shuns formal education. I can be my natural absurdist self with Cameron. He can be his natural absurdist self with me.

Months into therapy, having won his trust, I talked Cameron into visiting a psychiatrist for a medication evaluation. This was a big step, since Cameron had sworn off medication. On my day off, as prearranged, I showed up at his house and drove him to the psychiatrist's office. He walked away with drug samples that he was able to start taking immediately. Four months in, Cameron's mood is lighter. He works at his mother's accounting office two days a week, is less self-denigrating, and cooks for the family several nights a week. It would be a stretch to say Cameron is cured. He dabbles with, but mostly avoids, doing art. He has no libido (similar to before taking his SSRI), can't imagine ever having a girlfriend or getting married, and is indifferent to setting life goals. Yet, in my mind, the SSRI gives Cameron an emotional platform so that, over time, he might get traction in these areas in his psychotherapy with me.

Brian is a forty-year-old Argentinean immigrant. His wife, Joan, convinced him to see me under the guise of consulting about parenting their two daughters more effectively. It's patently clear to me that Joan yearns for Brian to take a liking to therapy so he might learn to be less curmudgeonly, irritating, irritable, and explosive with the children. Brian's resistance to therapy is so strong I get the sense that each visit might be his last. That is, until he decided it was time to get back on Prozac, which he has been taking off and on most of his adult life. On Prozac, Brian is less reactive, irritable, and irritating.

He smiles more. He appreciates that marriage is a give and take. He's more decent and accepts that everyday niceties are necessary to endear himself to Joan. Brian, though, is far from cured. He has few friends, because he perceives most people as pretentious and self-involved. He can be black-and-white in his thinking in ways that come across as overbearingly opinionated. And although he says he loves Joan and is even more affectionate with her than she is with him, his interactions with her in my office are mostly brusque.

Stella's case is more typical of my clients' SSRI experiences, where the benefits are ambiguous. She's a fifty-three-year-old public defender who has dedicated herself to the rights of battered women and impoverished people. Her soon-to-be ex-husband, Mitchell, runs a small law firm. Stella is an exercise fanatic and looks at least a decade younger than her chronological age. Despite being attractive, articulate, ambitious, and a dedicated mother to her college-bound daughter, Stella is highly self-doubting. Historically, she has deferred to Mitchell and felt defenseless against his accusations that she's cold and unloving.

A few years before beginning to meet with Stella alone, I saw her and Mitchell for marital therapy. To me, Mitchell was perpetually oblivious to Stella's need to withdraw for self-protective reasons, given his thinly disguised contempt for her. Mitchell also seemed unable to distinguish between Stella's benign wish for a fuller independent life, just to be personally satisfied, and a malicious desire to reject him.

Stella and Mitchell argued frequently about sex. Or at least Mitchell rattled off a litany of complaints that Stella earnestly tried to hear and acknowledge. Mitchell saw no reason why Stella, even as a woman in midlife, should not show up at the front door to greet him naked, just wearing a raincoat. Or be sexually revved up every other night for romance. Stella heard Mitchell out and made good-faith efforts to be more sexual. During marital therapy sessions, Mitchell showed little insight into how his compulsive work habits, scant few hobbies, and fears about aging and physical decline made him fixate on sex.

Before Stella and Mitchell mutually agreed to divorce, Stella was on Lexapro for about three years. It clearly gave her an emotional buffer. She was less weepy and woe-is-me. With her fitness goals and high level of professional responsibility, Stella seemed more able to maintain motivation. However, I always suspected that Lexapro kept her in a bad marriage, sapping her of that quotient of despair and frustration necessary to take decisive action. Or, depending on one's perspective, it helped her tolerate a bad marriage until her daughter was heading off to college and thereby less affected by parental divorce. Lexapro might have contributed to Stella's low sex drive, helping her avoid intimacy with Mitchell, whom she truly didn't love. Or Lexapro might have lowered her sex drive and impeded greater intimacy with Mitchell, whom she needed to love for the time being. Whatever the medication's role, at this moment she is off Lexapro and in a highly sexual relationship with a new boyfriend.

In my experience, the activation risks associated with SSRI use in young adults are valid. Recently I found myself in the middle of two cases involving harrowing events. Catherine is a nineteen-year-old woman who dropped out of college and became somewhat reclusive at home. She is, however, energized enough to take a long Metrolink train ride through downtown Los Angeles to a remedial writing class four days a week. She also exercises regularly and assists with household chores. Despite our weekly psychotherapy sessions, Catherine's inertia, irritability, and isolation lingered. In consultation with her parents, we decided it was time to pursue an antidepressant option. Catherine's long-term pediatrician put her on forty milligrams of Prozac. Out of the blue, within a week, Catherine started sneaking a steak knife to her bedroom and cutting her thighs, just below her buttocks, where the incisions could be hidden. She had never engaged in such behavior previously. Cutting became an odd obsession for Catherine. I upped her therapy sessions and carefully monitored the potential lethality of her actions. During sessions, she showed me morbid lyrical poems she had penned, glamorizing blood and death. I put a call into Catherine's pediatrician, who immediately titrated back her dosage to twenty milligrams. Catherine's cutting behavior faded as quickly as it had emerged.

The other case involves thirteen-year-old James, the adopted son of a professional couple. James comes across as arrogant and aloof, pulling out all the stops to get his way at home and at school. He is, nonetheless, whip smart and impishly charming. His progress in therapy is slow and incremental. The slow pace is to be expected, given that James's difficulties reflect challenging personality traits. Perpetually seeking untried solutions, James's well-meaning parents took him to his pediatrician, who wrote a script for Zoloft, unbeknownst to me.

Later that week, during a family therapy session, James recounted menacing thoughts he had been too frightened to reveal. Prodded by his parents, and with a wide-eyed, terrified look, James confessed that at home the night before, he had felt the urge to go downstairs, pick up a knife, and stab his mother. Some inquiry on my end revealed the Zoloft use. I mentioned the activation effects that can occur with Zoloft, about which James's well-educated parents were already privy. Within weeks of being tapered off Zoloft, James's menacing fantasies cleared up.

Two patients typify my experiences with clients on atypical antipsychotics. Both were prescribed Seroquel as teenagers, but now that they are in their early to mid-twenties, they no longer have a therapeutic need for it. Gwen, a twenty-six-year-old college graduate, was prescribed Seroquel from about age seventeen through nineteen. She has been in therapy with me continuously since age sixteen, and I have followed her through many trials and tribulations. During her teenage years, there were more trials than tribulations. Gwen and her parents had a very volatile relationship. Screaming matches were a common feature of family life back then. Gwen defied her parents and sneaked around with boys who were academic underachievers and known drug users. She switched high schools twice because conflicts with peers left her feeling socially alienated. On Seroquel, she was still explosive, but her rages were less frequent and less intense. She slept better, even though she felt sluggish in the morning. Once out of the house and away at college, she stopped using Seroquel, because of the logistics of attending psychiatric appointments and filling prescriptions. While she was in college, the explosive behavior of her teenage years greatly abated, and today it is almost unseen. Seroquel probably allowed her to adapt to a highly volatile parent-adolescent relationship, mitigating the emotional harm all the way around. Its therapeutic effects were bidirectional. The less emotionally reactive

Gwen was with her parents, the less counterreactive they were with her. It would not be wholly inaccurate to say that Seroquel effectively treated the relationship.

Brandon is a twenty-two-year-old grocery clerk whom I started seeing when he was a seventeen-year-old senior at a local Catholic high school. Until his teenage years, Brandon was an altar boy, a scout, a classical-piano player, and a general do-gooder. When his parents brought him to see me, he was dressed like a Goth. His eyes were obscured by his hair, his affect was glum, and he mumbled his responses. Some days, Brandon was upbeat, communicative, socially engaged, and friendly with his parents. Other days, he looked sullen and dejected; he isolated himself and was downright hostile with his parents.

One weekend, his parents became so alarmed by his behavior, they stuffed him in the car and drove him to a local psychiatric hospital. He was admitted and placed on an SSRI and Seroquel. The situation there deteriorated. Brandon was rehospitalized twice after this episode, each time his medications altered to fit the drug preferences of whichever psychiatrist happened to be on duty. For the better part of a year, Brandon was constantly in crisis. His moodiness, irritability, mental sluggishness, and nihilistic attitudes worsened. At one point, Brandon was on Seroquel, Risperdal, and Lexapro. When he turned eighteen and was nearing time to graduate from high school, he became enamored by the idea of joining the military. A recruiter hinted that Brandon might have trouble because of his psychiatric history. Legally an adult now, the young man pleaded with his psychiatrist to taper off his medications.

Fast forward to today. Brandon has been off all medications for about four years. He is gunning for a middle-management position at the grocery store he has worked at all along. He prides himself on being financially self-sufficient. He just broke up with his live-in girlfriend, whom he was with for two years. Brandon's mood is mostly stable. He can set meaningful life commitments and follow through with them and is a loyal, mostly kind son to his parents, whom he visits every weekend. Retrospectively, perhaps the drug cocktail that Brandon was taking had made him temporarily mentally ill, when before this, he had just been emotionally troubled.

Cases of long-term benzodiazepine use are nonexistent in my practice. The standard situation is usually a teenager or an adult who is facing sudden-onset trauma or a short-term source of anxiety and who needs immediate relief. Recently, for instance, Samantha, a thirteen-year-old girl for whom I provide family therapy, suddenly without warning refused to attend school. She went from being an emotionally explosive girl to an emotionally implosive one. She became uncharacteristically anxious, self-doubting, and overly concerned about the opinions of others. Some mornings, she writhed around on her bedroom floor, sobbing and complaining of fears of vomiting should she be called on by the teachers. Other mornings, she appeared stressed, but climbed into the car anyway, determined not to miss school, only to refuse to exit the car on arrival. Her parents, high-achieving doctors, were deeply concerned that Samantha would fall so far behind academically, there'd be no catching up. We all acknowledged these episodes were anxiety attacks without any apparent traumatic cause. Samantha's parents lobbied a colleague to prescribe a small number of Ativan pills for Samantha. They doled them out to her over a two-week period, only on the mornings or nights she seemed especially distressed and incapacitated. Within two weeks, the anxiety attacks passed and Samantha resumed normal attendance at school.

Over the years, I have treated hundreds of children and teenagers on ADHD medications, and I have written books and articles on the subject. Rarely do I see an adult on ADHD medications, and when I do, it's usually a young adult who was off drugs in the transition to college from high school and who hit a wall academically and quickly resumed usage. Typically, a young man with disorganized study and work habits and low test scores will confront the reality of his condition. Many teenagers who have true ADHD have spent much of their childhood years capitulating to parents' and teachers' demands to take their medications. In the transition to college, the young person can express freedom and individuation by toying with discontinuing medications he or she may really need. Once on ADHD medications again, that young adult often uses them more judiciously. For example, the student might take the medication only on heavy study days or when important quizzes and tests come up. Often, the real issue is client's getting a psychiatrist to agree to this scaled-back use of an ADHD medication.

In my experience, then, medications definitely have a place for people who manifest true psychiatric disorders or transitory collapses in their ability to function well, given the people and life situations with which they are stuck. Nevertheless, medications are massively overprescribed because the pharmaceutical industry's profitability depends on the casual abnormalizing of everyday unhappiness, sadness, shyness, aggression, forgetfulness, and distractibility. Of all the things an incapacitated patient can do, the best is to locate a medical doctor who will be a sort of pharmacological collaborator, someone who will suggest and experiment with options in light of their expertise, with full openness to hear about a person's good and bad experiences on a drug. And of course, this professional is willing to switch agents, adjust dosage, or discontinue usage, depending on a patient's solicited disclosures.

CHAPTER FOUR

Managed Care-Lessness

IN HIS 2008 BOOK, *Eleven Blunders That Cripple Psychotherapy in America*, the maverick mental health reformer Nicholas Cummings urged psychologists to take their heads out of the sand and confront troubling new health insurance trends that affected their professional autonomy: "Psychotherapy's decline has paralleled the ascendance of the biomedical revolution, and no lamenting and gnashing of teeth will bring back the golden era of psychotherapy, which, believe it or not, was in the 1950s. Ever since that dizzying climb, we have been sliding downhill like hapless snowboarders, a plunge that began escalating in the 1980s."[1]

One reason for the "dizzying climb" he refers to was the fortuitous impact of indemnity insurance plans on the practice of psychotherapy. Well into the 1970s and early 1980s, these plans dominated the health insurance landscape. They allowed practitioners to have a hands-off, fee-for-service arrangement with a health insurer. In other words, practitioners made clinical determinations—in concert with their clients—about the kind and amount of psychotherapy called for and billed the insurer directly. Coverage was largely unrestricted. Insurers mostly paid whatever the therapists deemed the value of their services were worth, as long as this figure loosely squared with industry standards. Clients were free to pick a therapist of their own choosing. Naturally, this system favored the professional autonomy of therapists and liberal amounts of therapy to those who viewed it as a means to a more fulfilling existence.

The plunge in quality and quantity of psychotherapy Cummings alludes to can be traced to the advent of managed-care health insurance plans. President Nixon signed the Health Maintenance Organization Act into law in 1973. It set in motion government and private sector financial partnerships to restructure the way health care was delivered and financed in the United States. In the 1980s and 1990s, large managed-care outfits arose, contracting with doctors and other professionals, ostensibly to provide services to patients more efficiently and more cost-effectively. So-called utilization procedures were implemented, requiring therapists to submit detailed treatment plans to reviewers so that psychotherapy sessions could be approved and paid for. By the late 1990s, the mental health services of more than 75 percent of Americans were being handled by managed-care insurance companies.[2]

An almost identical percentage of psychologists reported in a 1998 survey that managed care had negatively affected their work.[3] New bureaucratic requirements infringing on the professional autonomy of therapists became commonplace. Caps on the number of allowable psychotherapy visits were the norm. I remember when I was a newly minted licensed psychologist in 1998 having to fax treatment plans after each batch of three sessions to Good Samaritan Hospital in Los Angeles, with which I had a managed-care contract. I substantiated and identified a diagnosis, checked off levels of symptom severity, and commented on any suicidality or substance abuse problems. I also documented how due consideration was given to referring out for a medication evaluation and commented on how long therapy was projected to last. Finally, I wrote up a handful of treatment goals. My favorite treatment goal at the time was "decrease emotional constriction." It reflected my resistance to the behaviorally oriented managed-care zeitgeist. Identifying a goal that implied that human problems could be caused by repressed emotions allowed me to preserve a modicum of professional integrity.

Days would pass before I received a return fax authorizing the next batch of three sessions. The uncertainty of the outcome prevented me from really settling in with clients who had this insurance coverage. It curbed the formation of a real connection with these clients and kept the therapy shallow and practical. It also placed artificial pressure on me to *upcode*, or worsen, a client's diagnosis to maximize the chances that a utilization review bureaucrat would approve of much-needed additional psychotherapy. Some clients were profoundly uneasy about potential compromises in confidentiality by my supplying sensitive information to insurance personnel. A more severe diagnosis might get them the needed psychotherapy, but what if the information was being stored in a data bank that could be breached? Could the information be used in discriminatory ways against them?

Of the scores of calls and other contacts with managed-care utilization reviewers that transpired, I don't recollect ever having had one compassionate, meaningful, clinically rich exchange about a client. I developed the hardened assumption that the procedures in place to evaluate whether additional psychotherapy sessions were medically necessary were of the red-tape variety in the truest sense. It didn't seem to matter whether I conscientiously rewrote and submitted a treatment plan or kept the same information on it as before, just whiting out the old date and adding the new one. Most of the time, additional sessions were approved. That is, they were OK'd if I had documented the obligatory referral to a psychiatrist to get a client on medication or made a convincing case for why this step was not taken. Utilization review, in which a watchful eye was kept over the number of allowable psychotherapy visits, seemed to be a mere formality that was not in the best interests of the client or the treatment, and was not consistent with my preferred ways of ethically conducting psychotherapy. Rather, utilization review was a thinly disguised way of rationing care.

PROFITS OVER QUALITY CARE

Mental health remains the stepchild of the health-care system despite valiant efforts by state and federal authorities to enact parity legislation requiring insurance companies to fund mental health care using the same standards that exist for medical conditions. By mid-2017, it was unclear if, or to what degree, the Trump administration and Republican-controlled Congress would mandate coverage of mental health conditions in their health-care proposals. The latest data out of Harvard Medical School indicates that spending on mental health care in recent decades has grown at half the pace of regular medical health care.[4] The United States shells out about $113 billion a year on mental health treatment, with approximately half of that amount covering the cost of psychiatric drugs. Expenditures on mental health care account for only 5.6 percent of the total health-care budget. We are outperformed by Egypt, which allocates 9 percent of its health-care budget to mental health services. The 5.6 percent figure is substantially lower than what it was in 1986 (7.2 percent) and 2005 (6.1 percent).[5] Richard Frank, professor of health economics at Harvard Medical School, and his research colleagues have documented these trends and concluded: "Traditional mental health services are simply not sharing in the vigorous growth of the health care sector in the United States."[6] By "traditional mental health services," they really mean outpatient and inpatient psychotherapy, because whatever spending growth that has occurred in the mental health sector is largely attributable to prescription drug costs.

The underfunding of psychotherapy occurs at a time when average annual health premiums for families have risen by 20 percent from 2011 to 2016.[7] Meanwhile, medical insurers' earnings have skyrocketed. In 2014 alone, Aetna's profits soared 15 percent, to $594.5 million.[8] UnitedHealth Group's midyear revenues in 2016 totaled $46.5 billion, a $10 billion increase over that of the same time period in 2015.[9] Where, then, are employees' health insurance dollars going if so little of their premiums is allocated to their psychotherapy coverage? Elisabeth Rosenthal, the *New York Times* reporter whose "Paying Till It Hurts" column garnered attention for exposing abuses in the health-care system, cuts to the chase: "The biggest bucks are currently earned not through the delivery of care, but from overseeing the business of medicine."[10] She cites studies suggesting that anywhere between twenty and thirty cents of every dollar people spend on health-care premiums is absorbed as an administrative expense. That's about twice the administrative cost allocation of any other developed nation. In comparison, administrative costs absorb about only one cent of every Medicare dollar.

Administrative costs for commercial health-care insurers include everything from compensating accountants, investors, and lobbyists to protect profits; paying for the army of workers who review medical claims and the billing- and insurance-related paperwork this generates; and, of course, bankrolling CEO compensation packages. In his recent book *America's Bitter Pill*, Steven Brill, a Yale University public interest lawyer, describes the administration-heavy distribution of US health insurance premiums: "We've created a system with 1.5 million working in the health insurance industry but with barely half as many doctors providing the actual care."[11] The Physicians for a National Health Program estimates that $375 billion is wasted every year on billing and insurance-related paperwork, which would be eliminated if America shifted to a single-payer system of health coverage operated by the government.[12] Between 2012 and 2013, the average compensation package for the top nine health insurance CEOs climbed by more than 19 percent, to nearly $13.9 million.[13] Aetna CEO Mark Bertolini received an eye-popping compensation package of $41 million in 2016.[14] At a respectable fee of $100 an hour, that would amount to forty-one thousand psychotherapy sessions, or more than two thousand people getting a decent twenty-session dose of psychotherapy.

Of course, psychotherapy fees for practitioners who rely on managed-care payments are far from respectable. The current allowable amount that Blue Shield of California pays psychologists for a sixty-minute psychotherapy session is $70, which is about what a midlevel therapist charged in 1980.[15] In 2014, Medicare paid psychologists $86 for a forty-five-minute therapy session, down 35 percent from $102 in 2001.[16] Between 1990 and 2009, the average reimbursement rate for a psychotherapy session dropped from $81 to $54, a 33 percent decline.[17] When I was an Anthem Blue Cross provider several years ago, I was notified that the customary payment for a forty-five-minute psychotherapy session would be raised $2, to $94. This was the first rate increase in thirty years. These figures apply to psychologists, who typically are reimbursed by insurers $10 to $20 more

per session than are master's-level providers like licensed clinical social workers or marriage and family therapists.

The public is woefully unaware that behind the scenes, insurance
companies have substantially lowered reimbursement payments or
kept them flat. Employees are often bamboozled by employers who in
their attempt to bring down the costs of health insurance premium negotiate less expensive plans where the mental health coverage is carved
out. What employees, and even employers themselves, fail to realize is
that health-care organizations known as *behavioral health carve-outs* are
notorious for slashing psychotherapy reimbursement rates.

Carve-outs are the bad-debt buyers and used-car dealers of the
health insurance industry. Typically, a large insurer like Aetna, Humana, or Anthem Blue Cross will withhold 25 percent or more of
every health-care premium dollar for administration and profit and
negotiate a reduced rate with a carve-out to cover the mental health
needs of its subscribers.[18] Of that reduced rate, the carve-out then ex-
tracts its own amount for administrative costs and profits, leaving a
sparse sum of money to pay for the actual delivery of mental health
services. In the late 1990s, as behavioral health carve-outs prolifer-
ated, James Wright, an industry auditor, reported that he rarely encountered a managed behavioral-health-care company that kept less
than 50 percent of its negotiated amount with a large insurer for its
own administrative costs and profit.[19]

As expected, working with these lean figures, carve-outs were
compelled to aggressively underfund and ration care. They did this
with tactics like restricting an enrollee's access to treatment though
provider panels filled with less experienced therapists vulnerable to
accepting lower payments. When asked about this phenomenon, Steven Hayes, chair of the Department of Psychology at the University
of Nevada, once asserted: "The 'lowest competent provider' is now
the rule of the day."[20] Master's-level therapists on panels usually out-
number more-educated doctoral-level therapists by a ratio of five to
one.[21] Then and now, insurance industry bureaucrats know there will
be a revolving door, a ready supply of beginning-level, underworked
mental health professionals to fill their provider networks. The over-
abundance of practitioners in the field allows carve-outs to keep fees

low and oversight requirements stringent, knowing that disenchanted therapists who move off their network are replaceable.

Since the original insurer assumes responsibility for covering the cost of prescription medication, carve-outs push pills over psycho-therapy as the preferred intervention.[22] To this end, carve-outs bom-barded clinicians with preauthorization requests and strict utilization review requirements before approving and paying for psychotherapy sessions. Things improved somewhat with the passage of the 2008 Mental Health Parity and Addiction Equity Act and its expansion un-der the Affordable Care Act, making it unlawful to restrict mental health care more tightly than medical health care was restricted. Now-adays, the fallback strategies that carve-outs rely on to control costs involve pushing medications; insisting that mental health profession-als abide by evidenced-based treatments that underscore short-term, cognitive behavioral, solution-focused approaches; and skimping on reimbursement rates.

Several years ago, LifeSync, Humana's behavioral health carve-out, cut psychologists' rates from $80 to $54 a session in Illinois. This rate had the ugly distinction of being the lowest offered to psychologists of any private health insurer in America. The American Psychological Association (APA) stepped in and demanded that the Illinois Depart-ment of Insurance investigate whether this cut violated parity laws insofar as the slashed reimbursement rates decimated mental health networks panels, leaving patients without access to quality mental health care in a way that was dissimilar to patients seeking quality medical care.[23] Corporate greed was at play. In 2015, Humana's reve-nue was expected to rise 10 percent over the previous year's revenue, to $54 billion.[24]

A fee-related, breach-of-contract legal case initiated in 1998 by the Virginia Academy of Clinical Psychologists and the APA against the behavioral health carve-out ValueOptions and CareFirst Blue Cross/ Blue Shield was settled in 2003.[25] It involved a cut in psychologists' fees of greater than 30 percent, which resulted in more than one hundred therapists exiting the mental health panel, leaving some 360 patients without a provider. Again, corporate greed was suspected. The mental health coverage of about thirty-two million Americans is overseen by

ValueOptions, and projections of its revenue in 2014 edged upwards of $1.5 billion.[26]

Managed behavioral-health-care plans advertise their provider panels as being larger and more stable than they actually are. Magellan Health Insurance Company, a giant in the field, services the mental health needs of more than fifty million Americans and reportedly contracts with sixty-seven thousand providers nationwide.[27] However, in the words of Russ Newman, the APA's leading public-relations spokesperson, "when a consumer tries to access the promised benefit, he or she finds that many of the health professionals on the provider list are simply 'phantoms' of managed-care marketing and not really available."[28] In 2010, the *Wall Street Journal* ran a story in which an advocacy group called all thirty-four psychiatrists on Magellan's list of providers in Denver and Boulder, Colorado, with troubling results. Twenty-three either had dropped their contract or were unavailable. Four had moved offices or changed phone numbers. Two failed to return messages. One happened to be a kidney specialist, not a psychiatrist. Of the thirty-four, only four were actively taking on new Magellan plan members.[29] In another instance, a suit was recently filed in the Los Angeles County Superior Court against Anthem Blue Cross for selling plans touting large provider networks, when in reality the practitioners available for new appointments was much smaller.[30]

If you are a therapist, it stands to reason that if you are underpaid and overbureaucratized, you will only remain on a provider panel as long as it makes good economic sense. A colleague of mine told me recently that he only maintains his Magellan contract to add clients when his case load is frightfully low. The $70-per-session reimbursement rate ($20 of which is a client copayment) from Magellan is a disincentive to routinely take on new cases. Sadly, when he responds to a Magellan patient's request for treatment, the person on the other end of the phone is simply happy to have received a return call. Nine times out of ten, my colleague is quick to clarify that he is not taking on new Magellan clients. Sometimes, this brief conversation prompts my colleague and the disappointed would-be client to have a "strange bonding moment." My colleague can empathize with the trials of finding a Magellan in-network provider. An emotional connection is made over this difficulty. My colleague will then do something his Magellan contract forbids. He will probe to see if the caller is willing to pay a $20 or $30 administrative fee over and above the $20 copayment to compensate for Magellan's bottom-line reimbursement of $50. Given that the caller generally feels understood at this point, is aghast to learn how the insurance company shortchanges therapists, and feels desperate to find an in-network provider, therapy is launched. In my experience, these backroom deals shifting additional costs for psychotherapy to the client are more common than otherwise.

In addition, under managed care and especially managed behavioral health care, the practice of psychotherapy has been radically altered. Long gone are the days of indemnity insurance coverage when therapists had relative control over their own fees and the type and length of psychotherapy. University of Maryland public policy researchers Lisa Sanchez and Samuel Turner sum up the transformation, where neither outcome is really desirable: "The monetary and professional incentives have shifted from encouraging the delivery of more services to fewer people to encouraging the delivery of fewer services to more people."[31] From 1998 to 2007, the average number of annual psychotherapy visits in America dropped 20 percent, from 9.7 to 7.9 visits.[32] In 1988, an average therapy session lasted fifty-five minutes. Within fifteen years and under managed care, the average length of a therapy session was only thirty-four minutes.[33] In the past ten years, psychotherapy referrals by physicians have fallen by nearly 50 percent, even though figures confirm that mental health problems are on the rise.[34] Almost every patient discharged from a psychiatric hospital used to receive an outpatient psychotherapy referral. These days, only about 10 percent of these vulnerable souls received such a referral.[35]

Not only are Americans getting less therapy, but its quality is also declining. Forcing millions of people onto network provider panels takes the element of choice away from them. In one study of consumer preferences in service delivery, choice of therapist ranked second in importance, leading the investigators to assert that "selection of a compatible psychotherapist may be one of the most crucial decisions a prospective client can make given the well-established importance of the therapeutic relationship."[36] Choosing a therapist is not like choosing a mechanic, plumber, or carpenter. As with romantic relationships, there has to be chemistry, trust, and a good fit. A system that restricts a client's access to a broad range of well-compensated, available providers and that makes a person jump hoops to be seen in therapy lessens the likelihood an individual will find the right therapist for himself or herself.

A former APA president, Dorothy Cantor, faults managed care for turning the role of the psychologist into an active director, when it was once mainly an informed listener.[37] All the structural forces discussed above work against therapists' embodying the perennial ingredients of good therapy: empathy, patience, tact, and careful and caring listening. Instead, the circumstances compel therapists to embody a hasty, take-charge, teacher-like, and impatient approach to therapy. This tone is captured in the therapy guidelines that Optum (UnitedHealth Group's mental health carve-out subsidiary) distributes to its members: "A plan to achieve symptom reduction and rapid stabilization will be achieved."[38]

SHAME ON KAISER PERMANENTE

Frank had long since settled into retirement from a thirty-year career as a mental health professional at Kaiser Permanente by the time I interviewed him at his home during a particularly warm Southern California summer a few years ago.[39] He had been hired in the late 1960s, when Kaiser not only promised, but actually provided, a generous amount of psychotherapy to its subscribers. At that time, one of Kaiser's very own psychologists, Nicholas Cummings, had just released a landmark study of medical cost offsets. The study revealed how ready access to psychotherapy reduces costs related to medical and surgical services because a large percentage of people show up in the doctor's office without a recognizable physical illness. For these people, stress is the real culprit. Cummings concluded that access to ample psychotherapy reduces the overuse of more costly medical and surgical services.

In the 1970s and 1980s, Frank recalled facing no protest from administrators when he provided open-ended psychotherapy to many of the patients assigned to him. About a third of his case load paid a nominal fee to see him for twenty or more visits a year. Nearly one in five of the patients who crossed the threshold into his office obtained weekly visits with him lasting a year or longer. Frank was able to practice with relative autonomy, making his own clinical judgments regarding what problems were amenable to short- versus long-term individual therapy or to group therapy. Most of all, Frank remembered feeling at liberty to establish caring relationships with patients, to listen at length to their agonizing life stories. There was little top-down pressure to rush the therapy.

The treatment culture in Frank's psychiatry department changed radically in the 1990s. Frank summed up the transformation: "It became a medication-management, crisis-intervention model, not a real psychotherapy model." Clinicians were forced to allot more and more time slots each week for new patients. To absorb the increased volume, he had to schedule the days he met with existing patients further and further apart. When a patient was in a state of distress, Frank might schedule weekly psychotherapy visits for a month and ensure that the patient met with a staff psychiatrist for a medication evaluation. Beyond that, monthly or twice-monthly psychotherapy visits were the norm. Therapy often fizzled out, the long waits between sessions being insufficient to motivate patients to return.

During team meetings and clinical consultations, there was pressure to frame clients' life problems as manageable and solvable. Discussions about failed marriages, impossible bosses, being stuck in the wrong career, childhood trauma, or feeling empty and adrift in one's life were to be avoided. Better that the verbal exchange in the consulting room center on journaling and changing negative thought patterns, the importance of good sleep hygiene, and attending Alcoholics Anonymous meetings. Frank lamented the change: "When the pressure is on getting people out the door, you compromise your training. You don't invite patients to have any kind of relationship with you. You distort the nature of their problem by making it small and manageable, by sanitizing it and saying it isn't a big problem. You effectively discourage them from continuing in therapy."

With a look of consternation, Frank confessed he often found himself in the dubious role of convincing patients that brief therapy had solved their problems and that there was no need to continue. In truth, the patient needed more therapy, but the Kaiser system was not designed to provide it. He would have preferred to be honest, to tell his patients, "You need more therapy, but we can't give it to you here," rather than, "You're OK. You don't need any more therapy." Whereas Frank believed that the Kaiser mental health system was de facto one of crisis intervention and medication management (in his estimation performing this package of services well), this was not the type of product the marketing department pitched to subscribers. Typically, Kaiser insurance plans indicated that subscribers were eligible for twenty or more psychotherapy visits annually. Presumably, the marketing department was aware of the questionable ethics involved in putting anything on record suggesting Kaiser insurance plans discriminated against people with more serious, chronic psychological difficulties requiring long-term treatment. However, by adding more subscribers while keeping staffing low, Kaiser was forcing mental health professionals to turn over patients quickly. Frank recalled how only a small minority of patients ever actually received twenty psychotherapy visits a year. Even though the Kaiser plans were advertised as offering a full range of psychological services to individuals regardless of the severity of their problems, the system was not set up to make good on this promise.

During the latter years of his long tenure at Kaiser, Frank was perplexed, on a purely economic level, by the bias against long-term individual therapy: "There are those patients who need an attachment with a therapist. They don't get better, but they also don't get worse, because if they get worse, they enter the medical system, which is much more costly. It's better to offer long-term care to those who need it and use it well than to deny it to them, only to have them get worse and need hospitalization or seek out medical doctors—by far the more expensive options."

Since Frank's retirement a handful of years ago, Kaiser's mental health system of care has gone from overburdened to terribly overburdened. I have learned from multiple sources that the quantity and quality of individual psychotherapy offered has been seriously compromised. One of these sources, Anne, recently completed a year-long psychology internship at a Southern California Kaiser department of psychiatry. She informed me that it was standard practice for new patients to arrive for an intake appointment expecting a therapy session, only to have the intake worker, rather impersonally, pass out paperwork to be filled out. This paperwork was used to determine whether the client was in crisis and urgently needed a medication evaluation and an appointment with a therapist within a week or two, or whether he or she could be referred to one of the numerous groups available in the department. Each of the groups met weekly for two to three months and was highly structured, or what Anne called "psychoeducational": "The group leader took charge, passed out worksheets, and did most of the talking about what panic disorder, anxiety, depression, or some other clinical problem looked like and how to cope with it. There was very little real sharing about real-life problems going on between group members." Because every therapist on staff had to make room for seven or more new patients each week, conditions favored speedy group referrals to prevent therapists' caseloads from becoming completely unmanageable. Anne chuckled telling me about fellow therapists confiding in her they had trouble putting a face to a patient's name and keeping track of patients' personal information.

It turns out Anne's characterization of a Kaiser mental health environment dominated by impersonal intake sessions, brevity of contact, lengthy waits between therapy visits, high patient turnover, and speedy referrals to structured group interventions is widespread in the Kaiser system. It even led one Northern California Kaiser therapist to quip, "Kaiser treating clinicians are more like greeters than treaters."[40]

A spotlight was cast on these substandard care issues when the National Union of Healthcare Workers polled 350 Kaiser mental health providers and published the blistering results in a November 2011 document: *Care Delayed, Care Denied: Kaiser Permanente's Failure to Provide Timely and Appropriate Mental Health Services*.[41] Nearly 85 percent of responders indicated they were either "very dissatisfied" or "dissatisfied" with "your patients' access to timely mental health appointments." Regarding return appointment availability, 65 percent of clinicians were unable to schedule visits within ten days, the California state requirement since passage of AB 2179, the so-called timely-access

law. It required HMOs to provide initial and follow-up appointments
to mental health patients within ten business days. The average wait
time for return patients was seventeen business days. Upwards of 50
percent of those surveyed reported that patients were "frequently" or
"very frequently" "assigned to group therapy even though individual
therapy may be more appropriate." Many clinicians complained about
how curtailed and impersonal Kaiser's intake procedure for incoming
patients was, often involving the patients' being shuttled in groups
into a room to fill out forms for twenty or thirty minutes. One patient
went on record about her experience as a first-time patient:

> I *finally* got into the Kaiser Mental Health group in mid April. I was
> *so* relieved that day—Oh my God, I'm finally going to get help. It
> was the biggest joke of an appointment I've ever had and I left there
> worse off than I had been, which I didn't think was possible (basically
> the lady I met with, who was very nice, just read over the paperwork
> I had filled out and told me I had to go schedule appointments to see
> the "real doctors" that could help me).[42]

At Kaiser's Oakland, California, facility, an information sheet with
the following statements was being distributed to patients: "We offer
brief, problem- and solution-focused individual counseling. Research
shows many people improve in a single visit. For others, three to six
visits can produce desired changes." Apparently, Kaiser management
was becoming more bald-faced in publicizing its right to ration care.
Here was the implication that placing arbitrary limits on mental
health coverage visits was an acceptable practice. This was an affront
to the federal mental health parity laws that went into effect in 2010,
requiring that insurance companies refrain from imposing limits on
mental health coverage of the sort that did not exist in the realm of
medical coverage. Just as it was unthinkable to deny services to a kidney dialysis patient requiring ongoing treatment, the federal government wanted chronic mental health conditions to be equally treated.
John Grohol, a founding board member and treasurer of the Society
for Participatory Medicine—an organization that promotes greater
collaboration between patients and health providers—realized that

Kaiser needed to be called out. He sharply criticized the company in his blog: "Kaiser is one of those enormous health care providers that seems to have lost the plot—providing reasonable and timely health care for its customers."[43]

In June 2013, the California Department of Managed Health Care stepped in and issued the second-largest fine in its history against Kaiser—$4 million—for failing to provide mental health services in a timely manner and for circulating confusing and misleading information that "could dissuade an enrollee from pursuing medically necessary care."[44] Kaiser administrators may or may not have grasped how pamphlets promulgating the supposed benefits of single-session therapy would delegitimize the emotional pain and suffering of its psychologically troubled members. State regulators did. A cease-and-desist order was also issued to Kaiser, prohibiting the health plan from imposing limits on mental health coverage of the sort that did not apply in the world of physical health—limits that violate federal parity laws.

On September 10, 2014, Sal Rosselli, president of the National Union of Healthcare Workers, and Fred Seavey, the organization's research director, met with a gathering of mental health advocates at the National Press Club in Washington, DC. They assessed whether Kaiser had remedied the problems resulting in the sanctions levied against its health plan. Union officials claimed that Kaiser was falling far short of hiring more mental health professionals to improve timely access to therapy, especially given the four hundred thousand new enrollees entering the Kaiser system under the Affordable Care Act. They presented internal Kaiser documents showing questionable action plans for meeting California's ten-business-day mandate for first-time patients' initial intake appointments. Kaiser had devised "rapid access clinics" and "cluster intakes," forcing its already-overburdened clinical staff to free up time that could only be obtained by making appointments with existing patients less frequent. You might be able to get a first-time appointment quicker, but the quality of the clinical encounter and the rate at which a second or third appointment occurred would decline even further—there was the rub.

At Downey Medical Center in Southern California, the average daily wait for a follow-up appointment with a mental health profes-

sional was still twenty days. Sidestepping individual therapy and fun-
neling new patients into therapy groups, regardless of the nature of
their problems, remained commonplace. Seavey alluded to how Kaiser administrators were keenly aware of the huge cost savings associated with routinely passing over individual therapy in favor of group
approaches. During the meeting, Melinda Ginne, a retired Kaiser psychologist who specialized in the "hard cases," elderly patients whose
medical problems encompass a psychological dimension, described
the challenges for her patients. When she was compelled to do twenty-
five new intakes a month, the patients on her regular caseload were
obliged to wait three months for a follow-up appointment.[45]

In short, the consensus at the meeting was that Kaiser persisted
in offering substandard mental health care to its members. By early
2015, Kaiser mental health staff throughout California began hinting
that a strike was imminent. In my experience, psychologists, social
workers, and marriage and family therapists are usually an apolitical
lot. They tend to puzzle over people's internal psychological dynamics
rather than worry about socially manufactured forms of human suffering. Consequently, when twenty-six hundred Kaiser mental health
providers launched a week-long strike on January 12, 2015, I took the
strike as concrete evidence that the rights of patients under their care
were being seriously violated.[46]

One step Kaiser has taken to address shortcomings in its delivery of outpatient mental health services is to refer clients to Value-
Options (now known as Beacon Health Options) on a case-by-case
basis when psychiatry departments are overloaded. This front-runner
in the behavioral-health-care insurance industry prides itself on offering "time-limited, solution-focused" treatment and only reimburses
providers for shorter therapy sessions of between thirty and forty-
five minutes.[47]

Kaiser's failure to provide timely, quality care to its enrollees—
even long-term individual therapy when it is indicated—is a mystery.
Over the decades, study after study confirms that, regardless of the
severity of their psychological difficulties, only about one in five patients will engage in long-term therapy consisting of twenty or more
visits. Typically, people don't flock to therapy when liberal amounts

of it are offered. Besides, as Frank duly noted, if people with complex psychological problems are denied an ongoing attachment with a caring therapist, they are more likely to inundate emergency rooms and medical doctors' offices, running costs up.

Kaiser has the financial resources to turn back the clock and provide the laudable quantity and quality of care it did when Frank was a fledgling therapist on its team from the 1960s to the 1980s. In 2014 alone, the company reported $56.4 billion in operating revenue and an income of $2.2 billion.[48] With 9.5 million members, Kaiser is the largest health plan in the United States.[49] In a sense, as goes Kaiser, so goes the nation. Therefore, it is imperative that its low-grade mental health services be upgraded.

Maybe Kaiser should adhere to the quality of mental health coverage it offers its own administrators and physicians. In my private practice over the years, I have provided long-term, intensive, thought-provoking, emotionally evocative psychotherapy to umpteen Kaiser administrators and physicians seeking me out to address the same existential problems that, presumably, Kaiser members themselves experience. No group of people is immune to the misery of life after divorce, a pervasive feeling of guilt, the regret of paths not taken in life, or the omnipresent fear of sudden death. I perk up when I get the call from a Kaiser administrator or physician. I know their Harrington Health and Meritain benefits will pay me 75 percent of my full fee to see them for at least forty sessions a year. The rate redresses me for the cheap therapy I feel ethically drawn to offer the Kaiser members who become disenchanted with the quality of services made available under their health plan and who elect to self-pay me for treatment.

SCIENTIFICALLY SUPPORTABLE LENGTHS OF THERAPY INSURANCE PLANS SHOULD COVER

The psychotherapy effectiveness study that has stood the test of time and been cited in the formal psychology literature more than any other was released in 1995 by a not-so-formal publication, *Consumer Reports.*[50] A year earlier, embedded in the standard annual survey it sent out querying its 180,000 readers about appliances and automobiles was a host of questions tapping mental health concerns. Of the approximately 7,000 subscribers who responded, 2,900 had been in psychotherapy sometime in their lives and they disclosed very telling information about their experience. Long-term treatment (about two years) yielded better outcomes than did short-term treatment (six months or less). In other words, there was a positive dose–response curve. The more therapy a person received, the greater the improvement. Outcome was measured using global questions about overall emotional state, for example, "I have my ups and downs," "I have no serious complaints," and "I barely manage to deal with things." Responders whose choice of therapist and length of treatment were limited by managed-care plans demonstrated poorer outcomes.

Martin Seligman, the University of Pennsylvania professor credited with spearheading the positive psychology movement, was a consultant on the study. He hailed it as uniquely valid insofar as it reflected the experience of real-life people with real-world problems in open-ended therapy. His later critique of so-called efficacy studies is every bit as relevant now as it was then. Seligman highlighted some serious flaws with the preponderance of short-term therapy efficacy studies that were generated by academics and were relied on by leaders in the managed-care industry to minimize coverage.

First, typical efficacy studies of a fixed duration—usually ten to twenty sessions—may be eminently researchable because there is a discrete beginning and end, because they are easier to logistically manage and fund, and because the treatment is short. However, the findings of such time-limited studies have questionable generalizability. In the real world, most clients keep attending sessions until they experience some tangible, lasting sense of improvement. There are usually emotional peaks and valleys along the way, so that depending on when a therapist assesses client progress, fleeting positive or negative results can be generated. With the typical efficacy study, follow-ups with subjects beyond the designated small batch of sessions are rare, and there is no way to really know if positive results endure.

Second, efficacy studies of short-term therapy usually measure progress in terms of symptom reduction, not improvement in overall emotional well-being or everyday social and emotional functioning.

We forget that recovery from depression is not a lack of pessimism, hopelessness, and fatigue, but a presence of optimism, hopefulness, and enthusiasm. Narrowing the criteria for recovery to very specific, changeable thoughts or behaviors to be eliminated might make for tidy research, but most depressed people in therapy don't judge their progress in terms of having fewer pessimistic thoughts. They judge it in terms of whether they feel happier, are more creative and motivated at work, are having more sex, and are acting more lovingly with their spouse and children. Consequently, short-term therapy studies looking at treatment across ten to twenty sessions using symptom reduction alone to evaluate progress need to be read with caution.

A third common problem with studies of time-limited therapy is that the selected subjects supposedly exhibit pure cases of a mental disorder, such as generalized anxiety disorder, obsessive-compulsive disorder, or major depressive disorder. Yet rarely in the clinical world does one get a pure case of anything. I use discreet diagnoses because insurance companies require them to pay for services, and the diagnoses are useful global categories that enable psychiatrists to make practical medication choices. Beyond that, most clients embody a hodgepodge of psychological complaints that cut across diagnoses. The psychiatry establishment is finally coming to terms with this clinical reality. In 2013, Thomas Insel, the director of the NIMH, took a left turn and announced a reduction in funding for diagnostically driven research.[51] New studies released have both failed to find any unique underlying brain mechanisms linking up with specific diagnoses and failed to show in any scientifically convincing way that doctors usually agree on the accuracy of their diagnoses. It is difficult to know how this new information will all unfold with academics and managed-care executives who rely on outcome studies grounded in uniform psychological treatments for specific mental disorders.

At this juncture, asking a question like "What kind and length of therapy works with what type of diagnosis?" is problematic. Basing the number of psychotherapy visits on the present literature for a specific disorder is not supported by robust science. Such limits on visits may be useful for researchers, but are not helpful for suffering clients in the real world.

This is not to say that measuring treatment outcomes in psychotherapy is irrelevant. Rather, psychotherapy outcome research, in the spirit of the *Consumer Reports* study, needs to incorporate a long-term focus so that progress can be measured over time and assessed in global wellness terms. The research also needs to define psychological suffering less in terms of rigid diagnostic categories and more in terms of maladaptive ways of handling emotions and difficult personality traits and dynamics. Such studies are available. But they tend to be conducted in Canada and Scandinavian countries, where the health-care systems are publicly funded and do not operate under the specter of corporate profits.

One exemplary study of this sort was overseen by J. Christopher Perry and Michael Bond in the Department of Psychiatry at McGill University in Montreal.[52] They tracked the progress of twenty-one adult clients in therapy for five years. The clients had a blend of anxiety, depression, and difficult personality traits—representative of the prototypical client who presents for therapy. They were paired with experienced therapists and were offered a minimum of three years of therapy, free of charge, that they could terminate at will. Sessions were scheduled weekly, or twice weekly, at the discretion of the client and therapist. Rather than exclusively focus on symptom reduction as the index of progress, the researchers examined changes in clients' defensiveness over time: Was there less denial, repression, and avoidance of painful emotions? How apt was a client to point a finger at others when the individual had a role in his or her own misfortune? How much personal ownership did a client assume for making life changes? Was there less of a tendency to view the world in black-and-white and a greater capacity to think with ambiguity, to see the gray in situations? Was there more assertiveness and less passive-aggressiveness? What alterations were there in a client's ability to show good self-restraint, take critical feedback, or laugh at himself or herself? The study revealed that it took roughly two and a half years of therapy to significantly change clients' overall defensiveness. The change was long-lasting; it held up two and a half years later when clients were reassessed.

By and large, if therapy with people who display difficult personality traits or full-blown personality disorders is to be effective, it needs to last longer. Historically, insurance companies have openly refused to authorize psychotherapy for such people, because the conditions are perceived as chronic and needing long-term treatment. To adapt, most therapists pin a different coverable diagnosis, such as generalized anxiety disorder, on such clients. The clients might worry, expect the worst, and be keyed up and on edge. But their anxiety is often the product of deeper personality predispositions that cause them to emotionally underreact and overreact and that perpetually disrupt their social relations.

Surveys show that up to 50 percent of clients with generalized anxiety disorder have a personality disorder.[53] Roughly thirty million American adults, or 9 percent of the population, meet the criteria for a personality disorder.[54] Among young adults, the figure hovers around 20 percent.[55] There is an array of labels for these conditions, narcissistic personality disorder and borderline personality disorder being the most prominent ones. However, personality disorders share overarching features: a superior or inferior self-image; trouble recognizing the needs and feelings of others; extreme habits of either seeking out, or avoiding, attention and admiration; a tendency to perceive others' motives as malignant; and a susceptibility to become vindictive when feeling slighted. Not surprisingly, people with personality disorders universally have unstable social relationships. The most carefully constructed research on therapy with people with personality disorders indicates that they need anywhere between 50 and 150 sessions, or one to three years, of psychotherapy to achieve adequate, lasting change.[56]

Another realistic source of information about how long therapy takes with real clients exhibiting a complex blend of psychological problems is the clinical judgment of therapists in the field. Drew Westen, an Emory University researcher best known for his media appearances in which he psychologically analyzes key politicians, combed through 242 completed surveys by highly experienced psychotherapists (psychiatrists and psychologists with a median of eighteen years' postdoctoral experience). He asked them to describe their last completed psychotherapy with three patients who were predominantly anxious and panicky, anxious but not panicky, or depressed. Underlying problems with assertiveness, intimacy and commitment in loving relationships, anger management, and stable self-esteem were also probed. These experts in the field—from a variety of therapy orientations—reported that for any meaningful change to occur, a client needed at least fifty to seventy-five psychotherapy sessions.[57]

Michael Lambert, a leading expert on psychotherapy research outcomes from Brigham Young University, has proposed that, all things considered, the most conservative estimate of the number of therapy sessions required for 50 percent of clients to show short-term improvement is twenty-one.[58]

What, then, does sound science dictate about the length of therapy that insurance plans should cover? At a bare minimum, twenty sessions a year should be authorized. The upper end would appear to be about three years of weekly or twice-weekly sessions for people who exhibit personality disorders. For the large swath of Americans, who enter therapy for help because they're moderately anxious, depressed, and defensive, one to two years of weekly therapy appears to be indicated for meaningful and lasting change to occur.

WOODY ALLEN SYNDROME OR THERAPY-FLIGHT SYNDROME?

Over the years, the comedian and prodigious filmmaker Woody Allen has been the public poster person for perceived indulgent use of psychotherapy. We are a nation that venerates self-reliance. Going to psychotherapy one to five times a week for decades, as Allen has done, not only smacks of decadence, but also suggests personal failure, at least from the vantage point of American rugged individualism. But Allen is unrepentant about his heavy use of therapy, crediting it with keeping him creative, productive, and free from depression over the years. His heir apparent, radio talk-show host Howard Stern, once joked that his own main goal in therapy was to cut back to two sessions a week from his customary three, while Frank Gehry credits his thirty-five-year-long therapy for "liberating new energy" and turning him into a world-renowned architect.[59]

Distinguishing between ongoing psychotherapy that results in unhealthy dependence and long-term therapy for healthy upkeep of one's emotional life is no easy task. Still, in my experience, there are several red flags indicating unproductive long-term therapy. Some-times, a client is overreliant on safe, predictable, and compassionate interactions with a therapist and avoids entering into deeper commit-ments with outside family members, friends, and lovers. Other times, a client routinely seeks the counsel of a guru-like therapist before making any life decisions of weight. The clearest sign that therapy is having stagnating effects is when a client shows ample insight into his or her own troublesome behavior but repeats the behavior over and over anyway. Maybe a client remains short-tempered with authority figures after years of therapy. The individual can eloquently analyze the childhood roots of the problem: a sergeant-like, hostile father who instilled fear and a mother who accommodated this and modeled pas-sivity and fear. The therapist falls into the trap of repeatedly offering interpretations, which San Francisco–based counselor Marty Nemko cleverly calls "inaction-inducing balms": "Is it any wonder you went off on your boss, given that you grew up in a home with an intolerant father?"[60] The client may derive insight from these sorts of interpreta-tions, but there's little impetus to change the reactive behavior.

Strictly at a public policy level, however, the major problem is not that too few members of society are using up too much of our psy-chotherapy resources with doubtful behavioral progress. It's that too many members of society are using up too little of our psychotherapy resources for probable behavioral progress. Only about 3 percent of Americans ever enter psychotherapy, even though roughly half the population meet lifetime criteria for a serious emotional problem.[61] The statistics get grimmer from there. High psychotherapy dropout rates are one of the best-kept secrets in the mental health field. Up to 50 percent of clients who start therapy drop out after the first or sec-ond visit.[62] Scarcely 9 percent attend twenty or more visits.[63]

The high psychotherapy dropout rates have not only a human cost but also an economic one. The Centers for Disease Control and Pre-vention estimates that untreated depression alone costs employers $17 billion to $44 billion annually in lost productivity time.[64] A number of years ago, the McDonnell Douglas Corporation implemented an in-house counseling program for workers self-identified with emo-tional problems or struggles with substance abuse. Absenteeism rates among this pool of workers dropped 34 to 44 percent over the four years that the program was in place. Turnover was also lowered substantially, as were health-related expenditures. For every $1 spent on counseling, McDonnell Douglas ended up saving $4 in costs related to health care, absenteeism, and employee turnover.[65]

Decades of research on the offset of medical costs has shown that if ready access to psychotherapy is offered, overall medical costs are lowered. At any given time, between 50 and 70 percent of the patients on a physician's normal caseload have medical concerns that entail a strong psychological component.[66] Persons not receiving psychotherapy are roughly twice as likely as those who are to visit a physician for no clear-cut medical reason.[67] Psychotherapy is simply much cheaper than avoidable time spent in a physician's office, a hospital, or an MRI chamber. Collective estimates show a reduction in medical costs of 20 to 30 percent *above* the tab of the therapy treatment itself.[68] Medical patients who are concurrently in psychotherapy also tend to be more compliant with medical treatments, lowering the chances they will undergo relapse and pursue more expensive emergency-driven care.[69]

More liberal insurance coverage of psychotherapy is not only the humane course of action, but also the economical one. With the repeated efforts to repeal and replace Obamacare and restructure health-care coverage and delivery, government officials and health-care industry executives need to endorse access to quality psychotherapy both for the betterment of people's mental health and the fiscal strength of the health system.

CHAPTER FIVE

The Miseducation
of Psychotherapists

I SHOULD BE UP FRONT and confess that my educational background as a psychotherapist is a nontraditional one. Truth be told, I avoided traditional psychology classes as an undergraduate, preferring to roam around the philosophy, anthropology, history, human services, and American studies departments at California State University, Fullerton, in the early 1980s. I eventually obtained a degree in American studies because it allowed me to construct a major compiling coursework around the theme of culture and personality. This was a deeply personal educational choice. As a young man, I was torn open by the loss of my first love. I was also mired in confusion from acculturating to America after having spent my adolescence cloistered as a Catholic priest in training in rural Aberdeen, Scotland. I pursued coursework and devoured books that helped shed light on my sense of alienation and discontent. It dawned on me that my susceptibility to avoidance, self-denial, and compulsive action were all necessary ways to cope with the anxiety, shame, and self-fragility stemming from being a working-class immigrant raised in a Glasgow neighborhood rife with alcoholism and violence. The social alienation I felt at college was partly due to the false consciousness of many people I met—people with self-promotional personality traits adapted to the capitalist and consumerist way of life in America.

These insights came from books I read in my Freud and Philosophy, and Marx and Marxism courses offered in the philosophy department. Plays I read on my own, such as Samuel Beckett's *Waiting for Godot* and Eugene O'Neill's *Long Day's Journey into Night*, taught me about the tragic effects of false optimism and disjointed family communication patterns. They also taught me about how stubbornly we humans cling to familiar courses of action and resist change.

The one course I took in the psychology department, Personality Psychology, was not only uninspiring, but also downright boring. The litany of research findings to be memorized and regurgitated on quizzes and tests was both drab and tedious. It did not pull me in and inform me about *my* pain or about the suffering of legions of people who had undergone life experiences like me.

My own psychotherapy had been a lifeline. The calling I had at a tender age to be a Catholic priest mirrored the emerging sense, obtained from my personal therapy, that I was destined to be a therapist. By my midtwenties, I had a deep-rooted ethical commitment to become the best psychotherapist I could. That way, I might provide for others the transformational experiences I had derived from my own therapy. I had the dawning realization that my personality would be a sort of instrument of change as a practicing therapist; the more integrated and self-aware I pushed myself to be as a person, the better a therapist I would become. If I had more life experience, depth, and dimensionality as a person, I could relate better as a therapist to clients dealing with a variety of life problems. The more "been there, done that, felt that, thought that" sensibility I acquired, the greater my range of empathic relatedness to clients.

When it came time to apply to graduate school, I still avoided traditional psychology. I selected the master's program in existential-phenomenological psychology at Seattle University, one of only two graduate programs in the United States (the other being Duquesne University in Pittsburgh) that views psychology as a human science, not a natural science. Seattle University considered reading widely in existential philosophy and literature and engaging in self-growth experiences in group and ongoing personal therapy the ideal preparation to become a psychotherapist. So too was diving in and learning by doing while being supervised by a skilled mentor-therapist to reflect on and finesse one's emerging capabilities.

Nonetheless, I knew enough about the field to realize that if I wanted to enter a top-tier doctoral program in clinical psychology, I would have to accumulate the requisite undergraduate coursework in statistics, experimental methods, and research design. I completed these courses at the University of Washington in the late 1980s in light of the rational desire to have a reasonably successful career. I somehow compartmentalized the bewilderment I felt about the relevance of chi-square tests, multivariate statistics, experimenter bias, and construct validity to the work of psychotherapy; the work, I was becoming ever surer, instead required a therapist to draw from his or her own humanity and acquired clinical knowledge to enact the exquisite sensitivity and thoughtfulness necessary to help a suffering person.

This divided consciousness was honed during my years as a doctoral student in the clinical psychology department at Teachers College, Columbia University, in the early 1990s. Like the vast majority of clinical psychology programs across America, the department at Teachers College subscribed to the so-called scientist-practitioner model of training promulgated by the American Psychological Association (APA) at the Boulder Conference in 1949. Leaders in the field at that time sought to establish clinical psychology as a bona fide scientific endeavor. Psychotherapy was to be an applied science, its methods and techniques guided by scientific studies. Any clinical wisdom acquired in the act of performing psychotherapy could not stand alone as a knowledge base. This wisdom was merely raw information awaiting empirical research to verify its legitimacy. Among my cohort at Teachers College, most of the graduate students were reluctant, but compliant scientists. But the real meaty learning occurred in the reading and classroom discussion of psychoanalytic texts of all sorts, the performance of psychotherapy with clients in the department clinic, and the endless hours of personal therapy and clinical supervision obtained while fanning out to psychoanalysts' offices all over Manhattan.

Not once did I witness anyone question how the thousands of hours learning advanced statistics and experimental methods and gathering and running data for the almighty dissertation in actuality helped a person become a more effective therapist.

In my more cynical moments, I still muse over how my scientific training at Teachers College taught me about the psychoanalytic concept of dissociation. It pertains to the mental state people assume in powerless situations where, for survival reasons, they unconsciously adhere to the beliefs and demands of a dominant other and numb themselves to any feelings of unfairness or outrage. In my less cynical moments, I share the perspective that many of my fellow doctoral students held at the time. Using the scientific method makes you a better clinician because, when you are with clients, you have to be detached and hold competing hypothesis in your mind about why the client acts or feels the way he or she does before offering an insightful interpretation.

By the time I was a freshly minted, Columbia University–educated clinical psychologist in 1996, I was beginning to appreciate how any good psychotherapy was really a concentrated and specialized form of human relatedness. It involved the psychotherapist's active self-nurturing of time-honored human virtues such as forbearance, sensitivity, tact, even-mindedness, honesty, and emotional courage. It was not something categorically different, mimicking the field of medicine, where remedy and cure were predicated on faithful learning and precise application of scientifically backed techniques.

Yet as we will see, the new norm in clinical psychology and other mental health training departments and treatment centers around the country is to produce therapists who are well versed in the latest presumed scientifically approved or evidenced-based therapy techniques. Academic psychologists have unprecedented power ratifying what types of psychotherapy are deemed effective or ineffective. Too often, their focus tends toward researching and legitimizing cognitive behavioral methods aimed at reducing the symptoms associated with a clear-cut mental health diagnosis given to a client.

This approach plays into the hands of health insurance executives, whose main agenda is to keep psychotherapy reimbursements costs down and to maximize profits. This favors psychotherapy approaches that are time limited and track progress not in vague terms such as self-growth but in measurable terms such as symptom reduction.

The current zeitgeist is to train mental health professionals to vigilantly and efficiently address the thinking errors and maladaptive behaviors thought to produce depressed and anxious states of mind. This, even though most clients who seek out therapy, when they are given the space and time and are lovingly listened to, tend not to initiate any mention of clinical entities such as depression or anxiety. Rather, they are more likely to launch into heartfelt disclosures of everyday human problems such as questioning whether they still love their spouse, wishing they could angrily call out their boss, or feeling oppressed by having to care for an unappreciative, aging parent.

Contrary to the prevailing evidenced-based ethos championing the supposed unique status of CBT for treating a range of emotional disorders, the bulk of the scientific evidence actually supports a different conclusion. What works in therapy—and what most clients desire—is access to a practitioner whose education and clinical training prepares him or her to actively listen with great care, empathy, and genuine interest, affirming clients' shifting feelings and concerns, and probing for deeper meaning as to why a person gets stuck acting or feeling a certain way. Not only does the average client prefer this, but ironically, so does the average cognitive behavioral therapist pursuing his or her own psychotherapy.

THE COGNITIVE BEHAVIORAL THERAPY MAKEOVER AND TAKEOVER OF MENTAL HEALTH PRACTICE

Mary Sykes Wylie is a senior editor at *Psychotherapy Networker*, a leading trade magazine read by thousands of mental health professionals across America. She recently touted CBT as follows: "CBT is arguably the most successful therapy ever developed. In only about 40 years, it's gone from the almost accidental innovations of two disenchanted psychoanalysts to the most widely practiced and promulgated approach in the world."[1] An earlier *Washington Post* article added to CBT's esteemed status: "For better or worse, cognitive therapy is fast becoming what people mean when they say they are 'getting therapy.'"[2]

University of Pennsylvania psychiatrist Aaron Beck, the main orig-
inator of CBT, did just happen upon his approach and had no clear in-
tention of starting a school of therapy. In the 1950s and 1960s, unlike
his psychiatrist colleagues, Beck was a researcher at heart. By collect-
ing data and running statistical analyses, he sought to test the Freudian
notion that depression was caused by people either turning their anger
inward or protecting their parents—the true target of their anger—by
directing their anger at themselves instead: "It wasn't mother or father
who acted neglectfully or who rejected me; I myself was too needy or
incorrigible. I am bad and deserving of punishment."[3]

Beck instead discovered that his depressed subjects were highly
susceptible to negative and exaggerated thought patterns. He proposed that people's erroneous thoughts and beliefs about themselves,
their world, and their future fueled their depression. Depressed people might overgeneralize and, after small setbacks, reach absolutist
conclusions that they are a failure in life: "Since my wife does not
call me during the day, she must not love me. If she doesn't love me,
nobody will. Life is not worth living if nobody will love me." Beck's
cognitive therapy aimed at Socratically challenging such cascading
negative thoughts and beliefs: "Is it possible that your wife does not
call, because she is busy at work?" "Even if your wife does not love
you, is it possible that someone else might?" "Even if nobody will love
you, are there other passions and pursuits that might make life worth
living for you?"[4]

Beck borrowed from and elaborated on the so-called ABC model
espoused by Albert Ellis, the cofounder of CBT. A stood for activat-
ing event, B for beliefs about A, and C for consequence. Clients were
urged to keep a log of, and counter, the distorted beliefs caused by
distressing events that made them depressed. For instance, an acti-
vating event might be a boss who gives critical feedback. The client
jumps to conclusions: "My boss thinks I'm useless." The consequence
of this exaggerated belief is hurt feelings, depression, or avoidance
of the boss at work. Typically, homework would be given to document instances where the boss acted favorably toward the client: "My
boss gave me positive feedback today" and "My boss promised me
a pay raise." These more favorable ratings then support the more

wholesome belief "My boss thinks I'm a valuable employee," which contributes to the client's feeling more upbeat.

Beck identified a host of illogical thinking patterns that clients automatically engage in and that make them anxious and depressed. For instance, *black-and-white* or *all-or-nothing thinking* captures how clients cogitate in polarized ways: "I'm a loser," "My wife never listens to me." *Fortune-telling* pertains to the false assumptions clients make about the future as though their beliefs were actual realities: "Nobody hires a sixty-year-old truck driver. My career is over." And *personalizing* touches on how clients assume total responsibility for life outcomes without clear evidence: "I'm all to blame for my marriage failing."

A favorite technique of Beck's, and of a whole generation of CBT therapists to follow, involved prompting the client to rationally map out the probability that a feared or catastrophic event will occur. A client of his believed she would pass out and die if she entered a crowded store. Beck urged her to monitor and jot down the probabilities of dying each step of the way: leaving the house, one in a thousand; driving into town, one in a hundred; parking the car in the lot, one in fifty; walking to the store, one in ten; entering the store, two to one; and in middle of crowd, ten to one. Once she survived the trip, Beck asked her, "What do you think—right now—were the actual probabilities that you would have died if you had stayed in the store?" The client replied, "Probably one in a million."[5] Exposing herself to the feared event, surviving it, and rationally reassessing the probability of a terrible outcome alleviated her social anxiety.

Contemporary cognitive behavioral therapists would first probably teach Beck's client breathing exercises to employ during exposure to the feared event. Lead-up therapy sessions might focus on having the client imagine each step of the journey while engaging in calming breaths, before actually venturing into to the feared situation. A symptom checklist, like the Social Interaction Anxiety Scale or the Brief Fear of Negative Evaluation Scale, might be administered after every few sessions to monitor the lessening of social anxiety symptoms. Time would be taken up during therapy to fill out these checklists and discuss the results.

In short, the therapeutic stance in CBT is qualitatively different from that embodied by psychodynamic and humanistic practitioners. It is technique oriented, active, and agenda driven. Beck once told an audience of CBT learners, "The problem with non-directive counseling was that it was non-directive. The patients didn't really learn anything from it."[6] Clearly for Beck, there was little inherently therapeutic about listening intently, continuously taking the client's lead regarding what topics felt worthy of disclosure, and allowing for periods of silence to enable the client to access and reaccess emotionally laden experiences. In CBT, there's the seeming omnipresent need on the part of both therapist and client to be productive. One training video for Seeking Safety, a CBT-based program, underscores this need.[7] The therapist holds a sheet of paper, which presumably contains a list of steps to be followed, and asks the client, rather off-handedly: "How are you feeling today?" The client responds, "Today I'm feeling pretty hopeful." The session unfolds from there:

THERAPIST: OK. So there's been an improvement. What coping have you done over the last week?

CLIENT: This last week I used a lot of deep breathing, some grounding exercises that we learned. . . . I've been talking with a lot of my friends instead of isolating.

THERAPIST: Did you complete your commitment last week? What was your commitment?

CLIENT: To not drink. . . . I went four days without drinking.

THERAPIST: So you committed four times.

It is CBT's agenda-driven approach that makes it eminently researchable. Its techniques are specifiable, and its goals measurable. The focus on using identifiable techniques (e.g., challenging negative cognitions, checking in about desired behavior changes or commitments) to reduce symptoms (e.g., more positive self-statements; reduced isolation) over a short duration (ten to twelve weekly sessions) rendered CBT an ideal fit for randomized controlled studies—medicine's gold-standard research design. That's where clients with identical disorders are randomly allocated to groups that then receive different treatments. This random assignment of different treatments ensures that the effects of each treatment can be measured and compared. As early as 1982, Beck teamed up with a psychiatric resident, John Rush, and compared his psychotherapy methods to the effects of the antidepressant imipramine. CBT recipients rated themselves less hopeless and more positively minded than those ingesting imipramine. CBT went up against a leading medicine of the day, and won.[8]

With the imprimatur of science, CBT emerged as academic psychology's counterpunch to the heavily marketed wonder drugs, like Prozac, that threatened to sideline psychotherapy as a viable mental health treatment. There are now more than three hundred clinical trials of CBT, designating it as an effective treatment for various mental health problems, such as depression, anxiety, chronic pain, and marital distress.[9] While there's no question that clients benefit from CBT—especially those with discreet phobias like test anxiety and fear of flying—as we will see, its effectiveness as a treatment method with a range of client populations has been overstated. Moreover, CBT's streamlined therapy approach and simple treatment goals favor its adoption by academic researchers. Consequently, it has achieved exclusive status in graduate training programs around the country, undercutting trainees' needs for exposure to diverse therapy approaches.

CBT has quickly risen to dominate clinical and counseling psychology, as well as social work departments, shaping the therapy orientations of the upcoming generation of practitioners. Joan Cook at Columbia University led a nationwide study of 2,156 mental health professionals in 2010. According to the study, 79 percent of psychotherapists cited CBT as their main treatment approach. Thirty-six percent were mainly influenced by psychodynamic or psychoanalytic therapy, while 31 percent underscored the influence of client-centered/humanistic therapy.[10]

Nowadays, CBT has become so overrepresented in university psychology departments across the United States that alarm bells should be ringing about the lack of intellectual diversity in the training of graduate students in therapy. A 2013 article in *Clinical Psychology: Science and Practice* revealed that 80 percent of professors in clinical science psychology departments claim a CBT orientation, while only 7 percent view themselves as psychodynamic, and 4 percent humanistic/existential. Even among the professional schools of psychology attached to universities that offer the PsyD—a clinical psychology doctoral degree that allows students to emphasize clinical practice in their training over rigorous exposure to scientific experimentation—CBT heavily dominates faculties' research preferences: 48 percent CBT, 28 percent psychodynamic, and 12 percent existential/humanistic. The authors conclude that "an unfortunate effect of some otherwise positive developments in promoting clinical psychology as a science is the danger of a monoculture of ideas about the nature of psychotherapeutic change—specifically, a hegemony of cognitive-behavioral theory and therapy."[11]

There is even a movement afoot to reform all of clinical psychology and restrict training exclusively to evidenced-based treatments. CBT is often uttered in the same breath as evidenced based, the perception being that it stands alone as a respectable treatment to be researched and taught in graduate schools. Twenty-eight of the most prestigious doctoral programs in clinical psychology in the United States are enrolled members of the Psychological Clinical Science Accreditation System (PCSAS). In 2007, this organization formed itself in opposition to the APA, psychologists' largest governing body, because its adherents considered the APA too liberal in approving clinical programs across America. PCSAS members overwhelmingly favor CBT-based interventions. Its constituents rank among the most recognized universities in the country: Harvard University; University of California, Los Angeles; University of Southern California; Duke University; Emory University; University of Wisconsin–Madison; and Beck's very own University of Pennsylvania, to name but a few.[12]

But evidenced based is really evidenced biased. Burgeoning data indicates that clients don't really get better from the application of CBT techniques, but improve from contextual and relationship factors, such as the empathy, warmth, rapport, and active listening embodied by the therapist. Insofar as training programs fail to accentuate these more human qualities in their trainees, they fail the American public.

EVIDENCED BASED IS EVIDENCED BIASED

The public is unaware of what University of Wisconsin–Madison professor of counseling psychology Bruce Wampold coined "the great psychotherapy debate." This is no ivory-tower matter. The outcome of this debate affects the type and quality of psychotherapy that trainees obtain, and their training trickles down to the average consumer.

Within the field of psychology and related disciplines, camps are divided around what explains the effectiveness of psychotherapy. On the one side are those who privilege the role of *techniques* as the curative agent. Generally speaking, these are researchers and clinicians oriented toward more cognitive behavioral ways of thinking and practicing. The overarching model of psychotherapy they espouse is one of employing clusters of techniques (for example, activity scheduling, deep-breathing exercises, positive self-talk) to reduce the symptoms associated with a mental health diagnosis (for example, to reduce irritability, worrying, and poor concentration in a generalized anxiety disorder). Wampold considers this approach a medical model of psychotherapy because of the focus on specifiable treatment techniques aimed at symptom reduction.[13]

In the other camp reside the researchers and clinicians who privilege *relationship factors* as the curative agent in psychotherapy. Their body of work disputes the notion that effective application of techniques best accounts for favorable client changes. This camp believes that human factors common to all forms of therapy are the real ingredients of client progress: the degree of alliance and collaboration in the therapy relationship and the therapist's embodiment of empathy, positive regard, affirmation, and genuineness.

Meta-analytic studies pulling together massive amounts of data across research investigations strongly favor relationship factors as the driving force in effective psychotherapy. John Norcross, a past president of the APA's Division of Psychotherapy, catalogued these findings in *Psychotherapy Relationships That Work: Evidence-Based Responsiveness.*[14] One robust study drawing data from fifty-seven psychotherapy experiments, involving about thirty-six hundred clients, found that therapist empathy moderately predicted client success. At one level, it is a tad absurd that abundant resources have to be deployed to "scientifically" confirm the intuitive proposition that understanding clients' feelings, thoughts, and life dilemmas from their point of view is therapeutic. But in the science wars, perceiving human intuition as a knowledge base more than raises eyebrows. Another meta-analysis of information from eighteen studies found a similar effect for therapists' positive regard. This approach is what Carl Rogers defined as *nonpossessive love*, or continuously truly caring for clients and offering spontaneous, heartfelt, direct feedback. Yet another meta-analysis of the results of sixteen psychotherapy investigations showed that therapist congruence or genuineness had a significant effect on treatment outcome. The more that clients feel that their therapists are authentic—saying what they mean and meaning what they say—and genuinely invested in understanding clients' disclosures, the better the therapy outcome.

Good collaborative relationships or partnerships with clients, whereby the therapy relationship is infused with trust and respect and the parties agree on the goals of therapy (therapy alliance), garnered the most statistical support. Estimates show that the quality of the therapy alliance had a five to seven times greater correlation with positive client change than did any specific technique or set of techniques.[15]

These findings square with those of Wampold and his colleagues in their 2014 article "Expanding the Lens of Evidenced-Based Practice in Psychotherapy: A Common Factors Perspective."[16] According to their calculations, therapist empathy is about nine times more effective than any other technique is in helping clients. They found that the therapist's alliance-building skill, genuineness, and positive regard far outstrip the effectiveness of any technique he or she might employ.

The quality of medical-model research studies on psychotherapy are also coming under fire. Again, these short-term studies tend to attribute a clear-cut diagnosis to subjects and apply a specific method of treatment or set of techniques. Because the studies are overwhelmingly of the CBT variety, this type of therapy has become the signature evidenced-based treatment that has been singled out as effective.

In December 2014, Jonathan Shedler, a professor at the University of Colorado Medical School, announced some unexpected findings at a packed psychotherapy conference held at the luxurious Dartington Hall in Devon, England: "Evidenced-based treatments are weak interventions. Their benefits are trivial. Most patients don't get well. Even the trivial benefits don't last."[17] He was not booed off the lectern, because he rolled out some startling findings. Reassessment of the twenty-five-year-old NIMH Health Treatment of Depression Collaborative Research Program—which at the time put CBT on the map as comparable to SSRI antidepressants in the treatment of depression—indicates that only about 24 percent of those who received short-term, solution-focused CBT adequately recovered from depression. The remaining 76 percent stayed clinically depressed. A 2013 article in the *American Journal of Psychiatry* presenting the results of a large study of 341 depressed adults who had received sixteen sessions of CBT showed that only 23 percent achieved remission.[18]

Shedler also brought to the attention of the audience the little-known work of his friend and fellow academic, Drew Westen, from Emory University. Going back more than ten years, Westen had published several articles reviewing dozens of studies on short-term, empirically supported therapies involving more than twenty-four hundred clients. He concluded that overall improvement rates were low: about 54 percent for depression and 52 percent for generalized anxiety disorder.[19]

Extrapolating from Westen's work, Shedler went on to dismantle the evidence for the efficacy of CBT. In randomized, controlled studies, Shedler found that about two-thirds of subjects were excluded because they failed to strictly meet the criteria for the diagnosis the treatment was aimed at. If these subjects, who were presumably still depressed but had other life problems, had been included in the average study, CBT treatment would have been shown to only have lasting effects for about 5 percent of its recipients. Restricting subjects in research studies to those with clear-cut cases of major depressive disorder, generalized anxiety disorder, panic disorder, and the like, severely limits the findings' generalizability to real clients in everyday therapy situations. As mentioned earlier, psychologists like me who have been practicing for more than thirty years know that clear-cut cases of any single diagnosis are fairly uncommon. Typically, clients exhibit symptoms scattered across different diagnoses. They may have narcissistic or dependent personality traits, and they

can be both anxious and depressed. Science corroborates this observation. Almost 60 percent of patients with depression also meet the
criteria for anxiety disorder, and 50 to 90 percent of patients who
qualify for one diagnosis qualify for a second one. In short, the signature evidenced-based treatments fall short in being applicable to the
everyday client who enters therapy.[20]

A key point Shedler overlooked at Dartington Hall centers on
how measuring client progress strictly in terms of symptom reduction
falsely represents true recovery. So-called hard-science researchers
and managed-care utilization reviewers may see the value in framing
recovery in terms of symptom reduction. Reductions in irritability,
worrying, avoidance behaviors, and so forth, are readily definable and
achievable treatment goals. But practitioners think otherwise. The
top four goals therapists want their clients to realize in treatment are,
in order, "Have a strong sense of self-worth and identity," "Improve
the quality of their relationships," "Understand their feelings, motives
and/or behavior," and "Integrate excluded or segregated aspects of
experience." These findings are based on a poll of five thousand psychotherapists from all over the world.[21] While these treatment goals
might seem imperative and obvious to therapists and clients alike, they
are anathema to conservative scientists and profit-conscious health insurance personnel. Such goals are less definable and measurable and
raise the prospect of more open-ended therapy.

No doubt, Shedler was invited to speak at Dartington Hall and
commanded a large turnout because of his 2010 article "The Efficacy
of Psychodynamic Psychotherapy," in the top journal for psychologists, the *American Psychologist*.[22] For the legions of therapists, like myself, whose psychotherapy style is of the psychodynamic variety, this
article triggered a sigh of relief. First, it distilled in readable terms
some of the key concepts and practices of psychodynamic psychotherapy. For example, it describes the focus on providing clients ample opportunity to talk freely about their emotional experiences and thereby
gain greater mastery of expressing their feelings.

The article also discussed how clients knowingly and unknowingly
have relationship predispositions they superimpose onto the therapist
(transference). These repetitive patterns of relationship expectations

can be brought to light and undone, as they get enacted with the therapist. For instance, a client with a history of neglect might secretly expect the therapist to lose interest and be bored with him or her. The client learns that this expectation has more to do with painful past childhood experiences than with anything endemic to the therapist. Shedler also wrote about the importance of exploring clients' early histories to emotionally reprocess childhood traumas and address unmet developmental needs.

More importantly, Shedler comprehensively summarized all the available scientific evidence for the benefits of psychodynamic psychotherapy. This summary was long overdue. The prevailing sentiment among academics, health-care administrators, and the public was that psychoanalytically oriented therapy lacked scientific credibility and was all but defunct. A case in point is the insurer Health Net's treatment recommendation for adult depression: "Evidence regarding the use of long-term psychodynamic or psychoanalytic approaches is limited. There is better evidence to support positive outcomes from Cognitive Behavioral Therapy approaches."[23] In the popular press, it was sport to mock psychoanalysis, as reflected in a 2004 *Los Angeles Times* op-ed titled "Psychoanalysis Is Dead . . . So How Does That Make You Feel?"[24] It turns out that the evidence favoring psychodynamic or psychoanalytic approaches is not limited, and the approaches are not dead as a school of psychotherapy. Shedler reviewed the findings of seventy-four studies utilizing psychodynamic methods and concluded: "Effect sizes for psychodynamic psychotherapy are as large as those reported for other therapies that have been actively promoted as 'empirically supported' and 'evidenced based.' This was true across sufferers of depression, anxiety, eating disorders, and personality disorders."[25] Subsequent studies have shown that long-term psychodynamic psychotherapy may even be the treatment of choice for people with difficult personality traits and complex blends of emotional problems—the profile of the majority of people who seek out therapy.[26]

Alarmingly, scientific findings legitimizing and favoring such factors as good client-therapist relationships (therapy alliances) and therapist empathy and genuineness over the use of techniques do not find their way into the approved evidenced-based treatment databases that

government entities and health insurance companies use. And psychodynamic psychotherapy is conspicuously absent from these databases
as a supportable treatment. When you scour the data, you rapidly discover it almost universally lists short-term, goal-directed CBT interventions that are solution and workbook based. Arguably, the largest
such database that federal, state, and county departments of mental
health rely on to make recommendations to treatment facilities all
over America is the National Registry of Evidenced-Based Programs
and Practices. Overseen by the US Department of Health and Human Services, the registry has a website with a "Find an Intervention"
button, where you can obtain a list of evidenced-based interventions
for a given disorder. A search for "depression" yields a list of 121 approved treatments. Not once is there a reference to the importance of
the therapy alliance or therapist empathy and genuineness. Nor is the
word *psychodynamic* mentioned in any context.

Instead, there's an inventory of CBT-based, acronym-identifiable
interventions. Standouts included these: acceptance and commitment
therapy (ACT); cognitive behavioral social skills training (CBSST);
computer-based cognitive behavioral therapy—beating the blues
(BtB); dialectical behavior therapy (DBT); mindfulness-based cognitive therapy (MBCT); panic control treatment (PCT); Program to
Encourage Active, Rewarding Lives (PEARLS); and trauma-focused
cognitive behavioral therapy (TF-CBT).[27]

What might account for this state of affairs? These CBT treatments are protocol driven and workbook based. They outline steps
to take in therapy during each session, and there's an end point to the
work (typically after ten to twelve sessions). They often incorporate
worksheets and homework assignments for clients to complete. Progress is measured at weekly or monthly intervals through the use of
symptom checklists. There's an air of productivity, accountability, and
cost-effectiveness about it all. In short, these treatments have great
appeal to government and health insurance administrators focused on
tighter quality control and the bottom line. However, this biased selection of evidenced-based practices deprives clients of the first-rate,
intensive therapy they need to achieve longer-lasting gains in the
quality of their self-development and personal relationships. Nowhere

is this more apparent than in the handling of the mental health needs of former service members at the VA medical facilities and clinics, which train the largest number of mental health professionals of any organization in America.

COGNITIVE PROCESSING THERAPY:
THE VA'S FLAWED SOLUTION TO POSTTRAUMATIC STRESS DISORDER (PTSD)

On April 19, 2012, Eric K. Shinseki, secretary of the VA, publicly announced his department's renewed effort to beef up on mental health care for returning service members: "History shows that the costs of war will continue to grow for a decade or more after the operational missions in Iraq and Afghanistan have ended. As more Veterans return home, we must ensure that all Veterans have access to quality mental health care."[28] His commitment to adding almost two thousand mental health professionals to the VA workforce was on top of the eight thousand already hired since 2006.

Behind the scenes, a veritable army unto itself of high-ranking mental health administrators had been laying the groundwork for training new recruits in evidenced-based therapy for posttraumatic stress disorder (PTSD). This diagnosis applies to people who have faced a catastrophic or life-threatening event and exhibit these signs: recurring flashbacks of the event; avoidance of memories of the event and of people, places, or things that are evocative of the event; emotional numbing; and irritability from fatigue related to being hyper-vigilant. Studies conducted by the military put the estimated rate of PTSD among those returning from the wars in Iraq and Afghanistan at between 13 and 17 percent.[29] The top brass were learning what frontline mental health practitioners were directly witnessing: a large percentage of those afflicted with PTSD—as many as 40 percent—showed debilitating symptoms ten years after onset.[30] Also, a diagnosis of PTSD was a well-known risk factor for suicide. Effective PTSD treatments were sorely needed.

One of the main treatments aggressively disseminated, then and now, is cognitive processing therapy (CPT). This is a twelve-session therapy adapted for use with veterans by Patricia Resick and Candice

Monson from the National Center for PTSD at the VA Boston Healthcare System and Kathleen Chard at the Cincinnati VA Medical Center. CPT is a highly condensed CBT treatment tailored to therapeutically address the psychological effects of specific traumas. The central focus is talking and writing about the distorted beliefs a client retains regarding the causes and consequences of traumatic events. The manual outlines how therapists can effectively use Socratic questioning to help clients realize their thinking errors. The following vignette, presented in a report by Resick, Monson, and Chard, records the discussion between a therapist (T) and a service member (P) who survived an enemy attack by fleeing on an elevator out of a building in which some comrades perished. The service member had just been asked how he had made his decision during the attack:

> P : I just told you! No time! I just got in and went down! It was like I didn't even think! Suddenly I was on the elevator. It opened up. I got on.
> T : So, it was automatic?
> P : But I shouldn't have done it. I should have helped others.
> T : What would you say if a friend of yours escaped a burning building but others didn't? Would you blame him for not helping others get out? Would you assume he even had the chance or could help others?
> P : If a friend? . . . Like who? A friend? Well, I wouldn't automatically blame a friend for something. I guess not.[31]

Clients are urged to identify and keep a log of *stuck points*, or distorted automatic thoughts. In the vignette above, the client would be coached to see this as an example of survivor guilt and to categorize it as a *distorted sense of power* stuck point.

There is a strong psychoeducational component to the therapy. Early in the series of twelve modules, the client is taught about PTSD, the psychological and physiological effects of flight-or-fight reactions, and the various emotions people with PTSD experience. They are versed on standard CBT distortion mechanisms like all-or-nothing thinking, mind reading, jumping to conclusions, and emotional reasoning. This knowledge primes them to more confidently self-analyze for, and categorize, thinking mistakes in therapy and in their *impact statement.*

In an impact statement, the client, on his or her own time, writes a narrative of a selected traumatic event and later reads it to the therapist. The act of writing and reading aloud a detailed description of the traumatic event undoes the tendency to push out of one's mind the traumatic event and its effects. Throughout the treatment, the impact statement is continuously revised to incorporate less exaggerated self-recrimination.

Homework is assigned throughout in the form of worksheets. For example, on the Challenging Beliefs Worksheet, there are columns for clients to fill in to help them analyze automatic thoughts (e.g., "This can't be happening to me," "My life is over," "If only I had loaded my rifle better, I would have shot the person who shot my buddy George") for evidence of distortion (e.g., personalizing, emotional reasoning, jumping to conclusions). The Alternative Thought column allows for a more balanced, positive version of the original thought ("I'm nowhere near all to blame for what happened," "I can recover from this terrible event if I try," "You can't always predict when things will go wrong"). Usually, at intervals during CPT treatment, time is set aside to administer a symptom checklist, like the Clinician-Administered PTSD Scale (CAPS). If the CAPS is chosen, the therapist fills it out in direct consultation with the client over the hour or so it takes to complete it.

Beginning in 2006, Resick spearheaded a national VA initiative to disseminate CPT to locations across the United States. Through evidenced-based practice coordinators assigned to various VA medical facilities and clinics, CPT was promoted as a "first-line psychotherapy for PTSD."[32] By 2010, more than four thousand VA mental health staff had attended a CPT workshop. Today, at VA facilities as far apart as the Alaska VA Healthcare System and the Togus VA Medical Center in Maine, CPT training is a staple on the vast majority of postings for psychology, social work, and counseling internship positions and psychiatric residency slots.

Despite the bold initiative and ample resources allocated to implement CPT usage among mental health professionals throughout the VA system, attitudes toward this type of therapy are ambivalent at best.

The latest figures by behavioral health providers from the US Department of Defense reveal that more than half of the 60 percent of therapists who were trained in the VA system to execute evidenced-based interventions like CPT elect to not use them after the training.[33] A sizable percentage of VA mental health professionals question CPT's effectiveness. Hector Garcia, a staff member at the South Texas Veterans Health Care System, pooled data from a sample of clinicians across the VA system and published the results in a 2015 edition of the journal *Traumatology*. Only 12 percent rated CPT as very effective. About 53 percent considered it either ineffective or fairly effective.[34]

Les Greene, a senior psychologist at the VA Connecticut Healthcare System in West Haven, Connecticut, says that manual-driven therapies like CPT are ineffective for a substantial number of veterans because the therapies "are not relevant to the complexities and nuances of the real-world clinical setting, where the primary clinical question is what techniques and common factors will optimize treatment responsiveness for this particular patient at this particular time."[35]

Many combat veterans need more than short-term therapy aimed at altering unproductive thinking of the CPT variety. An intern (whom I'll name Jane, for confidentiality reasons) I interviewed at the West Los Angeles VA Healthcare Center raised this issue with me over lunch. As part of her training, she attempted to administer the standard twelve-session CPT module to an Iraqi War veteran who had a near-death experience dismantling an explosive device while on a military assignment. The client was frequently off topic from session to session. That is, he preferred to talk free-flowingly about matters he happened to deem relevant or of concern to him. On the surface, the emotional scars from being perpetually bullied as a child at school distressed him more than did his near-death experience in the military. Jane gave up trying to keep him on topic. She confessed that it felt terribly insensitive and inauthentic to shunt the discussion onto what topics a given session module dictated. Jane eventually convinced her supervisor to abort the CPT treatment because the complexity of the client's problems rendered CPT inappropriate. During our interview, Jane opined that CPT only works with "bright, motivated, self-aware, well-put-together clients, or it's a setup for failure."

Jane's experience brought to mind a quote I had earlier come across by the prolific British psychoanalyst Christopher Bollas: "People in breakdown do not need to have someone avert their gaze from the internal world to a self-help homework book; they need to be heard and understood from the depths of the self that are presented to them and that constitute their crisis."[36]

A clinical social worker I interviewed at New Directions for Veterans in Los Angeles also alluded to the awkwardness of trying to stick to the CPT workbook script: "A client came in and said, 'What's our next lesson?' I laughed and told him, 'This is not class time.' From then on, I changed my approach. I cherry-picked from the manual."

This cherry-picking approach to CBT seems to be a common one. The handful of psychology and social work interns I interviewed for this book all referred to feeling reassured that they could fall back on manuals and workbooks with clients. Since I was interviewing, not supervising them, I resisted mentioning anything about countertransference. I refrained from wondering aloud how much having a worksheet to stare down at and a tight agenda for each session served their own self-protective needs rather than any deeply meaningful therapeutic goals of the client. Insecurities for novice therapists abound: the need to feel productive, clever, and on top of it to prove one's educational credentials; a compulsion to do therapy the way a supervisor mandates, for fear of retribution; the desire to control the reverberating emotional effects of clients' chaotic, impossible, anxiety-ridden life narratives. All these insecurities get in the way of taking the clients' lead and truly listening to what's on his or her mind.

Might fidelity to the manual interfere with the therapist's desire to continuously help the client feel the unfeelable, think the unthinkable, and say the unsayable? I had to bite my tongue with one rather self-assured VA intern who smugly informed me that he lengthened a CPT treatment a few weeks to "do some psychoeducational work" about the emotions that often arise with PTSD. I so badly wanted to say the obvious: "Don't you see how teaching about emotions gets in the way of clients having them?"

Dropout rates for CPT patients in the VA system are staggering. One study of 351 veterans who initiated CPT treatment at a

VA outpatient clinic calculated a 38.5 percent dropout rate.[37] Four other studies yielded discontinuance rates of 31 to 50 percent.[38] Since the average dropout rate across clinical trials of PTSD treatments is approximately 20 percent, this should raise eyebrows among VA policy makers.[39]

In general, vast numbers of veterans fall through the cracks. They either fail to follow through with or prematurely discontinue the short-term, tightly packaged CBT or similar therapies offered. Among a sample of two hundred PTSD patients seen through a VA facility in Southern New England, only 12 percent attended all twelve sessions offered. Forty-three percent attended an initial visit, but never returned.[40] It is estimated that a meager 10 percent of veterans who embark on a course of therapy receive at least eight or nine sessions. And at least half those who complete PTSD treatment still retain the diagnosis afterward.[41]

The argument is frequently made that veterans are a tough population to treat. Instability follows them everywhere: struggles with drugs and alcohol, family dysfunction, unemployment, and homelessness. Rarely does the literature suggest that the deplorable follow-through and dropout rates might reflect the types and qualities of the therapy offered. Or that to engage and keep veterans in psychotherapy, we need to double down on training practitioners to hone their rapport-building, astute listening, and empathy skills. Clearly, there is a need to return to the wise concepts and practices promulgated by giants in the field of trauma treatment. The psychiatrist Judith Herman once wrote: "The therapist plays the role of witness and ally, in whose presence the survivor can speak of the unspeakable."[42] Trust building is not a single-session module to be checked off. It takes months, if not years, of therapy for clients to visit and revisit painful memories to access and fully express the mix of emotions that life traumas cause.

The traumatologist John Briere often talked about *therapeutic windows*.[43] These rely on the discerning power of the therapist to carefully read a client's emotional state. A window is open when a therapist can draw from the intersubjective emotional field existing in the moment, to know what to say, when to say it, and with what tone of voice to bring a client tolerably close to a traumatic memory. This is how trust is really built. There's a surgical psychosocial precision to these moments.

This form of relational sensitivity is nonexistent in CPT trauma work. A telling statement in the publication *Cognitive Processing Therapy: Veteran/Military Version: Therapist's Manual* addresses such sensitivity: "We are frequently asked if it is important to develop a relationship with the patient before beginning any trauma work. Our answer is no, this is not necessary."[44] The rationale offered is a thin one. It centers on how refraining from diving right into trauma work colludes with clients' avoidant tendencies. Surprisingly, there's scant appreciation for a client's *readiness* to confront a trauma in light of how the troubling events in his or her present life resemble what the past trauma psychologically put the person through. This is the stuff of real empathic sensitivity in therapy—approaches that seasoned practitioners in the field know about. As we will see, sadly, this sensitivity is often attained mostly in spite of a formal education in psychology, not because of it. Or, to quote the distinguished British psychiatrist Peter Lomas: "The forces that have moulded contemporary psychiatry and psychotherapy have, I believe, made it very difficult for two people to meet each other to discuss, in a natural and ordinary way, the problems of one of them."[45]

A SCIENTIFIC EDUCATION FOR A NONSCIENTIFIC CAREER

Nowadays, everywhere you turn, whether it's within the halls of academia or the mental health field at large, there's overwhelming pressure for psychotherapists at all levels to frame their training experiences under the mantle of science, as evidenced-based approaches. In the clinical psychology department at Stony Brook University, New York, the mission statement claims that students "are trained to embrace evidenced-based techniques across different therapeutic orientations in the interests of instigating behavior change."[46] In the graduate program in social work at the University of Arkansas, Little Rock, students are required to take a course titled Evidence-Based Social Work Practice in Adult Mental Health, in which they acquire "knowledge of evidenced-based practice approaches for adult clients who have a DSM-IV-TR diagnostic condition."[47]

A junior colleague told me recently that to remain competitive when applying to psychology internship sites, he had to attend as many evidenced-based treatment workshops as he could and highlight them in his application. We shared a good laugh as he prided himself on remembering all their acronyms: ACT (acceptance and commitment therapy), DBT (dialectical behavior therapy), EMDR (eye movement desensitization and reprocessing), and so forth. The acronyms seem to denote the scientific legitimacy of an approach; without them on an application or résumé, you risk rendering yourself unhirable. Not a week passes where I don't receive a brochure in the mail advertising an upcoming continuing education workshop touting some cutting-edge, evidenced-based set of techniques promising fast-acting, marvelous results. My favorite is a Treating Patients with Trauma course offered by David D. Burns, MD: "T.E.A.M (Testing Empathy Agenda Setting Methods) . . . is based on research on how psychotherapy actually works. . . . It helps therapists track therapeutic progress at every session and use 15 techniques to melt away therapeutic resistance."[48]

Something relatively unscientific yet of bedrock significance gets lost in the frenzy to teach and be taught evidenced-based skills and techniques—the need for therapists to acquire better relationship skills. Scott Miller, a well-regarded spokesperson for what works in psychotherapy and the founder and director of the International Center for Clinical Excellence, recently affirmed this viewpoint in an interview: "The best predictor of treatment outcome in mental health services is not the specific technique, but rather the provider of those services. In psychotherapy, for example, who provides the treatment is between five and nine times more important than what particular treatment approach is provided."[49] Elsewhere, he added to this observation: "The bottom line for those wishing to become more effective . . . is *work on your relationship skills.*"[50]

As we have seen, mountains of data, not to mention common wisdom, support the centrality of empathy building in the professional lives of therapists. Meta-analyses also zero in on the importance of other types of human know-how with clients: demonstrating positive regard and genuineness; being skilled at managing one's underreactions and overreactions in the consulting room (countertransference);

adeptly resolving conflicts or repairing ruptures in the therapist-client alliance; and adapting the therapy to the individual client. As for adapting one's practice to the client, the father of modern medicine, Sir William Osler, is reputed to have said, "It is sometimes much more important to know what sort of patient has a disease than what sort of disease a patient has."[51]

Psychotherapy graduate schools and training sites tend to be heavy on data-driven and book-knowledge sources of clinical learning. They see the correlation of empathy and client progress as just another fact. They are light on offering experiential sources of learning that cultivate trainees' evolving capacities to embody the nuances of knowing *how* to empathize with a suffering person. Philosophers call this the distinction between declarative knowledge and procedural knowledge. Knowing the citations of what studies provide empirical evidence for the clinical importance of empathy, or being adept at supplying an intellectual definition of empathy, is no guarantee that a would-be therapist can demonstrably be empathic.

Many graduate students and trainees are blindsided when embarking on clinical work, crossing the wide chasm between the classroom and the declarative knowledge they have amassed, into the therapy office, where procedural knowledge is demanded. The accounts of early-career psychologists in *Becoming a Clinical Psychologist: Personal Stories of Doctoral Training* are heart-wrenching. The following disclosure by Matthew Liebman, who was completing his predoctoral internship at Montefiore Medical Center in the Bronx, is all too typical:

> In graduate school it is easy to forget that everything you learn has to do with people. None of the theory is any good unless it can be applied to helping people in need. And when that person is sitting in a chair across from you, looking at you with a bizarre mix of depression and hope as if the next thing out of your mouth could potentially have the power to make it all better, the pressure may be enough to shake loose every bit of information you've learned in the past several years all at once, creating a flood in your psyche. Alternatively, everything you've learned thus far may simply disappear.[52]

It's therapeutic know-how that clients really need and want. This is borne out by the results of the 2004 Therapy in America Poll, which gathered information by phone from a large sample of therapy recipients on what led to success in their treatment. The two top-ranked factors were "therapist's listening skills" and "therapist's personality," endorsed by 63 percent and 52 percent of participants, respectively.[53] Arguably, it is these diffuse human abilities and qualities that are cultivated not in the classroom, but in the therapist's own personal therapy.

The distinguished psychologists Jesse Geller, John Norcross, and David Orlinsky succinctly define the core value one's personal therapy represents for most psychotherapists: "Our training, our identity, our health, and our self-renewal revolve around the epicenter of personal therapy experience."[54] Among therapists, there is an unspoken axiom that one's own therapy is the single-most important prerequisite for entering the field and performing meaningful work with clients. It is the basis for expanding our emotional thresholds. It familiarizes us with our darker human tendencies and pressing needs. Throwing ourselves into therapy in this way primes our capacity to be confidently present and compassionate with clients as they themselves reminisce, grieve, rage, lust, upstage, negate, appreciate, or tap into and articulate any number of awkward emotions and ideas. The more emotionally integrated and self-aware we become in our own therapy, the stronger our immunity against acting out with clients because of our own unresolved life traumas and basic needs (countertransference). Our therapists regularly become concrete models around which to construct our own fledgling therapeutic style.

The emotional turmoil of bearing witness day in and day out to clients' traumas, confusing accounts of their life experiences, and seemingly impossible relationship dilemmas can create burnout, vicarious traumatization, and compassion fatigue. Reaching out for professional help periodically throughout your career keeps you stable and capable of offering help.

Most therapists walk the walk. A national survey comprising a random sample of more than six hundred psychologists, counselors, and social workers concluded that 85 percent take part in therapy at some point in their lives.[55] Approximately 55 percent of therapists engage in two periods of treatment, and 20 percent three or more.[56] And when psychotherapists enter therapy, it is typically not short-term treatment, but long-term. The average number of sessions experienced by psychotherapists cited by one major study is about 222, or more than four years of weekly psychotherapy.[57]

Not surprisingly, when therapists seek out therapy, they don't scrutinize the scientific credentials of their preferred practitioner. A 2009 survey published in *Psychotherapy Theory, Research, Practice, Training* found that the top five qualities practitioners home in on when choosing a therapist are, in rank order, competence, warmth and caring, clinical experience, openness, and professional reputations. Research productivity was a distant twentieth, behind cost per session, gender, age, and religious affiliation. The authors of this investigation concluded: "Psychotherapists largely try to repeat a therapeutic relationship characterized by warmth, empathy, acceptance, equality, positive regard, and good listening with their own patients."[58]

Ironically, when CBT therapists engage in their own therapy, it is not of the evidenced-based CBT type they themselves were trained to perform. In a 2000 investigation of psychotherapists' therapy preferences, Anton Laireiter at the University of Salzburg in Austria discovered that 50 to 60 percent of CBT therapists enter psychodynamic therapies, and 20 to 30 percent humanistic ones, compared with a mere 10 to 15 percent who seek out their CBT brethren. Even the most hardened practitioners of what science has to offer about the effectiveness of CBT techniques seem to want for themselves what their scientific training cautions them against: to talk openly about whatever is on their minds.[59]

Disturbingly, the usefulness of one's own psychotherapy as an anchor to do the work is not required or otherwise pushed by university departments. Along these lines, psychologist Jonathan Shedler tells a story of a graduate student in Yale University's clinical psychology program. She asked a senior faculty member for the name of a reputable therapist she might look up. His response was shocking: "Why would you want to do that? Research shows it doesn't do anything."[60]

The good professor was obviously not up on the research about how important personal therapy is to the average mental health professional for their professional growth. In a well-regarded study of nearly five thousand psychotherapists worldwide who yielded information on their career development over their professional life span, 80 percent of the participants ranked their personal therapy as highly influential. This factor was only second in line to experience in therapy with patients, underscored by a hefty 97 percent of participants. The reading of relevant books or journals was seventh on the list of fifteen highly influential influences (50 percent endorsement), and conducting research was last (18 percent).[61]

Apparently, once they are ensconced in a life of professional practice, most psychotherapists turn away from any formative allegiance to research-based findings to guide their work. Instead, experiential learning in the context of their own clinical work and personal self-growth appear to be the main channels they rely on to maintain clinical know-how.

Academics like Timothy Baker at the University of Wisconsin–Madison stop short of saying that psychotherapists who fail to exclusively use evidenced-based treatments have an unethical practice.[62] Yet at a fundamental human level, the real ethical question is how a science-heavy curriculum in graduate school underprepares trainee therapists to develop the emotional intelligence necessary to assist with the emotional suffering of others in sophisticated ways. In *The Psychology Industry Under a Microscope!*, David Stein reviewed the course content of 115 doctoral programs in clinical and counseling psychology accredited by the APA. He discovered that almost 80 percent of them required students to take courses in research design, research methods, and advanced statistics. Only 2 percent offered a specialty course on case conference, where early in their graduate-school experience students acquire in-depth knowledge about specific client problems. Stein underscored a rather obvious but overlooked observation: "Research courses consume too much time and should be electives for those students who know they wish to be academicians or researchers. Medical students do not spend time studying research. They are exclusively devoted to mastering treatments for clinical problems."[63]

These days, fewer than 25 percent of doctoral students in clinical and counseling psychology become university professors or research psychologists.[64] The vast majority of doctoral students in these domains become practicing clinicians. Yet their doctoral education and training is highly abstract, predominantly preparing them for a career in clinical research, with scant focus on experiential learning opportunities that expand their personhood and relationship-building skills to give them depth and dimensionality as clinicians.

Ethical questions also arise when we narrowly define what constitutes a scientific education and omit sources of clinical knowledge that help trainees acquire expertise in psychotherapy for the betterment of clients. For example, in the push toward evidenced-based practice, case studies have been increasingly sidelined as less valid forms of evidentiary knowledge. For veteran psychologists like me, detailed case studies have always represented the most grounded, elucidating way of learning about clinical problems and personality dynamics and their treatment. The findings of large clinical trials are often abstruse and difficult to make relevant to any particular client I encounter. In a recent piece for the *New York Times*, "Why Doctors Need Stories," Peter Kramer put it this way: "The vignette, unlike data, retains the texture of the individual life."[65] Case studies often contain rich descriptions of client problems and dynamics, spelling out specific comments and identifiable actions taken by the therapist. Such treatment narratives become templates from which to derive a pragmatic understanding of past, present, and future clients. One's clinical know-how is boosted by the reading of a potent case study in ways that cannot be matched by the standard numbers-driven empirical study.

An education restricted to acceptable, evidenced-based practices and to an overemphasis on the renderings of the scientific method can also foreclose what the arts and humanities have to offer in understanding human nature and human change processes. We forget that Freud's theories were largely inspired less by his medical training than by his readings of *King Lear*, *Hamlet*, *Oedipus Rex*, *The Brothers Karamazov*, the philosophical texts of Plato, Mill, and Nietzsche, and the sculpture of Michelangelo. As one generation gives way to another, archetypal human dilemmas and life solutions show up anew in noteworthy works of art, fiction, and film. These productions have much to offer psychotherapists who desire a palpable familiarity with a range of disturbing states of mind. For instance, novels like *Filth*, by the Scottish author Irvine Welsh, and movies like *A Clockwork Orange* and *Bad Lieutenant* have implanted in me a working familiarity with sadistic states of mind, unsurpassed by any clinical literature I have read. And I perceive and appreciate resilience in clients more from having devoured Russell Banks's book-turned-film *Affliction* and periodic entrancement by the print hanging on my office wall: Ansel Adams's wind-battered but elegantly strong Jeffrey pine.

To be of real benefit to their clients, psychotherapists will need to abandon any rigid adherence to evidenced-based techniques inculcated in them in graduate school. They will need to reorient themselves to more fully appreciate practice-based evidence or knowledge acquired hour in and hour out while they conduct psychotherapy. And they must not only mine what psychological science serves up about problems in living, but also expand their informational paradigms to include the musings of philosophers, artists, writers, and filmmakers.

CHAPTER SIX

The Healing Relationship

LET ME BEGIN with a sample of my clinical work that illustrates how effective psychotherapy pivots on the therapist's human know-how, or wisdom in action. Using this wisdom, the therapist works to communicate ideas to clients with the right words and the right degree of emotion as a catalyst for real client change. This is closer to a form of *human expertise*—exquisite sensitivity and communicative finesse—than technical expertise, or some employment of a learned code of clinical behavior.

On occasion, my sixty-one-year-old retired police officer client, Jordan, amicably refers to me as his "bartender without the alcohol." My tendency to chuckle rather than stiffen up and make any number of standard therapeutic interpretations (e.g., "I think this reflects how uncomfortable you feel being in therapy with a trained professional and really opening up") indirectly conveys to him that I accept him for who he is and see the logic in his comment. An exchange with a bartender happens to be Jordan's blue-collar cultural reference point for a relationship where license is given to peel back the façade and speak more candidly about life's troubles.

Jordan is not, as therapists are wont to say, an insight-oriented client. He is not particularly psychologically minded. There's no painful confusion lessened by the search for a deeper understanding of why his life has turned out the way it has. There's little exploration of how his early life experiences have created problematic expectations for relationships in the present. Jordan is mostly indifferent to acquiring a richer understanding of why his two previous marriages ended in divorce, why he has no male friends, or why he has no bucket list of cherished life pursuits to pursue in retirement. But this is not to say that Jordan is immune to, and incapable of, learning from comments I offer aimed at deepening his self-understanding when I make the issue at hand fathomable to him, and I plead my case with the right words, communicated with the right degree of emotional expressivity. Or that our therapy relationship is not a productive one. Far from it. Let me explain.

One presenting problem Jordan had on entering therapy was that his daughter Marianne rarely spoke with or visited him. This was a constant open emotional wound for Jordan—trying to somehow cope with the psychological equivalent of having a dead child. Jordan had been a devoted father to Marianne in the years leading up to his contentious divorce from her mother, when she was about seven. But during her preteen years, Marianne lived almost exclusively with her mother and maintained only sporadic visits with Jordan. These visits dropped off drastically once she became a full-fledged teenager. After Jordan's former wife married a successful physician, Marianne was enrolled in an elite private school, where she became an accomplished show jumper. Even though Jordan was highly articulate and educated, he had been forced to pull out of a doctoral program in sociology in his late twenties, just shy of completing his dissertation, to work full time to provide for his wife and children from his first marriage.

He now wore a shaggy beard and identified as working class. This seemed to widen the divide between him and Marianne, who was primed by her mother's high-society lifestyle to view Jordan as a person of lower social status and the middle-class neighborhood where he lived as a ghetto. Her attitude dampened any motivation to maintain visits with her father. I deduced from Jordan's disclosures that his former wife might tend to demonize those she felt injured by and might strongly need others to share her absolutist negative attributions. In Jordan's mind, his former wife's psychology was one of "if you're not for me, you're against me." If there was any truth to this, it would be extremely difficult for Marianne to have a positive image of Jordan, particularly if her mother harbored a mostly negative one of him.

Despite the forces stacked against him, Jordan somehow believed that "family was family," assuming Marianne should simply override her mother's malignant image of him, disentangle herself from her privileged lifestyle, set aside her adolescent self-involvement, and commit to visits with him. His typical approach on the phone with Marianne was to launch into a lecture on the need to value family, to do the right thing, and to spend time with her father. The more Jordan felt shut out by Marianne, the more he demanded that she share with him information about her everyday life. This demand, however, hardened her perception of him as overbearing. It was as if Jordan believed his only recourse was to guilt Marianne into maintaining visits. In my mind, this attitude simply consolidated Marianne's image of Jordan as stodgy and unpleasant to be around, even though he genuinely loved her and was desperate for them to spend time together.

Noticing that a dysfunctional dynamic in his relationship with his mother was recurring with Marianne, I got worked up during one session and uttered, "Jordan, sometimes I think you turn into your mother, lecturing Marianne on how she needs to value family and visit more often. I remember this is exactly what you told me your mother would do. There would be the weekly calls where you would hold the phone away from your ear as she launched into a monologue about how neglected she felt as a mother who was entitled to, but denied, more contact from her children. Her approach might have worked for you and guilted you into keeping in touch with her. But this approach is not working with Marianne." Jordan sat back and absorbed what I had to say. The right mixture of forthrightness, affection, and timing allowed Jordan to truly digest what I had to say.

This insight paved the way for Jordan to realize that while he certainly deserved more contact with Marianne, he needed a different approach. It was not an insight that, once achieved, fundamentally altered Jordan's habit of guiltily lecturing Marianne. Mostly, he needed kindhearted reminders from me: "There you go again, Jordan, sounding like your mother and getting irate when Marianne inevitably wants the phone conversation over in a hurry!" Over time in his conversations with Marianne, he was better able to catch himself midstream and take a different tone with her. He was less apt to demand she commit to visits. He invited her to reach out to him when she was so inspired and when her busy school schedule permitted. Despite his best efforts, Marianne largely shunned any contact with Jordan.

In the early phase of therapy, Jordan railed at the unfairness of it all. He clung to an image of how his relationship with his daughter should be—regular visits actively encouraged by her mother, invitations to show-jumping events, friendly phone conversations. This unrealistic picture fueled his bitterness. Gradually, Jordan accepted the emotional truth that he was essentially powerless to turn the tide in his relationship with Marianne *for now*, because of the seemingly impossible psychological and family dynamics at play. For Jordan, a former college football player and law enforcement officer, to acknowledge feeling powerless was no easy feat. At opportune moments, I pressed to see if, behind the anger, there was grief over missing out on seeing his daughter grow up, the same daughter he had held in his arms as an infant. Tears welled up in his eyes, and in mine also.

Jordan's emotions about the situation with Marianne came to be less monopolized by anger. In time, his mind-set was a mixture of sad resignation and hope for a future in which Marianne might decouple herself from her mother in the transition to college and show an interest in resuming a relationship with him. He became less obsessed with exerting time and energy trying to correct his relationship with Marianne to no avail. Or, as I put it, he gave up the futile pursuit of trying to draw water from a dry well. Jordan, who could be quite lyrical, had his own versions of this realization: "Yeah, Doc, like shoveling sand against the tide or making a perfect swan dive into an empty pool." Instead, he turned his time and attention to his adult children from his first marriage and their grandchildren, who were responsive to his overtures and enjoyed his visits.

Another problem Jordan brought to therapy was the complicated nature of his marriage to his current wife, Betty. There was every indication that Jordan was ambivalent about the marriage. He was adamant that he had agreed to the marriage for reasons of convenience—to pool their financial resources. He joked that even though they lived under the same roof, they didn't live together. (He lived above Betty in a duplex.) They both seemed to prize solitude and were overly attached to their personal routines. Jordan complained that he desired more companionship with Betty, more conversations, more travel, more physical intimacy. Yet rarely did he initiate and persist in the actualization of intimate get-togethers, travel plans, or other activities. Instead, he secretly kept relationships going with several female friends he met online, rationalizing that, in truth, he was not married and needed more companionship than Betty was willing to offer. Invariably, Betty would catch on to Jordan's outside female friendships (he claimed they were nonsexual) and understandably withdraw in self-protection. The outcome left Jordan feeling emotionally neglected by Betty, justifying his need for other women friends.

In my work with Jordan, I waited for openings to call attention to how the demise of his first two marriages may have soured him on the whole idea of marriage. As emotionally constricted as Jordan was—which probably limited the quality of intimacy he could offer his wives—he nonetheless prided himself on being a loyal, self-sacrificing husband and father. That his former wives fell out of love with him and angled for their own financial interests and child-custody conveniences during and after the divorces not only hurt him emotionally but also fractured his value system. By staying ambivalently married to Betty, Jordan was no doubt safeguarding himself against reexperiencing the rejection and demoralization he had previously experienced with his former wives.

For all his difficulties with Betty, the one virtue she indisputably wore was loyalty. I confirmed this quality for Jordan in the concrete details of his disclosures to me: her willingness to accompany him to his medical appointments and care for him after his multiple surgeries; her eagerness to include him in her family events; her conscientious and fair handling of their finances. Once, drawing from Jordan's and my shared reality as lapsed Catholics, I asked, "Is it fair to hold Betty responsible for the sins committed by your exes—their disloyalty, their self-interest—when Betty really seems to have your back?" Jordan's perception of Betty as a loyal partner was strengthened by my confirmatory feedback. A healthy feeling of guilt emerged—he did not want to hurt Betty anymore by keeping outside women friends. He cut off all ties with them, and if any women resurfaced, he vowed to tell them he was married and to include Betty in the details of any interactions. I could even discern that Jordan was more likely to let Betty know he appreciated having her in his life.

Thornier issues remained in our therapy. Jordan can be passive, and his lack of initiative and persistence were Betty's main complaints about their relationship. Give Jordan a list, a scheduled event, or a family obligation, and chances are he will follow through. Ask him what dreams he has in his life with Betty, whether travel or music or other activities would make him feel more engaged in his life, or what he can do to jump-start his sex life with Betty, and Jordan is speechless. Some of this silence is explainable in terms of Jordan's preference to live a simple, unencumbered, relatively solitary life in retirement as a welcome countermeasure to his overly social, overcommitted career in law enforcement. However, we laugh that he is forever the Catholic altar boy, wired to live a life of duty and obligation, as if there's sin in pursuing personal enjoyment and satisfaction. As a former altar boy and Catholic seminarian myself—both of which I told Jordan early on in treatment—I could profoundly relate to his struggle. A dimension to my ongoing work with Jordan remains niggling and nudging him about identifying and persisting with what he really desires, what might make his life fuller, more fulfilling.

As of this writing, Jordan has been in weekly psychotherapy with me for almost four years. Our therapy relationship could easily have failed before it even started. In the beginning, Jordan was a reluctant client, brought in under duress by Betty, who was exasperated by his lack of real commitment to her. He had never been in therapy before. He carefully guarded his privacy because of his undercover work in law enforcement. He was used to doing the inquiring, the investigating, the detective work. He is a burly man, a pull-yourself-up-by-the-bootstraps type, not given to shows of emotion other than angry rants. What made the relationship viable and, then, therapeutically productive?

The answers are myriad. Jordan clearly needed an egalitarian arrangement, not a hierarchical one. He needed to sense that we both basically encountered the same existential predicaments, muddling through life facing problems common to all humans. I asked Jordan once what he would have done if, rather than joining in with him briefly in discussing British soccer, sharing my views on religion as requested, or responding to his concerns about whether I could relate to his challenges as a father, I had responded like a typical therapist: "Jordan, this is your time to talk about you, not to avoid that and get me to talk." Jordan remarked that such a comment would have ended the therapy right then and there.

Session in and session out, Jordan incrementally learned he could count on me to be sincerely interested in, and emotionally engaged by, whatever was on his mind. He learned to expect that I would apply whatever wisdom I could muster to zero in on something of emotional relevance, said as best I could in a way he might truly hear—me exercising due diligence to avoid being a stilted professional using alienating clinical jargon. These conditions fostered greater emotional vulnerability and prompted Jordan to talk less self-consciously about his troubles. The more credibility I gained in his eyes because of my style of relating to him and genuine regard and affection for him, the more I could lean in and confront him when necessary.

My relationship with Jordan is a prime example of how effective therapy actually works. It reveals that the healing properties of the therapy relationship reside in the client's persistent and confident expectation of empathy, confirmation, confrontation rooted in loving concern, usable psychological insights, and affirmation of the need to live life more actively, happily, and deliberately.

EMPATHIC IMMERSION

Empathy's rise to prominence as a basic therapeutic stance is a testament to clients who implore their therapists to just stick to the task of listening to and accurately understanding their personal experiences. Both Heinz Kohut and Carl Rogers—the two theorists credited with according central importance to therapeutic empathy—have humbling stories to tell about how they finally learned to value the act of tuning in to clients' subjective experiences more carefully and caringly, eventually systematizing their own schools of therapy.

Treating a middle-aged professional man harmed by religiously based parental intolerance, Kohut rather candidly spells out his own epiphany:

> The patient, as I finally grasped, insisted—and had a right to insist—that I learn to see things exclusively in *his* way and not at all in *my* way. And, as we finally came to see—or rather as I finally came to see, since the patient had seen it all along—the content of *all* my various interpretations had been cognitively correct but incomplete in a decisive direction.[1]

Rogers is almost apologetic in his epiphany:

> Very early in my work as a therapist, I discovered that simply listening to my client, very attentively, was an important way of being helpful. So when I was in doubt as to what I should do in some active way, I listened. It seemed surprising to me that such a passive kind of interaction could be so useful. . . . The most effective approach was to listen to the feelings, the emotions, whose patterns could be discerned through the client's words . . . [then] "reflect" these feelings back to the client—"reflect" becoming in time a word that made me cringe. But at that time, it improved my work as a therapist, and I was grateful.[2]

It was the misuse of Rogers's method of reflecting back clients' moment-to-moment feelings and concerns that made him uneasy—the therapists who simply mouthed back clients' words in a rote fashion:

CLIENT: I'm irritated with my wife because she mistakenly took my car keys in her purse this morning and I had to take the bus to work.

THERAPIST: So you are irritated with your wife because she mistakenly took your car keys.

Nevertheless, both Rogers's person-centered and Kohut's self-psychology therapy approaches underscore how psychologically restorative it is for clients to have their shifting feelings and ideas tracked and reiterated with genuine care and attentiveness. For Rogers, ready access to consistent empathic recognition helps clients avow, express, and integrate feelings, thereby making them more congruent as people, or more emotionally grounded.

Kohut believed that meeting clients' "mirroring needs" was critical to their attainment of a viable and vital sense of self. Therapy rich in mirroring experiences allowed clients a second chance at development. Clients visiting him complained of feeling depleted, void of ambition, or prone to drastic downturns in their self-esteem when falling short of their goals and aspirations. Kohut thought that these vulnerabilities grew out of inadequate mirroring of their basic emotions during their childhood. In particular, he believed that such a client felt the consistent absence of a caregiver's love—that special gleam in the adult's eye—in response to the child's display of talents and abilities. Or the client's childhood caregiver had been unavailable to help the child process grief, shame, and rage during the inevitable disappointments all kids face.

In the self-psychology model, the therapist's sustained and predictable focus on sensitively handling clients' moments of elation, chagrin, sadness, fear, or even rage at being misunderstood has profound remedial effects. Mirroring affirmation of clients' proud moments can remedy thwarted self-esteem. Repeatedly seen as worthy, the clients more resolutely see themselves as worthy. Over time, reliable access to sensitive attunement when there are upsurges of intense emotion lessens the potential for clients to get emotionally flooded by such experiences. Emotions such as anger, sadness, and elation are avoided less and become acceptable aspects of clients' self-experience, which makes clients feel more alive and energized.

Many beginning psychotherapists—especially in the current quick-fix zeitgeist—shy away from upholding an empathic stance with clients. They often believe they are not being productive enough if their primary mode of relating to clients centers on reflecting, or mirroring clients' subjective experiences. They assume that mirroring lacks sophistication and devalues their vast education and training. I often remind my trainees of the implications of Rogers's and Kohut's ideas. I reassure them of the therapeutic value to settling in and becoming absorbed in the subjective experiential lives of their clients; of yielding to and following along with clients' moment-by-moment disclosures; of accepting the free-flowing, nonlinear nature of the endeavor; of starting sessions without any conscious agenda, trusting that something emotionally relevant always presents itself. The ideal state of mind to inhabit is cleverly captured by Sheldon Roth, a psychoanalyst from New England: "What we are always striving for is to be at the edge of the patient's most immediate experience and awareness. When our patient walks through the door, we have no real idea of what this might be. We want to behave as if excessive movement puts all of living nature into hiding, as it does at a woodland pool."[3]

Much that is wholesome about therapy involves the clinician's covert automatic imitation of clients' verbal and nonverbal behavior. Empathically immersed therapists give themselves over to the organically unfolding interaction, unconsciously and preconsciously adapting their behavior to that of their clients. Synchronized, well-timed nods, frowns, grimaces, leg folds, and chin rubs lubricate and embolden client disclosures. There is abundant, barely conscious facial dialogue in good therapy, the sort of dialogue that leaves clients feeling attended to and understood.

Sometimes, empathic responses encompass short phrases the therapist uses to convey that he or she is tracking what's on the client's mind or to pithily sum up what the client feels. The brevity of the expression reflects a respect for the tempo of the client's communications, a desire not to markedly interrupt him or her midstream.

Adam, an emotionally constricted pharmacist, arrived flustered for his therapy session. We had the following exchange:

ADAM *(with frustration in his voice)*: There was a road crew blocking traffic with cones in both directions in my neighborhood this morning. I was stuck in my own driveway! There are no shortages of fools out on the road.

GNAULATI: The circus is in town!

ADAM: And the clowns are out!

Mary Anne, a busy executive and mother of three daughters, bemoaned having no time to herself:

MARY ANNE: I'm clocking about a fifty-hour workweek right now, on top of all that's expected of me at home. I'm not eating right or exercising. Everywhere I turn, I have to put out and put out, just keep on giving. You can only imagine how I feel. . . .

GNAULATI: Depleted?

MARY ANNE: Exactly. I'm so unbelievably worn out and exhausted.

Empathy can have evocative effects for clients. It can act like an emotional stimulant, freeing up clients to access and more fully articulate dimly felt emotions.

Because Janet's aunt had had no children of her own, Janet had felt compelled to step in and help out while her aunt had been dying in hospice care. Janet earlier confessed to me that she had been repulsed by her aunt, an alcoholic who had watched soap operas all day:

JANET: Who am I to judge? Maybe my aunt was content with her life.

GNAULATI: It sounds to me like, in retrospect, you feel guilty for not having had more compassion for her while she was dying.

JANET: I suppose so. I feel bad. I could have made her final days a little easier.

GNAULATI: How?

JANET: Sneak her cigarettes, buy her better booze. I don't know.

GNAULATI: I can tell you have some regrets. . . .

JANET: Yeah. I guess I just feel bad about the life she had and wished I had not been so put off by her.

Sticking with and teasing out the implications of clients' word choices and metaphors in ways that draw out underlying feelings is another form of empathy. My client Liam made every effort to reach out to neighbors and friends to make his home a desirable place for their kids to gather, so that his kids had companions. All too often, however, his invitations were ignored or turned down. He frequently felt that adult family members and friends failed to match his zeal to spend time together. When he was growing up, Liam's home had been a veritable neighborhood hot spot where kids and their parents convened. This all changed suddenly during his preteen years when his mother died. He spoke with me about his longing:

LIAM: I feel like I'm losing at the game of life. I'm not sure what I'm doing wrong or if I'm doing anything wrong. Friends are getting together and not including me. My son is definitely not part of the in group at school. It is very different from how I remember my life as a kid. It's all overwhelming, like there's a big hole in the plane and I'm trying to cover it up.

GNAULATI: Planes usually crash when there's a big hole in them.

LIAM: I'm going to cry, but I can't. I want to get back to the point I was making. . . .

GNAULATI *(softly)*: Maybe the point is, there's a lot of sadness and loneliness that's hard to just go with . . .

LIAM *(sobbing uncontrollably)*: Before my mother died, our home was the hub. Family and friends came to us.

Therapists also use their empathic understanding to turn an implicit impression within the client's narrative into more of an explicit realization.

Lydia, who elected to homeschool her children, was demoralized because her husband, Marlon, frequently underappreciated all it took to both raise and educate their children.

LYDIA: When I tell Marlon I'm essentially working two full-time jobs—running a household and educating our kids—he claims I'm exaggerating and making excuses for myself. He calls me lazy and disorganized. Then when I push back and tell him he's being mean, he accuses me of being too sensitive.

GNAULATI: So Marlon doesn't see himself as too critical, and he sees you as too sensitive. It looks to me like you think Marlon has a blind spot for how critical he can be.

LYDIA: He really does. It's getting to the point where I feel I need to swallow my feelings when he starts up and just say something to appease him.

As should be evident from the above clinical examples, empathy only truly validates client experiences inasmuch as the therapist feels moved by, not removed from, the client. Real empathy is far from sterile affirmation. It's not an applied technique or a function the therapist provides. It involves genuine emotional engagement from the therapist. When therapists empathically give from their humanity, the client feels not only heard but also confirmed. His or her pain and suffering, hopes and aspirations, fears and anxieties, attributes and foibles are not just observed but also authenticated.

As we are about to see, confirmatory feedback plays an important role in normalizing the feelings, self-perceptions, and other attitudes that clients abnormalize. Of course, sensitive confrontation in therapy also has its place. There are always those moments in the office when the conscientious therapist might need to hold clients accountable for the betterment of their social and emotional well-being.

SENSITIVELY CONFIRMING AND CONFRONTING CLIENTS

Several lines from Walt Whitman's widely acclaimed poem "Song of Myself" capture quite lyrically the quality of personal involvement that distinguishes confirmatory therapeutic gestures:

I do not ask the wounded person how he feels, I myself become the wounded person . . . (It is you talking as much as myself, I act as the tongue of you . . .)[4]

In clinical terminology, Martha Stark, clinical instructor in psychiatry at the Harvard Medical School, claims that the appropriate state of mind is one where the therapist remains "centered within her own experience, allowing the patient's experience to enter into her, and taking on the patient's experience as her own."[5] Being fully and wholly present to clients in this way is especially important to normalize needs and desires clients tend to abnormalize.

Coming out of a long-term relationship with an abusive, possessive boyfriend, twenty-eight-year-old Sara went through a period in her life where she welcomed casual romantic relationships with men. She restored some confidence in her ability to live life independently. As the novelty of rediscovering her freedom wore off, she secretly longed for a close, monogamous relationship with a man. She didn't want the type of monogamy marked by enmeshment and possessiveness that had existed with her abusive former boyfriend. Rather, she wanted a relationship in which both partners gave each other space and showed mutual regard for each other's independence. It was more than her recent string of boyfriends had to offer. On the face of it, her wants were perfectly legitimate: texts and phone calls returned in a timely manner, romantic dates planned and followed through with, initiation shown to give her gifts and suggest travel locations she might enjoy. In short, Sara wanted clear signs that she held a special place in the heart of whatever boyfriend happened to be in her life.

Sara delegitimized her legitimate romantic needs. She berated herself for "weirding out" when she became hurt and irritated with a given boyfriend when it took him days to respond to her texts. She saw herself as needy for wanting a man to initiate a date. It was "psycho" of her to be jealous when she discovered that a new, reportedly committed boyfriend refrained from putting pictures of the two of them on his Facebook page, even though pictures of his former girlfriend remained there. It was in this context that we had the following exchange:

GNAULATI: It seems hard for you to gauge what's OK to expect from a man.

SARA: I just need to be more chill and focus on me and my own life. The last thing I want is to be the jealous weirdo girlfriend.

GNAULATI: Maybe you're jealous, hurt, and irritated for good reason. As I see it, it's a baseline requirement for any serious romantic relationship to want a man to treat you special, make dates, and follow through with them. Don't you agree?

SARA: I guess so.

GNAULATI: I wish you would know so! You lost good years in that horrible relationship with your ex-boyfriend, and a big part of me thinks you deserve so much better than you're getting with men.

SARA *(with sadness in her eyes)*: You're right.

Clients need to know we not only can encounter them, but can also counter them. Not only face them, but also face off with them. Client-centered therapists (like child-centered parents) lose credibility if their expressions of sympathy and positivity are staid and overly predictable. More often than not, the issue is not *whether* to confront clients when they get stuck behaving egregiously or selling themselves short, but *when* and *how*. This decision involves therapeutic tact, described by Yale University psychologist Jesse Geller as follows: "the capacity to tell clients something they don't want to hear in a manner in which they can hear it."[6] The struggle entails benignly standing against the client, prepared to stand your ground and withstand any ire the confrontation creates, or as the prolific British psychoanalytic essayist Adam Phillips put it, "the analyst has to be tenacious without being authoritarian."[7]

Generally speaking, when clients act out (e.g., engage in unselfconscious impulsive, reckless, and blameworthy behavior), the therapist's job is—*in a good-natured way*—to engender in them an awareness of the negative consequences of their actions. They take too little responsibility for their actions. As counterintuitive as it sounds to the average caring therapist, healthy guilt needs to be aroused but in a way that doesn't make clients feel all bad. The focus is on the bad deed, not the badness of the doer of the deed. The following clinical vignette will illustrate.

In the early years of their marriage, before children came along, Bob and Joanne agreed that they had much love for one another. Bob wrote sweet notes to Joanne recognizing her cleverness, sincerity, and quick wit. Joanne made picture books of memorable times they shared together. In couples therapy with them, I had a palpable sense of the love and respect they had for each other despite the testiness and brittleness in their interactions.

Bob was prone to being boorish, making crass and critical comments that stunned Joanne. In turn, she would withdraw and respond coldly to Bob's subsequent makeup overtures.

Two months into treatment, we had a session in which Joanne described to me the photo book she had compiled early on in the marriage, documenting the paths her and Bob's lives had taken, culminating in their meeting and falling in love. I suddenly found myself tearing up and cobbled together a response:

> GNAULATI: That's so sweet and tender. . . . There's love that you have for each other that has gotten baked over by ways you get caught injuring each other. Bob, too much of the time I think you can be unselfconsciously critical and harsh like your mother. This then aggravates a tendency that you, Joanne, picked up from your father to withdraw and appear indifferent when Bob excitedly shares his workday with you. . . . You injure each other and risk eroding a love that has always been there.

Bob and Joanne appeared caught off guard by my tears, as was I. They were riveted by my comments and demurely nodded their heads in agreement. The following week, they reported that the session had been a "mini breakthrough" and that Bob was kinder, asking Joanne if she needed more help around the house. Bob thought Joanne was more lighthearted and more engaged with him.

Some clients are poised to disavow positive things said to them. They are overly invested in their distorted negative self-perceptions and attributions. A therapist must tenaciously verify what positive things they obviously have going for them to challenge their hardened self-deprecatory image.

Alan, a twenty-eight-year-old graphic artist with disabling social anxiety, had dropped out of college and was living with his parents. He often blithely launched into a litany of his failings with me:

> ALAN: Let's face it, I'm incompetent. There are the competent ones who do well in college and make something of their lives.

Then there's people like me with nothing going for them who sponge off their parents.

GNAULATI: What are you talking about, Alan? Granted, you may not have a college degree and you may be going through a transitional time in your life, having to live with your parents and struggling to conceive of some form of gainful employment. But I find you to be incredibly bright and articulate, an autodidact who is interested in literature and philosophy for its own sake, and someone who has a knack for seeing through pretense. That's not incompetence!

The examples I have provided should clarify that real empathic confirmation draws from the therapist's humanity. It involves emotionally diving into and divining clients' painful life stories. Professional aloofness and detachment cannot be therapists' routine fallback position to keep themselves from getting mixed up in their clients' psychological afflictions. We do well to heed the advice of the existentialist psychologist Emmy van Deurzen: "As therapists and counselors we need to be capable of letting our lives be touched by those of our clients. It is no use occupying the higher moral ground from which we can look down with mere empathy, interpretation, or judgment: we have to struggle with our clients' problems."[8]

FEELING WITH, AND FEELING FOR, THE CLIENT

There's a long-held belief in the field that disturbing emotions are like psychic forces lodged in clients' unconscious minds awaiting excavation through correct identification by the therapist. With this line of thinking, the therapist mostly subdues his or her emotionality, reflecting back what the client feels: "I can see that being passed over for the promotion at work makes you mad." Once correctly labeled and accurately mirrored by the therapist—and then vented by the client—the disturbing emotions somehow no longer disturb.

However, this more *intrapersonal* view of emotional experience is increasingly being replaced with an *interpersonal* one. A convergence of knowledge from fields as diverse as relational psychoanalysis, infant research, attachment theory, and affect regulation theory is beginning to change our thinking about emotional experience. The so-called intersubjective model, which I subscribe to, underscores how the content, intensity, duration, and outward expression of client emotions are inextricably linked to how they are responded to by the therapist. How quickly a client's feelings emerge and are recovered from; how lasting and intensely they are experienced; and how adept a client will become at finessing their outward expression—all these manifestations are contingent on the therapist's verbal and nonverbal expressions of mutually generated feelings in the room.

Because emotions are relationally contagious, therapists need to allow themselves to feel these contagious effects. An unfortunate carryover of the rule of abstinence, or neutrality, as a therapeutic stance is that clients are deprived of the potentiating effects of therapists' expressiveness. If clients are to be put more in touch with underlying feelings surrounding a painful disclosure, it sometimes takes a therapist to amplify his or her own mutually generated reactions to clients' disclosures. To take a reserved approach out of the belief that the therapist's expressiveness could contaminate the client's access to fully formed, self-contained, pure emotions is misguided.

There's a performing—not just informing—dimension to putting clients in touch with underlying feelings. The therapist must be skilled at knowing how and when to amplify versus dampen a response, prolong or foreshorten an emotional reaction, react animatedly or sedately, make a point loudly or quietly, and make eye contact or avert it. All these decisions must be coordinated as authentic expressions while the therapist rapidly processes verbal and nonverbal interactional information in the room. These skills provide the sort of receptivity and sensitivity clients need to effectively access, articulate, and elaborate their own unformulated emotions.

Along these lines, Allan Schore, a national expert in affective neuroscience at UCLA, writes: "For a working alliance to be created, the therapist must be experienced as being in a state of vitalizing attunement to the patient; that is, the crescendos and decrescendos of the therapist's affective state must be in resonance with similar states of crescendos and decrescendos of the patient."[9] Schore has published voluminously on the importance of therapists standing in as "psychobiological regulators" for clients, using their more expanded emotional repertoires to arouse and dampen clients' feelings along therapeutic lines. This regulation is more of a naturally occurring process arising out of therapists' acute attunement to, and sensitive handling of, clients' shifting emotional states, rather than some established technique.

Sometimes, a therapist and client are so in synch in the joint venture of fleshing out all the underlying thoughts and feelings a client experiences surrounding a troubling life event that the therapist can flit back and forth from feeling along with the client to feeling for the client. The therapist can sometimes even actually speak for the client in more elaborate ways that enlarge the client's emotional potential. Some examples are warranted.

Twenty-six-year-old George told me of an interaction he had while out at a fancy restaurant with his high-powered attorney parents and their wealthy friends. The discussion turned to an app one friend was designing to lure people into gambling at younger ages. George, a very perceptive, interpersonally astute, though extremely self-conscious man with a knack for seeing through pretense, responded, "Do you have to make money at other people's expense?" The family friend sneered at George's presumed naïveté, claiming that in a capitalist society, exploitation and moral ambiguity were inherent in the whole enterprise of accumulating wealth.

George confided to me that the family friend designing the app was brash and self-centered. He was cruel to his wife, who once confessed to George's mother that she only stayed married to preserve the opulent lifestyle her husband's career afforded her.

My anger mounted as George told his story. Noticing him shut down, I felt a pull to defend and emotionally invigorate him. I leaned forward in my chair and raised my voice:

GNAULATI: You didn't feel like pushing back when he called you naive? Like saying, "I might be naïve, but you are about as self-centered as they come, with a wife who is unhappily married, who only stays with you for the money, a wife who is wearing golden handcuffs. The two of you pursue wealth and

status, life feeling emptier by the day, yet falsely believing you
are happy"? What the heck!

GEORGE *(laughing, seeming to feel protected and understood,
half-shocked, yet half-emboldened)*: I'd never say that!

GNAULATI: I get it; I'm being over the top. But don't you believe
it and at some level wish you could say some version of that?

GEORGE *(blushing, but using a firm voice)*: Of course I believe it
and wish I could have been honest with that pompous ass.

In the words of the prolific York University psychotherapy researcher Leslie Greenberg, this interaction was my way of "changing
emotion with emotion"; or "emotionally addressing the withdrawal
tendencies in fear and shame by the thrusting forward tendency in
newly accessed anger at violation."[10]

Another example will help. A middle-aged college professor named
Gustavo came to see me after an incident in which his wife accused
him of being unfeeling in his reactions to a non-life-threatening medical procedure she needed. He had arranged for her to see a local expert in the field; escorted her to various preparatory appointments;
talked to the doctor on her behalf because her anxiety interfered with
her cogently representing herself; and ensured that she had a dose of
Valium on the morning of the surgery to diminish her anxiety. All the
same, Gustavo agreed with his wife's sense that he was oddly detached
and lacking compassion for her. Why was he not more loving toward
his wife in her hour of need? Maybe his wife was right that he was a
"cold fish," a "vain man" who valued professional accolades over family attachments.

As we explored their marital relationship, it came out that Gustavo had worked hard to put his wife's children from a first marriage
through private school and college; their father was well off but had
refused to pay child support. The first husband was highly manipula-
tive in his custody dealings. Nevertheless, Gustavo's wife insisted that
this difficult man be included at all holiday events and family functions
involving the children. At the same time, she frequently chastised
Gustavo for being unsupportive and overcommitted to his academic
research. Curiously, Gustavo was convinced his wife was spot-on in

seeing him as unforgivably coldhearted. In the context of one of these exchanges, I showed my irritation:

GNAULATI: Gustavo, you seem to represent your wife's point of view very well and underrepresent your point of view, or any feelings you might have, about being called unsupportive. *(Gently pounding fist on the chair)* I'm noticing that I'm more angry at your wife than you are right now! There's not a voice inside your head that wants to say, "Honey, I know I can let you down by not being more emotionally involved; I know you need more from me emotionally; but working hard to put the kids through school and college is the main way I've shown my support. So too is putting up with your unbearable ex-husband for the sake of the kids. It's downright hurtful to me that you not only don't appreciate that, but see it as me escaping from the family!'"?

GUSTAVO *(laughing loudly, segueing into obvious irritation)*: When I stop and look at it, that's actually how I feel. I need to get better at not letting my wife get into my head and see me as being selfish for working hard at my career. I did it mainly to put her kids, whom I adore, through school and give us all a good life!

Obviously, being gesturally animated and emitting somewhat leading comments like these can be risky (although, strictly speaking, we are talking about emotionally leading comments the therapist is led to by the client). I'm not endorsing wild, anything-goes therapy. Ruptures in the therapeutic relationship can ensue if clients perceive that the therapist has fixed biases about what and how they should feel. I'm proposing that therapists strive to embody *disciplined spontaneity*. They should use their intimate knowledge of any client to make rapid, intuitive judgments about what therapeutic exchange they could make with the client and how to draw him or her out emotionally. Disciplined spontaneity works when the client chimes in, picking up on saying more about the underlying emotional reactions the therapist channels for the client. Or at face value, it is effective because the accuracy of the therapist's emotional channeling of the client's unconscious affects is consensually validated by the client.

INSTILLING
PSYCHOLOGICAL MINDEDNESS

Emotionally enlivening clients and leaving them feeling understood is only one component of the therapy relationship. Another is facilitating their acquisition of greater self-understanding, or *psychological mindedness*. The latter term can be traced back to an obscure paper penned in 1973 by the now-deceased psychoanalyst Sheldon Appelbaum, of the Menninger Foundation.[11] In a nutshell, the term pertains to people's capacity and willingness to seek links between their current troublesome and troubling behavior and unresolved events in their past, as well as deciphering their own and others' motives and intentions. The use of the term *psychological mindedness* among mental health professionals, as well as in popular culture, has dwindled. This decline is largely because of the presumption that Freudian insights are arcane and don't lead people to change their overreactivity, irrational habits, and self-defeating tendencies. There's truth to this, but it's not all true. Some personal reflections of the benefits of Freudian insights in my own life will clarify.

My teenage son's bedroom is a disaster. A year or two ago, each time I saw wet towels on the floor and dirty dishes on his desk, it took every ounce of energy I had not to go apoplectic. My silent anger completely disabled me from saying or doing anything constructive to inspire him to keep his room clean. If anything, my anger inspired him to keep his room dirty because—in his normal, adolescent way—he had found my Achilles' heel: a ripe issue he could defy and oppose me on to express his autonomy.

Why did this particular issue emotionally undo me? My own adolescence was far from normal. From about age thirteen to seventeen, I lived away from home in a Catholic seminary in rural Aberdeen, Scotland, studying to be a priest. I had my own cubicle with scarce room for a bed and a chest to keep my clothes in. I kept my space immaculate. I had to. I was a prefect in charge of checking the cubicles of other seminarians to ensure they were clean. Leaving my own room unclean was unthinkable.

So one reason for my anger was my tacit sense that my son should adhere to my authority just as the other seminarians whose cubicles

I checked had. What's more, I had essentially bypassed my own adolescence, conforming to what the adults in my life expected of me, deluded into thinking that any normal acts of adolescent rebellion were signs of intolerable disobedience. The lingering effects of this mind-set were intolerance of one of my son's favorite ways of rebelling—keeping a dirty room.

In time, this realization gave me some flexibility in thinking about, and responding to, my son's behavior. It lessened the intensity of my anger, but certainly did not make it go away. It made me ignore the mess sometimes, to keep the peace. At other times, I came on strong, imploring him to respect the need to be cleaner and more organized in his life. The realization made me step back and wonder if my son's room was his regression zone, his place to let it all go in reaction to his demanding private school, where he had to compete academically and keep it all together.

My point is that helping clients hit on historical explanations or hidden motives for their undesirable behavior doesn't make it vanish. Instead, they now have a context for understanding their behavior and a newfound flexibility in responding.

There are other therapeutically useful Freudian notions besides that of history repeating itself if we don't recollect it and come to terms with it (*repetition compulsion*). Over the years, I have found that calling attention to clients' reliance on prototypical Freudian defense mechanisms has personal and interpersonal benefits. For example, in the case of projection, a therapist can shed light on a client's unawareness that he or she shares the same unlikable qualities the person found objectionable in another. True insight into acts of projection can have humbling effects and leave the client more annoyed with himself or herself than with a significant other.

My client Maria attended a nontraditional high school and was eager to graduate as quickly as possible by taking a high school equivalency test. Her stepbrother, Wally, had recently graduated from high school but lived at home with no regular job or realizable life plan. Maria frequently complained to me that Wally was disorganized, lazy, and uninspired.

MARIA: I'm so disappointed in Wally. He spends most of his day in his room on his computer. I feel like barging in and telling him, "Dude, go get a life."

GNAULATI: I know you are disappointed in Wally because he's not doing more with his life. Maybe you're worried that Wally's life is in *your* future and you are disappointed in yourself for not doing more with your life?

MARIA: It bothers me that I don't have more motivation at school and just want to be done with it all.

Psychoanalysis is not the only school of thought offering therapeutically meaningful insights. In the humanistic tradition, clients' behavior can be demystified in light of the struggles with the existential realities of the human condition: death, loneliness, freedom, nothingness. I find myself gravitating toward existentially oriented interpretations and quips that are rooted in the common concerns clients bring to me:

"Maybe you allow yourself to get caught up in compulsive action as a way to ignore the big changes you would need in your life to be happier. It's easier for most people to follow a script than write a script."

"When you are on your deathbed, I doubt you are going to regret not having racked up more billable hours at the law firm! You're probably going wish you had had more quality time with the ones you love."

"You seem to feel like your priorities are all off. What are your *real* priorities?"

"I wonder if what keeps you in this unsatisfying relationship with your girlfriend/boyfriend is the fear of being alone."

"I can tell you'd rather be alone than around conventional people living conventional lives."

"You sound like there should be some absolute purpose to your life outside of yourself that you need to discover, as if you don't have to define that and act on it for yourself."

In fairness, cognitive behavior therapy (CBT) has its own brand of psychological mindedness it tries to instill in clients. At its core, CBT helps clients step back and think more clearly about *how* they think (versus *why* they think the thoughts they have). Pointing out cognitive distortions—such as polarized thinking (inappropriate all-or-nothing or black-and-white explanations for events); personalization (assuming too much responsibility for negative outcomes); overgeneralization (basing a false general conclusion on a single piece of evidence); and catastrophizing (exaggerated negative expectations)—to clients can be helpful in alleviating anxiety and depression. Teaching clients to catch themselves when thinking in extreme (for example, replacing "Nobody loves me" with "Lots of people care about me, but I wish I was in love") can make a person feel slightly less demoralized. But when therapy comprises an exclusive and systematic analysis and correction of problematic thoughts and habits, it can be limiting, becoming more of a sterile educational experience than an emotionally evocative, personally transformative one.

In humanistically oriented psychotherapy, pointing out clients' thinking errors doesn't occur in a didactic or systematic way, as is the case in traditional CBT. The process of making clients aware of the cognitive distortions they automatically employ occurs more naturally, as the distortions sporadically occur in the flow of a therapy session. The therapist is not using an intervention so much as offering tidbits of reflective personal feedback on questionable assumptions the client makes when talking with him or her.

For example, forty-nine-year-old Charles, a devout Catholic, entered therapy to address the depression that set in after his divorce. I questioned one of his assumptions in this exchange:

CHARLES: I feel so alone. It's at its worst on the weekend, when I don't have my kids with me. I failed the marriage.
GNAULATI: I failed, or *it* failed? You seem to be taking exclusive responsibility for the marriage not working out.

Brandon, a young adult client of mine, took a gap year from college. He did not anticipate how lonely he'd be apart from his girlfriend and male buddies, all of whom went to college straight out of high school:

BRANDON: I'm starting to think that when I eventually go on to college, I'll be lonely and have no friends.

GNAULATI: I think you're overgeneralizing because of how isolated and lonely you are right now. If you remember, it was not that long ago that your weekends were packed with social gatherings.

BOLSTERING A SENSE OF PERSONAL AGENCY

In 1933 Freud issued his famous quote on the aim of psychoanalysis: "Where id was, there ego shall be." In *Freud and Man's Soul*, Bruno Bettelheim clarifies that the correct English translation from the original German encompassed less jargon: "Where the experience of it-ness was, there shall be an experience of I-ness."[12] In broad terms, Freud meant that a sense of personal agency—of feeling in control of and having control in one's life—requires us to familiarize ourselves with and appropriate our emotions, especially our "primitive" ones. Time and again in therapy, accessing, articulating, and having a therapist confirm our propensity for anger, lust, grief, envy, pride, and so forth, helps us feel as if we are the subject of our emotions, not simply subjected to them.

This is not to say that any of us can achieve supreme control in our emotional lives. As the respected Boston psychiatrist Arnold Modell once claimed, "we cannot control what we feel any more than we can control our heartbeat. Our feelings simply happen to us. What we can control, at least potentially, is our interpretation of those feelings."[13] We can try to more deeply understand why we feel the way we do. As I earlier indicated, doing so can give us more flexibility in the way we respond. We can also work at modulating and finessing our outward expression of emotion. We can gauge the right amount of intensity needed to make a point, use less accusatory language, and refrain from belaboring a point. We can move faster out of negative emotional states and respond to, rather than perpetually react to, others' emotions. This is part of the emotion work that clients commit to in therapy, and in life.

Continual acceptance that life needs to be lived more actively than passively also bolsters our sense of personal agency. This often makes the difference between living a life that makes us happy, not just content. Along these lines, Daniel Russell defines a happy life in *Happiness for Humans*: "Living a happy life means actively living, engaging the world, finding things to live for and then living for them."[14] At work and with their families, clients raised to accommodate to the needs of others and comply with adults' demands can passively default to overprioritizing what they should do and underprioritizing what they might enjoy doing. Such clients can benefit from reminders to prioritize and actively pursue sources of personal enjoyment:

> "I know you need doses of solitude to function best. You don't seem to be making that enough of a priority in your life right now."
>
> "Is that really what you want to be doing with your time?"
>
> "I can tell that you are struggling to use your free time wisely, but it's a struggle that probably needs to be owned more."
>
> "With all you have going at work and home, it must seem like there's no time for you. I worry if you don't *make* time for you, doing what replenishes you, your depression will worsen."

Personal agency involves not only living life actively, but also living it purposefully. Russell adds, "There are ends we act for, then there are ends we *live* for: ends that give our existence direction and purpose, that make the difference between a shapeless existence and a complete *life*."[15] In *When Nietzsche Wept*, America's leading voice on existential psychotherapy, Irvin Yalom, puts it more bluntly: "Not to take possession of your life plan is to let your existence be an accident."[16] Therapy can be a domain for clients to clarify, assess, and commit to pursuing life commitments that are in line with their own true talents, preferences, values, and ideals. This is a decidedly subjective process. What applies for one person doesn't necessary apply for another. Clients sometimes wish there were objective standards for living they could adopt wholesale. They refer to other people in their lives who have it all together—if my clients could only be just like them. In those moments, refocusing their attention on who they are, what they are genuinely good at, and what gives their life meaning and purpose is indicated.

In the transition to parenthood in his early forties, Marco, an accomplished physics professor, put his career on hold to be more available at home as an involved dad. Now that his son was in preschool, he felt freed up to invest more time and energy into his academic life.

Marco was a brilliant, divergent thinker who could perceive the pros and cons of many ideas. This ability is what made him an accomplished scientist. But it also could prevent him from making career choices in line with his overriding academic interests, as the following vignette shows:

MARCO: I'm really not sure what I should be emphasizing in my career. Should I pursue my own start-up company using some of the commercial applications of my research, like several of my colleagues? *(laughing)* I could buy a yacht. Should I put additional time into mentoring my postdoctoral fellows? I have my hand in so many research projects right now, I don't know if I'm coming or going.

GNAULATI: Not a pleasant state of mind to be in . . .

MARCO: Javier, my colleague in South America, flies all over to conferences, is laser-focused in the lab, and still has time to play trumpet in a band. I wish I was more organized and productive like that! Maybe I should take up the trumpet!

GNAULATI: He is he, and you are you. I remember you told me that his wife is a stay-at-home mom who places few family demands on him. He may have free time that you don't. Now that you are reprioritizing your career, what's really of value to you?

MARCO: Good question. I don't have the foggiest.

GNAULATI: You don't have any idea?

MARCO: Well, I do wish I had more time to just hang out with my postdocs and dialogue about new ideas in physics.

GNAULATI: Maybe taking you back to your own graduate-school years when you had intellectual fervor for physics.

MARCO: *Yes.* I feel too much like a bureaucrat and a manager running the lab. At heart I'm a people person who gets the most out of engaging in organic social interactions with like-minded thinkers in physics. I need more of that in my life.

Clients afflicted with debilitating emotional problems and unfavorable life circumstances often feel they have no choice but to passively resign themselves to their fate. There are times in therapy with such clients when a caring, careful processing of despair and grief takes on significance. Other times, their defeatism needs to be challenged. Existentialist philosophers and writers often observe that we are thrown into a world not of our own choosing, but we somehow have to carve out a life as best we can. Existentialist philosopher Albert Camus's *Myth of Sisyphus* is an allegory of how life can be lived with "the certainty of a crushing fate, without the resignation that ought to accompany it."[17] Sartre once said, "Freedom is what we do with what is done to us."[18] A specific quote by the Irish playwright Samuel Beckett is worth bearing in mind when you are digging in with clients mired in resignation: "Ever tried. Ever failed. Try again. Fail again. Fail better."[19] (This aphorism is tattooed on the forearm of my favorite professional tennis player, Stan Wawrinka!)

Clarissa's mix of social anxiety, obsessiveness, and autism spectrum symptoms meant she needed to attend a nontraditional high school. Upon her graduation, Clarissa's parents insisted—despite her vehement protests—that she live in an assisted-living boarding school that enabled her to take college courses and learn skills of daily living. She did the everyday tasks, like taking the bus across town and preparing meals with peers, under great duress. Mostly, she was content cloistering herself in her room, reading and expanding her prodigious knowledge of history, politics, and philosophy through Internet searches. Moments like the following were common in my work with Clarissa:

CLARISSA: I should just be left alone to stay in my room. I don't see the point in having to make meals and hang out with people I have nothing in common with.

GNAULATI: I know you prefer to be left alone in your room, Clarissa, but how is that going to help prepare you for life in the future when you need to live on your own? I suppose every little step you take being social adds up.

CLARISSA (crying): That's pathetic. Like taking the bus and cooking meals are successes. Successes are getting straight A's in college, like my sister.

GNAULATI: I know you wish you had her life, but you don't. You have your life, and it's filled with overwhelming hurdles. With your social anxiety, taking the bus across town *is* a success, and if you pooh-pooh that, it's going to be very hard for you to believe in yourself.

We find, in therapy, that many clients have rarely, if ever, been in relationships marked by sustained empathy, genuine and abiding concern, and persistent encouragement to live life actively and purposefully. Thus, the therapy relationship can be new, emotionally invigorating, and personally meaningful in and of itself. Confident expectations that they will be listened to and sensitively responded to *largely on their terms* can awaken long-since-foreclosed memories, desires, grievances, and aspirations in clients. For clients who have lived lives of self-effacement and conformity, which leaves them susceptible to feeling demoralized and depersonalized, the therapist and the therapy can even be a veritable emotional life-support system to make a true self viable. We should not be surprised if such clients become acutely attached to their therapists and immensely invested in therapy. It represents an ontological endeavor for them—an invaluable experience to become authentic persons more connected to the emotional wellsprings of their lives and the sources of meaning and purpose that ultimately make life worth living.

CHAPTER SEVEN

Practicing with Personality

ALL TOO OFTEN, the training and education of psychotherapists sets them up to be excessively directive or nondirective—too hands-on or too hands-off—in their approach to clients. The directive therapist employs techniques and clinical agendas that can get *in the way* of freeing clients up to articulate what really troubles them. The nondirective therapist strives to get *out of the way* of clients to free them up to articulate what really troubles them. In both approaches, there is scant attention paid to how the therapist can use his or her personality or any subjective experiences in the room to allow clients to get *with the way* they are troubled and to express this more resolutely. Therapists need to be actively attuned, authentic, and authoritative to encourage clients in this way. These are human qualities with human applications in psychotherapy. They require that the therapist become acquainted with, and know how to enact, time-honored virtues such as sincerity, forbearance, forthrightness, tact, discretion, and mirth.

AWAY WITH THERAPEUTIC DETACHEDNESS AND PROFESSIONAL ALOOFNESS

Sophie Freud, the granddaughter of Sigmund Freud and a long-standing faculty member at Simmons College School of Social Work in Boston, was once asked for advice about how to best conduct psychotherapy. Her answer was plainspoken: "Be yourself, I tell them. Act as if this relationship were a friendship, without the usual reciprocity of attending to each other's needs one expects of friendship. Reciprocity lies instead in the privilege of making a difference to another person."[1]

We assume that Sophie's grandfather would roll over in his grave at such a proposition. After all, the iconic psychoanalytic stance is that of a *blank screen*, in which the therapist is sphinxlike, or stalwart in controlling his or her emotions so as to train all powers of concentration on the client's disguised feelings and inner motives. However, we know from the historical record that Freud was an ambivalent adherent to his own method. We get a window into a more nuanced view of how Freud conceptualized the role of the psychoanalyst as early as 1895 in *Studies in Hysteria*: "One operates, as best one can, as an enlightener, as a teacher, as the representative of a freer or superior philosophy of life, as a confessor, who by his continuing compassion and respect for the confessions that are made, as it were grants absolution. One tries to do something for the patient in human terms, as far as is allowed by the capacity of one's own personality and the degree of sympathy that one can find for the case in question."[2]

Freud was fond of issuing scientific-sounding exhortations about the need for psychoanalysts to be "abstinent," muting their own subjectivity in the pursuit of purer objective interpretations about the client's real wishes, feelings, and intentions. Nonetheless, in the dark recesses of his own psyche, that Freud was apt to perceive the therapist as a sort of tribe elder who was equal parts confidant, confessor, and life coach—a careful listener and purveyor of wise counsel. Despite this more humanistic rendering of the therapist's role, variations of the blank-screen model still shape the method many therapists are trained to utilize. By *blank screen*, I mean a stance in which the therapists are encouraged to neutralize their personality whenever they are with clients, to optimally perform a method, technique, or intervention.

In the world of CBT, it is the intervention, not the interventionist, that matters. Like the good scientist, the good cognitive behavioral therapist embodies an *ethic of dispassionate detachment* to best do his or her job. Subjective experiences in the room with clients are not crucial sources of therapeutic data, at least not when evidence-based practice is followed. What matters is standardized application of technique: doing therapy exclusively in the format for which it was scientifically validated. In this model, therapists should really be interchangeable if there is strict adherence to treatments protocols.

For those who practice a more conservative version of psychoanalytic psychotherapy, an ethic of dispassionate detachment also prevails. Back in the mid-1990s, when I was a graduate student in New York City, the bastion of psychoanalytic psychotherapy, I was chastised by a supervisor for sitting face-to-face with a client. The supervisor was adamant that this reflected my "countertransferential" need to be liked by my clients, an insecurity on my part. He counseled me to sit adjacent to the client, facing away from him, and to be relatively stone-faced.

This seating arrangement was necessary, he said, for the transference to emerge—that is, for the client to come at me with expectations and disappointments that were rooted in past painful relationships with caregivers. If I showed too much of myself, I would contaminate the process. If the client got angry with me or began acting seductively, my actions in the room would be the cause, not the client's unconscious distorted perceptions of me. This supervisor seemed to construe every attempt on my part to affirm clients' feelings and perceptions as rooted in my personal insecurities. In reassuringly nodding at clients or paraphrasing for them what I sensed was of emotional significance, I was committing the sin of countertransference. I was infantilizing my clients by keeping them dependent on my approval. My supervisor spoke about these matters with utter conviction.

I eventually parted ways with this man because of what I experienced as his icy disregard for the effects of his supercilious behavior. He seemed oblivious to how the dispassionate detachment he counseled me to assume (and which he himself embodied in his supervisory role with me) covertly incorporated attitudes and behaviors that were far from neutral. Being a blank screen with clients was tantamount to being unselfconsciously aloof. In most human contexts, aloofness begets distance, guardedness, and irritation—hardly an atmosphere conducive to therapeutic acceptance and openness.

In contrast to the ethic of dispassionate detachment that imbues CBT and traditional psychoanalytic work, Carl Rogers championed an ethic of *compassionate detachment* in his client-centered approach. In *A Way of Being*, Rogers highlights a Lao-tse quote that best encapsulates standards he believes therapists should strive for:

> If I keep from meddling with people, they take care of themselves;
> If I keep from commanding people, they behave themselves;
> If I keep from preaching at people, they improve themselves;
> If I keep from imposing on people, they become themselves.[3]

Although Rogers was a champion of therapists being authentic as a means to actualize similar tendencies in clients, he privileged a nondirective therapeutic style—one in which therapists subdue and bracket their own subjectivity. In his model, therapists self-detach in the act of empathically tuning in to clients. The therapist becomes a sort of human mirror, listening to and fleshing out the client's feelings. One can think of it as a sensitive way of being objective or accurately perceiving the client for who he or she really is.

But the caricature of the Rogerian practitioner selflessly reflecting a client's feelings is a real trap into which inexperienced therapists can fall. Empathy that is not thoroughly grounded in the therapist's own subjective experience can come across as artificial. It's postured empathy. True empathy involves deep emotional engagement and identification with clients' life problems. It's an experiential blend of finding oneself in the other while simultaneously discovering the other in oneself. The therapist is emotionally moved by the client from within his or her own emotional center. There is a meeting of two subjects. To use an awkward metaphor, the therapist bleeds along with the client. However, there is a distinction between empathically engaging clients and sympathetically overidentifying with them. The therapist still strives for *differentiated relatedness*, that is, the ability to find oneself in the client's experiences without making oneself the focus. I'll cover these topics in greater detail in the next chapter.

The corollary ethic for the type of therapeutic stance I am proposing is one coined by James Bugental, an American existential psychotherapist. *Disciplined compassion* gives genuine care and concern its rightful, central place in therapy.[4] It suggests that what fundamentally makes psychotherapy auspicious is the therapist's abiding devotion to the client's emotional welfare. In the words of Jerome Frank, in his landmark book *Persuasion and Healing*, disciplined compassion is a "determination to persist in trying to help, no matter how desperate patients' conditions or how outrageous their behavior."[5] As we will see, a therapist's sincere and eager desire to help has more in common with how people comport themselves and interact in everyday relationships than with a specialized scientific or medical practice.

AUTHENTIC CARE

Among humanistically oriented psychotherapists, it is axiomatic that therapist authenticity begets client authenticity. For instance, Lewis Aron, in *A Meeting of Minds*, proposes: "Emotional honesty, accessibility, directness, openness, spontaneity, disclosure of the person of the analyst—these create in the patient heightened naturalness, forthrightness, access to the repressed, recognition of and sensitivity to the other, increased self-esteem, and greater realism about, and hence depth, in relationship."[6]

Likewise, David Elkins, former president of the Humanistic Psychology Division of the APA, asserts, "In the presence of an authentic therapist, the client's being, no matter how repressed, will resonate and respond."[7] The vast majority of psychotherapists probably believe in the importance of authenticity in dealings with clients. But embodying that authenticity is a completely different matter. I've yet to hear of any graduate course offered on authenticity training. Yet the work of being authentic is arduous. It involves being in the moment with clients without the safety of a script or a rigid role. Self-discipline, tact, and sensitivity are involved in saying the right thing, in the right way, at the right time so that the client feels understood and responded to as a unique person. Without these three attributes, the therapist risks saying the wrong thing, in the wrong way, at the wrong time, harming the client and potentially ending the therapy. By comparison, being emotionally present with a client to say the right thing, in the right way, at the right time, can be psychologically invaluable and make therapy critically important as a venue to make him or her feel understood.

Therapists are left to draw from their own humanity to learn how to be authentic with clients. A prerequisite is the general integration of the therapist's personality. Adequate familiarity with, and acceptance of, one's primal emotional states is a must—pride, shame, grief, rage, envy, lust, and greed, for instance. To practice more authentically as a therapist, you first have to be sufficiently congruent as a person; generally speaking, your outward behavior has to align with your inner intentions. It is an acquired capacity—to say what you mean and mean what you say. You must be a credible person to establish yourself as a credible psychotherapist. These personal-psychological achievements then get finessed and tailored to the clinical situation. Correspondingly, acting naturally and valuing transparency over mystification, directness over indirectness, spontaneity over constraint, tact over tactics, a more egalitarian therapist-client arrangement, and common speech over clinical jargon now all become relevant.

A key way therapists can manifest authenticity with clients is through the use of ordinary language or common speech, instead of clinical jargon, during therapy. Speaking with clients this way makes the therapy more personal than impersonal. Spontaneous conversation that matches the client's way of speaking not only makes the client feel special but also emotionally enlivens the therapy.

The use of everyday speech also avails clients with terms they might use out in the world when they are trying to make themselves understood. Not that the therapist is in the business of prescribing language. In therapy, as in real-life interactions, we all organically and tacitly pick up words and phrases that have poignancy for us. Insofar as the therapist's utterances are littered with common words, rather than clinical jargon, the client has covert and overt access to phrases that if adopted, are generalizable to everyday life. People tend not to use words or phrases like *projection*, *cognitive distortion*, or *identification with the aggressor* in ordinary contexts. Accessible comments like "I think it's really you who is sad, not me; maybe that's an exaggeration" and "I think you are slipping into being overbearing like your dad without thinking about how this might hurt your daughter" are more utilizable. Some clinical examples will drive home my points.

Keith, a thirty-one-year-old Asian American man, saw me for depression. He had been passed over for promotions at work and was unable to end a dissatisfying long-term relationship with his girlfriend. Keith's father had wielded a strong hand in making all the son's major life decisions for him. The father had picked out which college Keith had attended, the profession he had entered, and the neighborhood he lived in. Not surprisingly, Keith was overly compromising in his romantic and professional life. I interpreted his situation in everyday words: "I can tell it's incredibly difficult to stand your ground, since you grew up with a father who didn't give much ground." The theme, as well as the phraseology, of "standing one's ground" and "giving ground" subsequently became important in my therapy with Keith.

Monica, a forty-one-year-old mother of three young children, often berated herself in my office for not being an attentive-enough mother. Juggling career and family demands kept her in a constant state of exasperation, being unable to do either job well, at least in her mind. Monica's perfectionistic tendencies and predisposition to compulsive action interfered with her being fully engaged with her children. Days before Halloween, Monica's six-year-old daughter, Lucy, announced from the backseat of the minivan that after school, she wanted Monica to go shopping for materials to make costumes. Lucy had loved making costumes with Monica last year, the little girl told her. Monica cried as she related this story to me. I softly replied, "I think you should stop and be thankful that you've done something right as a mother with a daughter wanting to relive a special moment. It's like Lucy is your conscience reminding you to slow down, hit the pause button, just be."

One of the most underrecognized forms of inauthenticity masquerading as good clinical practice pertains to the therapist's need to be clever. Not infrequently, this need arises from the disquieting effects of the client's repetitiousness and "stuckness." Many clients tell and retell painful life events in therapy and repeat troubling and troublesome behavior, despite their best intentions to change. We therapists are often haunted by the feeling that change should happen faster, galvanized by a more sophisticated interpretation or skillful application of technique. Countertransferential cleverness becomes a risk. We impatiently leap in and offer explanations for the underlying causes of clients' behavior and propose solutions, when perhaps all they need in these moments is to have their agony witnessed yet again.

Taking clients at their word, truly entering and residing in the manifest content of their narratives, the warp and weft of their everyday lives, of what they feel actually matters, requires that we therapists give ourselves over to the ordinary. I am both amused and intrigued by the seeming banality of the topics many clients bring to therapy: sleeping in separate beds because a husband snores, standoffs over which restaurant to dine at, home remodels that threaten to lead to divorce, friction over contrasting disciplinary styles with children, personality conflicts with coworkers. We can delegitimize what for clients are legitimate concerns when we are too eager to read into the deeper meanings behind their attitudes and actions.

Sometimes our need to be clever is rooted in our unwillingness or inability to give ourselves over to the ordinary. Our interpretations and interventions become disguised ways of coaxing the client to talk about what we think should actually matter, to justify the potency of our education and training, or to simply stave off boredom. This is not to say that clients do not need, yet resist, deeper meaningful linkages. When a client is irked by his wife's perceived stonewalling, we can't always be clear whether a nod acknowledging his frustration is in order or a deep interpretation is needed: "Antonio, I think your wife's stonewalling gets to you because it is reminiscent of how your mother treated your father."

Many therapists intellectualize the therapy to stay mentally stimulated in the face of hour-in, hour-out client disclosures of everyday struggles and conflicts. Seeing ourselves as master decoders of meaning can give us a sense of higher purpose about the profession, at least in an intellectualized way. The habit of thinking up a clever interpretation, musing on linkages in the content of the client's disclosures, or assuming more of an observational than participatory stance can speak to our own difficulties in being emotionally present, tracking and matching the client's transitory feelings and gestures. There is

intimacy to this. There is also the professional hazard of depersonal-
ization, as well as emotional and mental exhaustion. Intellectualizing
the therapy can be a means to cope with these hazards.

The exquisite receptivity and sensitivity required in practicing with
authentic care is nothing short of a labor of love. It's also the labor
therapists get paid for. Knowing why, when, and how to do or say
something truly therapeutic involves ample mental acuity and interpersonal sophistication.

Most salutatory interactions in psychotherapy occur at a sublimi-
nal or an implicit level. Moment to moment, the well-attuned therapist is naturally modulating his or her nonverbal behavior to enhance
client engagement and understanding. Facial expressivity, eye contact,
speech prosody, voice cadence, and animation are subliminally coordinated against what the client seems to need and can tolerate. The
therapist has to have one eye trained on whether his or her expressiveness is too little or too much for the client to assimilate, and recalibrate
accordingly. A smile, a sincere frown, raised eyebrows, eye rolling, or
a calm demeanor—any of these physical embodiments of thought and
emotion, deployed in the right way at the right time, can have therapeutic benefits, even though they mostly occur outside both the therapist's and the client's awareness. We have to quickly and smoothly
decide which words to use and in what tone, backed by which gestures,
in ways a client can both ingest and digest. Practicing psychotherapy
well is akin to manifesting sublime levels of discretion, which the British philosopher A. C. Grayling defines as "knowing when to speak,
what not to say, when to stop, and how to deflect a conversation when
a doubtful turn has been taken."[8] There is love in this kind of work,
and work in this kind of love.

Finally, a feature of authentic client care is the ability to remember
the memorable aspects of the client's life. I'm often surprised when
clients are surprised by my ability to bring up relevant historical information or noteworthy life events they formerly disclosed. I find that
when I truly care about clients and become completely engrossed in
their life stories, the memorable events in their lives become etched in
my own memory banks.

THE THERAPIST'S AUTHORITATIVE VOICE

As real persons striving to be themselves, albeit more muted, professional, other-directed versions of themselves, therapists strive for clarity and candidness of expression that sets the tone for therapy. One
way to achieve this goal is through linguistic authorship, that is, by
wording your interpretations and clinical comments to reflect how
these observations—nothing more and nothing less—are the renderings of your own mind. They are your formulations, predicated on
whatever human and clinical wisdom you possess.

Therapists are often uneasy about personalized use of language—
the use of the first-person pronoun *I*—resorting more frequently to the
second-person pronoun to deliver more impersonal *you*-statements.
Third-person pronouns are commonly selected to give an air of professionalism (e.g., "It's hard to get a husband to listen who seems so
caught up in himself"). It's as if *I*-statements put the therapist and client in a sort of friendship zone and are thereby anathema to the need
to provide a medical or scientifically backed service. To demonstrate
expertise, many therapists use *you*-statements to make interpretations
like "You seem stuck reacting to your wife in the very ways your father
reacted to your mother"; "You say your husband is the angry one in
the marriage, but this might be partly a projection as you yourself
struggle to manage your anger"; or "You seem to be holding back
from saying what you really feel." Personalized versions of these are
more prone to be underutilized: "It looks to me like sometimes you
get caught reacting to your wife in the very ways your father reacted
to your mother"; "One thought I find myself having is that it seems
easier to see your husband as struggling to manage his anger than to
see yourself struggling to manage your own anger"; or "I can see you
are having some feelings that are hard to express."

The assumption may be that it is more clinical or scientific sounding to avoid *I*-statements. Still, no matter how much we linguistically
dress up our therapeutic utterances to make them seem objective and
rooted in sound theory or science, we are the authors of our own re-
marks. They bear the signature of our subjective filters or what we consciously and unconsciously deem experientially and clinically relevant.

Prefacing our interpretations and clinical comments with *I*-statements allows us to be authoritative without being authoritarian. We can take a stand on clients' struggles and say something plausible, something that derives simply from one person's perspective (who happens to be us) and that can be considered by both client and ourselves and legitimately denied if found wanting. Such statements are not something that should be swallowed whole because of their supposed veracity and that, if denied, are taken as an indication of defensiveness.

Linguistically putting ourselves into the therapy can also make it more emotionally evocative, enlivening the therapy session and leaving clients feeling we are personally invested in them. Here is a sampling of my standard ways of prefacing clinical comments: "One thought I have is . . ."; "As I see it . . ."; "This may say more about my biases here, and if so, let me know, but . . ."; "Of course, where my mind goes when you tell me this is . . ."; "I would be careful doing that . . ."; "Hold on a minute, I'm confused"; "It occurs to me that . . ."; and "Something tells me that you . . ."

There are even occasions where I speak for clients or offer phrases that are refined versions of what they vaguely communicate or hint at. The emotional texture of the interaction is usually synchronous so that, in a manner, the client and I are speaking in one voice. I am speaking for the client while I'm speaking with him or her. Some case snippets will clarify.

Two years into therapy, forty-seven-year-old Magdalena recalled a disturbing exchange with her father. The incident dated back to when she was an impressionable young woman. Her father had driven across town to her apartment to reassure her that he still loved Magdalena's mother, despite having had numerous affairs during the marriage. Unselfconsciously macho, he had announced to Magdalena, "I remember the animals I have killed while hunting more than I remember the women I have fucked." Magdalena had replied, "Wow, that's deep, Dad."

Alarmed at her recollection, I piped up. "Deep?" I asked. "Any other words come to mind? How about, 'Dad, that's so callous and cruel. Could you be any more coldhearted?!'" As if he were oblivious to the fact that his flesh-and-blood young daughter was sitting next to him and would be harmed, not reassured, by such a comment.

Magdalena wept as I fleshed out with words and affect what was in her preconscious experience. She had recalled this disturbing exchange after having shared a conversation with her movie-star husband about the importance of monogamy. He flippantly remarked that monogamy was a false ideal for powerful men exposed to sexual opportunities. He cited evolutionary reasons for this. While on location, he had had multiple opportunities for casual sex and had acted on the opportunities, later trying to convince Magdalena that these weren't a threat to the marriage. The conversation with her husband about monogamy was Magdalena's indirect way of trying to obtain reassurance about his love and fidelity.

"He didn't pick up on your need for reassurance, eh?" I asked. Then I paraphrased what I imagined the husband was saying by his actions: "'I'm not wanting to have an intellectual conversation about the pros and cons of monogamy. I'm telling you this because I want you to accept that I'm the one you love, and you want to be with me and only me.'"

"I do want that," she told me. "Yes, that's what I really wanted to tell him."

We assume that if clients are to progress, they need to be accountable to their own *ego ideal*, that is, their own better self, to act on acquired insights. But it's the rare client who is self-motivated in this way. Most of us muddle through life, vexingly reenacting the same old bad habits, even when we have insight into our behavior. When emboldened, we can act auspiciously on our own behalf. But often we do right by our higher aspirations because people whom we know and trust nudge us in the right direction at the right time. We are more dependent on others to create tipping points for change than we want to believe—more so than the American cultural ideal of rugged individualism permits.

Potent psychotherapy sometimes requires the therapist to use his or her authoritativeness to call clients out and push them beyond themselves and to keep them from repeating the same bad decisions, even though they have some insight into why they do it. The therapist needs to shake clients out of their emotional slumber, that is, he or she needs to counteract what Freud called the *death instinct*—the expectable inertia we all encounter against actively existing.

By authoritativeness, I mean the therapist's reasonable degree of human responsibility for the client's well-being and betterment: the therapist extrapolates from his or her intimate knowledge of the client, acquired clinical knowledge, and life philosophy to wholeheartedly share with the client something that is a stimulus for action. The therapist is so moved by the client that he or she takes a stand, hears the call from the client's better self, and speaks up in its defense. At key moments, the therapist is the steward of the client's better self and needs to be judiciously active in its defense. Along these lines, Maurice Friedman, whose 1977 book *The Healing Dialogue in Psychotherapy* presaged many issues raised by contemporary relationship-oriented psychotherapists, asserted: "The therapist may be wrestling *with* the patient, *for* the patient, and *against* the patient."[9] Yet in these declarative moments, we therapists still have to be sensitively assertive. Irwin Hoffman, a distinguished psychoanalyst, aptly captures this obligation: "Whether we like it or not, we are inevitably involved in some measure as mentors to our patients. . . . We also have to try to act wisely even while recognizing that whatever wisdom we have is always highly personal and subjective."[10]

For example, Dan, a forty-six-year-old lawyer prone to be overly dutiful and perfectionistic in his work habits, mentioned to me that if his supervisor refused to give him Thanksgiving week off, he would unilaterally decide to go out on sick leave. With good humor, I replied, "Maybe this is your way of saying that because you work so hard, you deserve time off on your terms. But hold on! This seems to me to be one of those occasions when you risk morphing into your mother—stepping on toes, putting your foot in your mouth, and possibly getting yourself in hot water at work. You don't need to come out swinging like your mother. Just be persistently assertive, stand your ground about needing Thanksgiving week off, persist, insist. Use your good lawyer skills!"

Francesca, a forty-year-old homemaker with three children, caught her husband having an affair. She immediately felt impelled to file for divorce. Francesca tended to be impulsive and action oriented and, when hurt, often went on the offensive. She was no stranger to betrayal and infidelity in her life. Her brother was addicted to drugs, and his denial, lies, stealing, and failed promises were excused by her parents. Her father took off suddenly, but briefly, with another woman when Francesca was a teenager. Several key boyfriends had also been unfaithful.

During therapy, I used my authoritative knowledge of Francesca and my professional skills to advise her. "Francesca, I think it's premature to file for divorce," I said softly. "I know Alan betrayed you, and this is especially devastating because he knows your history. But this has to be bringing up old hurts and injuries, and you and I need to take all the time necessary to sort this out emotionally before you make any life-altering decisions. From what you have told me, Alan typically is trustworthy and you have had a solid marriage up to this point. Filing for a divorce may make you feel powerful, refusing to put up with lies and betrayal, and having an out like you didn't have as a kid. But I think it's premature."

Brian, a thirty-nine-year-old gay client of mine, was tired of arguing with his fiancé over the travel and after-work dinners that were an integral part of Brian's job. They were not, Brian repeatedly had to reassure him, a concerted attempt to avoid and reject him. Reportedly, his fiancé's mother had died when he was eleven years old and his father had left him with relatives to immigrate to and start a new life in America. Brian's fiancé seemed unaware of how his history set him up to expect rejection and sudden abandonment. Brian often felt attacked by his fiancé for not being devoted or attentive enough, for not making him his one and only life priority. During a session when Brian seemed dejected and defeated, he announced to me that after the marriage, he was going to quit his job and travel with his husband for a month in Europe.

With a concerned look, I pushed back: "Right now, I'm feeling protective of you. Quitting your job and touring Europe might solve some short-term problems—end your job dissatisfaction and prove to your fiancé that you are committed to him with a capital *C*. But you have very little money in savings and no job options to replace the one you have, and you guys are determined to adopt kids after the wedding. I'm starting to think that this decision reflects how defeated you feel standing up to your fiancé about the importance of your career and the need to travel. I'm thinking that it is probably high time your fiancé get therapy to take a close look at how his abandonment history places unfair demands on you to be the uber-devoted, all-good parent he did not seem to have."

Sometimes a straightforward, kindly worded, and affectionately expressed admonition can simultaneously convey deep understanding of a client's core struggle and support a positive change of attitude and behavior. Mark, a forty-two-year-old pediatrician, in keeping with his upbringing as a devout Catholic, experienced a vague, omnipresent sense of guilt that leaped out in situations where his personal enjoyment and satisfaction warranted attention. It was far easier for him to identify and pursue activities out of a sense of duty than for desire. At the start of a session, Mark apologized for having to rearrange the cushion on his therapy chair to make himself comfortable. I quickly commented, "There's no need to say you are sorry for wanting to be comfortable." We both smiled knowingly.

All too often, our therapy models and manner of practicing presume that clients should be their own source of motivation, communicativeness, and behavior change. To rely on the therapist for motivational energy, communicative finesse, and input about advantageous changes is viewed as a form of unhealthy dependence. This harkens back to the Freudian notion that inside us all, at an unconscious level, is a greedy infant holding out to have its needs met by others so we can avoid growing up and taking initiative regarding our needs and wants. This notion falsely pathologizes any adult need for outside reassurance and validation. It belies how even self-reliant clients with a strong inner compass still need their therapist to say a hearty "good" or "I like the sound of that" to reaffirm something well said or done.

SELF-DISCLOSURE

The rules for being neutral and abstinent, or displaying simple empathy, are clearer and easier to follow than those for being human in the room with clients. When urged by clients to share their own attitudes toward child-rearing, relationships, and the like, many therapists deflect. Remaining neutral, interpreting the underlying motive, or reflecting back underlying feelings are the typical fallback responses many therapists are trained to generate when clients put direct questions to them. The anxiety of being put on the spot leads many therapists to routinely sidestep direct questions and recoil from uttering anything resembling a personal or professional opinion. On the other hand, there are risks of overstepping one's role in a chummy, talkative way. The client's need for feedback gets eclipsed by the therapist's need to share. There are no uniform rules pertaining to when, how, and why to self-disclose to clients. But there are some general rationales.

Normalizing Perceptions the Client Is Convinced Are Aberrant
Perhaps the clearest indication for therapist self-disclosure is to resoundingly normalize experiences and perceptions clients unselfconsciously think are aberrant. Self-disclosure is especially beneficial for clients raised in homes where so-called mystification has occurred. The controversial Scottish existential psychologist R. D. Laing wrote voluminously about the damaging effects of mystification in families. *Self and Others* and *Sanity, Madness and the Family* are two of his books that have stood the test of time in this domain. Periodically I encounter clients whose perceptiveness and deftness at seeing through pretense was undermined and disconfirmed early on by caregivers. Their need for confirmatory feedback from me, as a trusted therapist, to verify the accuracy of their perceptions is paramount if their hardened self-doubting tendencies are to be undone. To do this, I might animatedly reframe as a personal asset what the client believes is a liability.

Gertrude was one such client. Growing up, she cherished solitude, which her mother judgmentally misconstrued as evidence of her being a social misfit, a loner, and depressed. During a session when Gertrude was maligning herself for being an oddball, in agreement with her mother, I retorted, "I don't think your mother gets you, Gertrude. I see you as a complex person who is an introvert by temperament—someone who would rather be alone with her own thoughts than around people who jabber for the sake of jabbering. I know because I'm like that myself. Your mother seems to have maligned your need for solitude instead of seeing it as a wholesome thing, a personality trait that speaks to your depth as a person."

Catalyzing Deeper Client Revelations

Spontaneous therapist self-disclosures can also catalyze more penetrating client revelations. We can issue the usual reminders to clients to refrain from holding back, to be candid and upfront with their communications. Yet sometimes it takes risky displays of honesty and frankness on the therapist's part to give clients license to shoot from the hip.

In a recent session, I had the following exchange with Barry, a thirty-five-year-old music industry executive in turmoil over large-scale changes taking place in his profession and considering his next move:

BARRY: What do you think I should be doing right now to set myself up for a better future?

GNAULATI: Right off the top of my head? Full disclosure, based on how I see you and what I know about you?

BARRY: Yes!

GNAULATI: I see you as an intellectual who has made compromise after compromise in your career to mold yourself into a businessman, which you are ambivalent about being, at best. When I stop and fantasize what life could be like, I imagine you getting a master's degree in English and teaching at a reputable private school, using your executive skills to work your way up into a high-level administrative position over time.

BARRY: You are so right on. But if my colleagues and friends heard I was going back to school to get a degree in the humanities, they would see it as a go-nowhere degree. *(with pronounced frustration)* I really need to figure out what to do!

GNAULATI: OK. Now it's your turn. No holds barred, total fantasy. What would you love to pursue?

BARRY: Full disclosure?

GNAULATI: Yes!

BARRY: A job with the Washington Redskins.

From there, Barry spoke free-flowingly and intoxicatingly about his love of this football team and his determination to look into a marketing job with them.

Tactfully Expressed Social Feedback

Social living requires a generous amount of pretense, nicety, and politeness that at its outer edges becomes socially acceptable falsity. I suspect we all secretively crave honest feedback, to see ourselves as others see us, so long as it is provided by a credible source. Opportunities for candid, fairly objective, tactfully communicated social feedback that we can learn from are rare. Clients often invite and welcome this. The average therapist is neither trained to provide it nor armed with a clinical rationale that it is beneficial. Regardless, as therapists, we are uniquely suited to provide tailored feedback to clients, given our intimate knowledge of their personal histories and psychological vulnerabilities.

During a couples therapy session with spouses who were separating and wanted my help executing this plan with the least amount of emotional fallout, Frank seemed hard-edged in his interactions with his wife, Kathy. I leaned in and had this exchange with him:

GNAULATI: Frank, what you just said and the way you just said it sounded bossy to me. It's interesting. It seems stylistic, like a typical masculine way of communicating, where you are just imparting information. You get confused when Kathy is irritated with you. To me it seems you really don't mean to be brash—that's the word that comes to mind. But whether or not you intend any harm, that's the effect it seems to have on Kathy.

FRANK: I'm not disputing that. I am finally starting to see how hard it is for me to show empathy.

Frank happened to be one of those clients whose logical and officious communicative style did not reflect defensiveness so much as a traditional masculine way of relating. He took direction well about how to listen better, though not because he was passive or pathologically dependent. Pragmatically speaking, he accepted the need to be more understanding with his soon-to-be former wife, and since he did not have the skill set and valued my expertise, he welcomed the opportunity to acquire it.

Advice Giving

In the Freudian and humanistic traditions, advice giving is largely thought to promote inappropriate client passivity and dependence. For some clients, a childlike form of dependence is reinforced when they ask for and receive advice from therapists. The rule of thumb is to put it back on the client to articulate what he or she identifies as preferences, goals, and solutions and thus to promote a sense of healthy personal agency. In my experience, however, I make exceptions when it comes to child-rearing advice. We live in an age where parental investment in optimal child-rearing is at an all-time high. There is really no fundamental psychological preparation for the transition to parenthood. The lifestyle and mind-set changes associated with new parenthood happen rapidly and mostly subliminally, and the average parent is caught perpetually playing emotional catch-up between the life that was and the life that is. Knowledge about child-rearing from therapists who keep up on it and happen to be conscientious parents themselves is valuable beyond belief to clients.

Jennifer and Jamal visited me to figure out how to understand and deal with their thirteen-year-old son's sudden refusal to be home alone with Jamal. Lukas, the son, had been legally adopted by Jamal when the child was about five years old. Lukas's biological father had died from an aggressive form of melanoma before he was born. There were no indications that Jamal was being abusive, intrusive, or overbearing with Lukas in any acutely problematic way. If Jamal was guilty of anything, it was occasionally letting his anger spike because of his high-pressured job and Jennifer's health problems. By temperament, Lukas was shy and reserved, unacquainted with angry feelings. Jamal's rare angry outbursts seemed to throw Lukas off balance, even though they were not directed at him. Lukas subsequently developed an all-bad perception of Jamal, canceling out all the good the father had instilled in the boy's life over the years—the hours of Lego play together, being read to as a child, the fun family vacations. Lukas simply wanted to avoid being around Jamal at all costs. As best as I could understand, I construed the issue as Lukas unconsciously grappling with his biological father's death, an aversion to anger, and a reawakened desire to have his mother all to himself as he did for the first five years of his life before Jamal came along. Jennifer and Jamal were well-educated, so the Oedipal reference was a source of amusement.

I advised the parents as follows: "Until we know more about what is driving all this, I would respect Lukas's need to be apart from you, Jamal, as much as can be allowed, given the exigencies of family life. That said, I don't think either of you should play into Lukas's all-bad perceptions of you, Jamal. When Lukas shuns you, Jamal, I'd show him in reasonable ways how hurt and confused you are, while giving him space. In these moments, Jennifer, it is probably good for you to gently come to Jamal's defense so that you are aligning with him and not playing into the whole Oedipal dynamic—to not let Lukas divide and conquer, so to speak. There has to be a way where you, Jennifer, can be Lukas's loyal advocate, while being Jamal's also."

Admitting to One's Core Biases

Therapists' core biases have a way of manifesting themselves, whether overtly or covertly. It's better to be transparent about them for the clients who will readily perceive the biases anyway, as long as your transparency hurts their experience of you or the therapy in any way. A client can feel mystified if he or she indirectly senses of your bias, but you deny it. Under the best of circumstances, if a client tacitly knows where a therapist stands on an issue of personal importance, and the therapist concurs, it can free the client up to speak more openly about it, leading to greater therapeutic rapport, a sense of kinship that can enrich the therapy experience. If the client does not share your bias, there can be an agreement to disagree. For many clients, this understanding can be a psychological achievement. They can go on feeling positive about the therapist and therapy, despite differences in opinions, lifestyles, and beliefs. That said, occasionally in therapy, a client demands that the therapist completely agree with him or her to preserve the client's own beliefs and values that the client thinks are essential for him or her to go on living. Such a situation can be a Faustian bargain, where to dance around answering in the affirmative or to openly acknowledge disagreement means the therapy is over. On the other hand, lying to placate the client means the therapist's personal integrity is compromised.

More than a decade ago, Karen, a long-term client of mine, was admitted to a local hospital to deliver a baby daughter. She was overjoyed at the prospect of being a mother and supplying her extended family with its first grandchild. Her marriage was rocky, but the pregnancy had brought her closer to her husband. Tragically, Karen's baby was stillborn. We scheduled an emergency session to process this horrendously tragic event. Karen was understandably distraught. She wept bitterly and pleaded with me to agree that she would see her daughter in heaven:

KAREN: Tell me that I'll see my baby daughter in heaven.

GNAULATI: Karen, it must be devastating to think that your baby girl is gone forever and you might not ever see her again. I can't even begin to imagine how painful this must be.

KAREN (*getting more and more distraught*): I need to know that you think I'll see my baby daughter in heaven.

GNAULATI: I know how badly you wanted to be a mum. There was every indication you would give birth to a healthy baby girl. It is all so very, very tragic what happened.

KAREN: So you're telling me I'll never see my baby daughter again. I can't deal with that (*sobbing bitterly*).

GNAULATI: I guess I am saying she's gone and this is awful beyond belief. The grief and loss may be too much.

It should not surprise the reader to discover that Karen did not return to therapy. I gave her a referral to a Christian counselor, per her request. In her distressed state of mind, a shared concrete belief in an afterlife was crucial to prevent her from hemorrhaging with grief. Since I do not believe in an afterlife, I could not, in good conscience, give her the concrete reassurance she desperately needed. I focused on standard therapeutic ways of helping Karen face her unbearable loss.

This was not enough. To this day, no matter how I rationally substantiate the professionalism and therapeutic sensitivity I showed during that session, I still feel traces of Karen's devastation.

Let me offer some final thoughts about therapist self-disclosure. There is always the specter of self-aggrandizement and self-gratification when therapists choose to self-disclose. Questions need to be asked of ourselves: Are we looking for attention or focused on the client's betterment? Are we reassuring and affirming client experiences or stealing the focus? Are we enlivening the therapy experience for the client or are we staving off our own boredom?

During moments of self-disclosure, therapists need to be concise and on point. Clients should be well aware that the therapist is self-disclosing for poignancy reasons, to emphasize information that is mutually considered to be of value to the client. A quick return to what is on the forefront of clients' minds is important.

HUMOR IN THERAPY: CULTIVATING AN APPRECIATION FOR THE ABSURD

Many disorders and psychological afflictions are characterized by an underdeveloped sense of humor, especially a dearth of appreciation for the absurd. In the *Myth of Sisyphus*, Camus writes: "What is absurd is the confrontation between the sense of the irrational and the overwhelming desire for clarity which resounds in the depths of man."[11]

Anxious and depressive mind-sets can be perpetuated by an unrelenting propensity for clarity, rationality, order, efficiency, or obedience in the face of life events, relationships, and work commitments that are messy, cumbersome, have ambiguous outcomes, and/or defy logic. Being on edge, bitter, resentful, or envious can be the emotional consequence of not surrendering to the absurdity of it all, accepting life as it is, rather than life as it should be.

Many clients repeatedly get ensnared trying to make an irrational world conform to their rational expectations. Some of these clients embody schizoid tendencies, intellectualize, are overly concrete in how they understand themselves and others, or have a compulsive need for order and efficiency. They include the so-called type A personalities and those with obsessive-compulsive or autism traits. These tendencies can be seen as taking oneself too seriously. The goal of therapy is, to borrow a quote from French philosopher Jean-Paul Sartre, to overcome the "spirit of seriousness." Or to piggyback on Camus, to relinquish our "appetite for the absolute" and our "nostalgia for unity."[12]

To some degree, we all are afflicted with a spirit of seriousness. We are prone to totalize, dogmatize, and personalize. Existentialists like Camus would have us believe that a sense of the absurd is necessary to live with less deception and more humility in the postmodern world, which lacks any all-encompassing meaning system, any cosmic plan, any prime mover or divine presence quarterbacking life for us.

At times, depression is really apathy. It results from a person's having sacrificed his or her autonomy, passively living a scripted existence, and unsuccessfully trying to ignore a dawning awareness that the social or religious conventions that ought to instill meaning in actuality have lost all meaning, all relevance.

As the evolutionary story goes, humans were not designed to live to be octogenarians. Antibiotics, cancer-busting drugs, high-tech life-saving medical devices, and the like, have greatly extended the human life span. As recently as 1800, few countries in the world had life expectancy rates above forty.[13] Currently, the life expectancy in industrialized nations worldwide hovers at around eighty. Marriages and work lives that once averaged twenty or so years now average fifty years or more. Coping with the same old, same old is unavoidable. Depression can indicate existential boredom or being in a career, job, marriage, or family situation that feels inescapable and that has become staid, monotonous, and overly predictable. Taking flight and reinventing oneself are quintessential ways Americans typically respond to existential boredom. But individuals bent on acting responsibly refrain from rashly abdicating family and professional obligations. Having it in our repertoire to somehow find a way to adapt to and accept the monotonous, banal aspects of life is an existential imperative. An appreciation for the absurd involves a lightness of being that renders somehow more livable the seemingly inescapable life situations we find unfair, irrational, or banal. An appreciation for the absurd helps us laugh off these unavoidable and unpleasant aspects of life.

Humor and a keen sense of the absurd also help us accept the precariousness and arbitrariness inherent in human existence. A core dimension of our benign human denial system involves blinding ourselves to the role that randomness plays in the unfolding of life events. Yet all too often, chance governs life outcomes. According to one theory, the French probably lost the Battle of Waterloo because Napoleon happened to have a fierce case of hemorrhoids that morning and could not mount his horse to command his troops.[14] The *Titanic* might not have sunk had the crew member in charge of the crow's nest not forgotten to drop off the key to the chest that held the binoculars on the morning of the maiden voyage. Without the key, the crow's nest crew had no binoculars to look out for dangers. It is humbling to contemplate how much being in the right place at the right time with the right person has dictated the ups and downs in our professional and love lives. Mirthful humility about this can stave off anxious and depressed feelings.

I recently finished a ten-year course of therapy with a middle-aged woman who credited my use of absurdist humor as instrumental in helping her overcome depression. Cynthia was a fifty-five-year-old public defender who had dedicated her professional life to representing poor and marginalized clients. She prided herself on being rational, reliable, dutiful, and efficient in her work life and maneuvering every day in the byzantine bureaucracy of the criminal justice system. Cynthia was disenchanted with the young public defenders; they were apolitical and had no sense of mission, preferring to jabber on about *Walking Dead* episodes than adequately serve their clients. She railed at the support staff who seemed incapable of putting files in the right places. She frowned on the hubris of the translators she relied on with her Spanish and Mandarin-speaking clients. She was paralyzed going up against judges who followed the letter of the law in bizarre ways that dehumanized client after client.

This work environment filled Cynthia with a sense of futility and demoralization; she felt trapped in her job. She couldn't conceive of exiting the practice of law in the public sector for political reasons (in college, she had become acquainted with leftist politics) or personal ones. Having grown up in poverty and been raised by a mother who had burned through six marriages (with all the attendant instability), she needed bedrock security in all areas of her life.

Cynthia lived with her mother and supported her financially. This arrangement also left her feeling trapped and demoralized, because her mother was insufferably talkative. Cynthia was a self-avowed introvert; she had even seriously flirted with the idea of becoming a nun. Her ideal job was being a librarian at a nunnery. Therefore, one can only imagine the psychological effects of living with a mother who talked nonstop and collected rescue Labradors and tchotchkes and whose abrasive tendencies emptied out her social life, leaving Cynthia to be daughter, companion, caregiver, and provider all in one.

Years of grieving and expressed frustration in therapy gave way to acceptance and an awareness of the unavoidably absurd aspects of both her home and work life. We increasingly engaged in humorous word play that was mutually satisfying and promoted lighthearted acceptance, a counterpoint to Cynthia's usual melancholic resignation.

One day, Cynthia divulged her irritation at the courtroom support staff who misplaced files. I commented, "I guess they would rather file their nails than nail filing the folders." We both laughed, with Cynthia eventually softly chuckling and saying, "Well, what do ya do, what do ya do?" I added, "If the choice is between murdering them and putting up with them, I guess you'll have to put up with them." Cynthia laughed again, then conceded, "I guess I'd go out of my mind if I was filing files all day long for years on end. . . . I should cut them some slack."

Another time, I noted, "The thing you can count on with your mother is you can't count on your mother."

It was true, and it was funny, and a little sad, and over time, the humor and the perspective helped Cynthia react less seriously to her mother. This type of banter enabled Cynthia to build anticipatory disappointment, that is, to refrain from expecting the impossible.

Off and on during treatment, we revisited a vexing exchange between Cynthia and her sister. The sister was a devout Catholic who nonetheless had done very little financially or otherwise to help Cynthia out in taking care of their mother.

One day, Cynthia told me that her sister had condescendingly said to her, "There's a place for you in heaven."

I shot back, "No wonder Sartre said hell is other people. Hell is other people telling you there's a place in heaven for you as a way to rationalize their own unwillingness to take responsibility."

I had tapped into and amplified Cynthia's muted feelings about her sister's hypocritical statement. My feeling, the word play, the philosophical reference, all made her feel understood—both in terms of her value system and how she defined herself as a person (her intellectual sophistication, her ethicality) in addition to tapping the truly difficult circumstances of her life.

On another occasion, Cynthia brought up the "There's a place for you in heaven" comment and added, "I don't know what the Lord's going to say when he discusses how she hasn't sent a birthday card to Mom in over thirty years." I quickly chimed in: "I do. He's gonna say something like, Whoops, it's a few years in Limbo for you, dear lady!" We both laughed uproariously. There was spontaneity, intimacy, resonance, and deep confirmation in the interaction. Cynthia's laughter tacitly revealed that she had made peace with her sister's hypocritical religiosity. And Cynthia had witnessed me enjoying my work, enjoying her, and grasping her life struggles more resolutely.

A humorous comment can be a cut-to-the-chase experience, entailing an instantaneous, rapid, and preconscious processing of interpersonal events eventuating in a joke or quip that leaves the client feeling soundly understood. At an implicit level, when we joke with clients, it is indisputable evidence we enjoy them. Laughter is an intelligent way of accepting the unchangeable, and when we laugh with others, we feel good together. We therapists need to remind ourselves that humorous interactions with clients can cement a tacit connection and add a quotient of compatibility that benefits the working alliance in psychotherapy.

PROFESSIONALISM RECONSIDERED

The personal development of mental health professionals has a bearing on the effectiveness of the services they offer in a way that rarely applies in other careers. If our dentist or accountant seems even-tempered and discerning as a person, it's a bonus. We hire them for their technical knowledge, not their human know-how. It's an entirely different matter in the mental health field. The effective psychotherapist some-how must have the presence of mind to immerse himself or herself in an array of client problems without undue doubt and insecurity. Clients need to steadily and confidently expect that the upsetting stories they tell and retell will not emotionally rattle the therapist in fundamen-tal ways. Most of the time, we therapists must tolerably suffer clients' feelings that they consider insufferable. We carry clients' unborn grief, sadness, elation, rage, envy, pride, and shame. This capability requires great depth and dimensionality of personhood.

Psychotherapists have a professional duty to psychologically work on themselves. Our therapeutic instrument is our personhood and how we use this clinically in the room with clients. Emotionally speak-ing, we can only take clients as far as we have gone ourselves. If we disavow aspects of our humanity, it will be hard to help clients avow these same qualities in themselves. Blind spots for our own thwarted grief necessarily impede our ability to prompt clients to see and dwell in their own grief. The same applies to other emotional states.

These days, the professional duty to continuously work on ourselves psychologically has been eclipsed by a barrage of other priorities. In the frenzy to get established in the field, many new psychotherapists seem compelled to distinguish themselves as specialists of one sort or another. Typically, they tout these specialties as evidenced based. Not a week goes by that I don't receive an email from my local profes-sional organization looking for a referral for a practitioner who has a specialty with clients or clinical entities. The specialties the organiza-tion is seeking include transgendered youth, eating disorders, parent alienation syndrome, divorce, domestic violence, children with poor executive functioning, teen suicide, borderline personality disorder, and depression in midlife homemakers. Of course, it's important to keep up on the literature in these areas, have a working familiar-ity with a range of diagnoses, and acquire discrete skills over time. However, there are overarching psychological dynamics and human frailties common to most clinical entities. It would be refreshing to receive an email from my local professional organization requesting a practitioner who specialized in tolerating and working with such phenomena as despair, contempt, healthy pride, obsessive jealousy,

dysfunctional vanity, or out-of-control greed. For therapists to become familiar with these core human concerns, they must personally
struggle with traces of these matters within themselves.

Multicultural competence, an acquired knowledge base to treat
clients across a variety of racial and ethnic groups, is receiving renewed attention in psychiatry, psychology, and social work graduate
schools and training sites across the United States. The attention is
highly understandable. It is estimated that by 2050, the percentage of
racial minorities in the country will increase to about 50 percent of
the population.[15] In some urban settings in the next decade, upwards
of 80 percent of therapist-client pairings will comprise cross-racial or
cross-ethnic dyads. It is important for mental health professionals to
have a knowledge base of what is common and normative across racial
and ethnic groups, but it is not enough. For instance, therapists need to
read up on the role of filial piety in the Asian American community—
the deep cultural obligation to respect and be loyal to one's parents and
elderly family members. Therapists can learn that second-generation
young adult Asian Americans frequently live a dual life, being more
Westernized in public and more deferential at home.[16] Awareness of
this different norm keeps therapists from pathologizing such behavior.

Nor is it enough for therapists just to strive to avoid color-blind
racial attitudes in which the harm some clients face because of covert
or overt forms of racial privilege and institutional discrimination are
glossed over. A racially unaware therapist, for instance, might pathol-
ogize the justifiable anger and suspicion of racism at work on the part
of an African American client passed over for a promotion at work.

To take the all-important step of acquiring multicultural competence in clinical work, a therapist must examine his or her own racial
and ethnic identity. A red flag for therapists to watch out for is either
the overvaluing or devaluing of cultural attitudes and behaviors with
which they have been raised. For instance, a Caucasian therapist might
idealize the need for adolescents to individuate from parents. He or
she may minimize a Latina mother's complaint that her son is being
unacceptably disobedient. Or, conversely, a Latina therapist might idealize an adolescent's need to be compliant with parents and minimize a
Caucasian mother's complaint that her son is being overly submissive.

Therapists also need to watch for cultural insularity in their personal lives—a narrow outlook that subtly reinforces values and attitudes they think are normal for all people. More so than in other professions, we have an obligation to build cultural competency by regularly putting ourselves in contact with members of various racial and ethnic groups. When we see clients from racial and ethnic groups other than our own, we have to feel comfortable not only in our own skin, but also in their skin. We need to look at them looking at us and be accepting of and at ease with their otherness, with simultaneous confidence that we can understand their concerns because of our shared humanity. Along these lines, Adrian van Kaam, founder of the Institute of Formative Spirituality at Duquesne University in Pittsburgh, aptly claims: "True therapeutic concern is, at the least, an implicit awareness of the inalienableness of my client's life."[17]

Finally, now more than ever, there's pressure for therapists to conform to bureaucratic protocol, which, if not *actively resisted*, can result in substandard client care. Ironically, therapists are instructed to follow many procedures that are considered commensurate with being an ethical professional but which, if overprioritized, can lead to unethical behavior with clients, in the human sense. During our initial visits with clients, we are supposed to go over our office policies and procedures and set the formal rubric for therapy. We are asked to talk about fees, cancellation policies, reporting requirements, diagnoses that go on insurance forms, and treatment goals and objectives. Therapists feel the top-down pressure to be formal during the initial psychotherapy visits, whereas clients are longing for us to be informal and just listen. I often wonder if the current 50 percent dropout rate after the first few psychotherapy visits is abnormally high because too many therapists inappropriately yield to top-down bureaucratic requirements and thereby lose the client.[18]

Typically, when clients enter therapy, they are in a state of real need. Any stigma associated with pursuing therapy can easily win out. If anything, the burden of proof is on the therapist to represent therapy as a worthwhile venture. Our full presence of mind and breadth of authentic care must be engaged during these initial visits. To enter therapy is to cross the threshold into a healing relationship, one where the therapist uses human virtues—sincerity, forbearance, forthrightness, tact, discretion, and mirth—for clinical purposes, so that whatever emotional breakdown the client experiences, in time, will achieve the psychological status of an emotional breakthrough.

CHAPTER EIGHT

Psychotherapy and
the Social Good

ACADEMIC AND POLITICAL PUNDITS usually disparage the social worth of psychotherapy. American Enterprise Institute scholars and authors of *One Nation Under Therapy: How the Helping Culture Is Eroding Self-Reliance*, Christina Hoff Sommers and Sally Satel declare: "The fateful question is: Will Americans actively defend the traditional creed of stoicism and the ideology of achievement, or will they continue to allow the nation to slide into therapeutic self-absorption and moral debility?"[1] Sociologist Frank Furedi echoes this sentiment: "Despite its celebration of the self, our therapeutic culture is hostile to behavior patterns that demonstrate self-reliance and self-control."[2] McGill University psychiatry professor Joel Paris insists: "The more people focus on the self and inner feelings, the less sensitive they tend to be to others. In this way, talk therapy runs the constant danger of supporting narcissism, at the individual and cultural levels."[3]

The assumptions embedded in these viewpoints resemble those contained in Christopher Lasch's seminal book *The Culture of Narcissism*, penned almost forty years ago. Therapy and therapy culture, Lasch says, promote self-preoccupation at the expense of true interest in and love for others. He also says that therapy encourages dependency on others for approval and admiration over self-reliance, a lack of personal responsibility by blaming others and one's psychiatric afflictions for one's reprehensible behavior, and moral relativism.[4]

Does psychotherapy indeed undermine democratic values and the social good? Do the beliefs and practices circulating in the psychotherapy world merely perpetuate toxic narcissistic tendencies, leaving people overly focused on their own personal amusement and pleasure, devoid of any duty to do right by others or society? Does it teach people to rely on others for admiration and approval?

Clearly, these criticisms represent neither the aim nor the tenor of the practice of psychotherapy I map out and subscribe to in this book. Too much bad press has been meted out exposing the underside of humanistic psychology—the self-help therapies and encounter groups that sprang up during the 1960s counterculture and beyond, celebrating the unfettered expression of emotion, "free love," and a narrow ethic of self-fulfillment. There's a need for good press highlighting how humanistic therapy methods actually advance democratic values and the social good.

Psychotherapy imbued with humanistic ideals instills a capacity for empathic concern in clients who then become citizens opened up to greater caring for the emotional well-being of others. It also engenders the type of authentic self-development that renders an individual psychologically equipped to truly feel, think, and act like an individual while also assuming responsibility for the quality of his or her relationships. We forget that exercising autonomy and relating with sensitivity are not psychological givens, but hard-won psychological achievements. Moreover, psychoanalytic and existential therapies are uniquely suited to treat the psychological vulnerabilities that attract people to the compulsive pursuit of extrinsic sources of happiness—wealth, status, popularity, and attractiveness—so rampant in our consumer culture. Instead, the therapies uphold intrinsic sources of happiness, as Princeton University psychologist Robert Woolfolk reminds us: "If anything, psychotherapists are on the side of genuine caring, spending time with one's family, leading a balanced life, and challenging the worth of acquiring more social status and material possessions at the expense of people who love you and whom you should be making time for and loving back in return."[5]

CORRECTING THE EMPATHY DEFICIT

While Barack Obama was still a US senator from Illinois in 2006, his address to graduates at Northwestern University became newsworthy: "There's a lot of talk in this country about the federal deficit. But I think we should talk more about our empathy deficit—the ability to put ourselves in someone else's shoes; to see the world through those who are different from us."[6] He was reiterating a message contained in his book *The Audacity of Hope*: "A sense of empathy . . . is one that I find myself appreciating more and more as I get older. It is at the heart of my moral code, and it is how I understand the Golden Rule—not simply as a call to sympathy or charity, but as something more demanding, a call to stand in somebody else's shoes and see through their eyes."[7]

It turns out that Obama presaged a current threat to the health of our democratic culture: an empathy deficit. Research out of the University of Michigan tracking the empathy ratings of nearly fourteen thousand college students over the past thirty years reveals that almost 75 percent of students today perceive themselves as less empathic than the average student in the 1980s. The sharpest declines in empathy appear to have occurred over the past decade. Nowadays, students are approximately 40 percent less empathic than those who attended college just after the turn of the twenty-first century. They are less likely to endorse statements like "I often have tender, concerned feelings for people less fortunate than me."[8]

The importance of empathy to a healthy democracy cannot be overstated. We need an ever-expanding number of citizens with greater empathic capabilities, or an abiding inclination to feel their way into the lives of others, to want the same care and respect for others as is desired for oneself. The philosopher Martha Nussbaum states the problem succinctly: "A democracy filled with citizens who lack empathy will inevitably breed more types of marginalization and stigmatization, thus exacerbating rather than solving its problems."[9] Political scientist Michael Morrell shares a similar concern in *Empathy and Democracy*: "Without the process of empathy, it is highly unlikely that citizens will demonstrate the tolerance, mutual respect, reciprocity, and openness towards others vital for a deliberative democracy to fulfill its promise of equal consideration that is central to giving collective decisions their legitimacy."[10]

We can educate our citizenry on multicultural diversity. School-based and workplace information sessions can increase people's understanding of problems like racial prejudice and sexual harassment. But one still needs to be psychologically capable of high degrees of empathic concern to really care about the life predicaments of others—perhaps especially when their backgrounds are very different from one's own. Citizens need to care about caring. On this matter, psychotherapy embodying the empathic methods outlined in previous chapters fills an important social vacuum.

Among other things, therapy sensitizes clients. It positions them psychologically to feel at one with others, to feel "the me in you" and "the you in me." The greater the spectrum of emotions a client is freed up to experience and verbally master in therapy, the more fully and confidently he or she can enter the emotional life of others. To put it another way, psychotherapy enlarges one's humanity. The issues affecting another person—unemployment, a promotion, racial discrimination, coming out as gay or lesbian—may not have direct relevance to your personal experiences. But the underlying emotions—humiliation, pride, rejection, anxiety—might be relevant. It is at this more primal emotional level that people relate to and care about each other's life situations.

Furthermore, therapist empathy tacitly begets client empathy. Being recognized is foundational for showing recognition. Outside therapy, clients are apt to model the empathic concern they receive from a therapist, because they have learned firsthand what it feels like to be deeply listened to and seen.

A VITAL DEMOCRACY
REQUIRES AUTHENTIC SELVES

In the aftermath of World War II, many psychoanalysts raised public awareness about the insecurity of democratic societies and the specter of fascism unless an ample number of citizens attained a good measure of authentic selfhood. The ever-colorful British psychoanalyst D. W. Winnicott asserted, "Of a true democracy one can say, 'In this society at this time there is sufficient maturity in the emotional development of a sufficient number of the individuals that comprise it for there to exist an innate tendency towards the creation and recreation and maintenance of the democratic machinery.'"[11]

In his widely read book *Escape from Freedom*, Erich Fromm spelled out how the average person is not as freedom-loving and self-directed as he or she believes. People tend to relinquish their freedom, succumbing to social convention and public opinion: "Modern man lives under the illusion that he knows what he wants, while he actually wants what he is supposed to want."[12] Embracing the anxiety associated with making up our own mind and taking action that might buck social convention and public opinion are, in Fromm's view, tasks "we frantically try to avoid by accepting ready-made goals as though they were our own."

Fromm's proposition was an existentialist one: we humans are inherently inclined to avoid the anxiety and creative energy in the risky enterprise of defining and acting on true personal desires, goals, and aspirations. Our avoidance causes us to slip into inauthentic ways of living, or what existentialist philosopher Martin Heidegger labeled a state of *fallenness*. We reflexively accommodate to what we think others and the social roles we inhabit demand of us. We acquiesce and live life as if we are an agent of someone else's intentions.

Overconformity of this sort is antithetical to a healthy democracy, which thrives on an ample citizenry showing individual integrity. High-functioning democracies need large numbers of people who are anchored to an authentic sense of self and infused with enough internal fortitude that they can think both with and against tradition. These people are prepared to see the good and bad in themselves, in others, and in their nation's history, social arrangements, and cherished ideologies. These people have a strong sense of personal agency. They evolve into, and work at being, the subject of the life they live rather than feeling subjected to the life they live.

Psychodynamic-humanistic approaches to psychotherapy warrant special consideration for the health of any democracy because they privilege greater client authenticity as a treatment goal. The central therapeutic agenda, session in and session out, pivots on prompting clients to reclaim their subjective voice—feeling, thinking, desiring, and acting from a locus of real selfhood. The emphasis on honest expression of spontaneously occurring experiences grounds and vitalizes the self. Recognized and accepted by the therapist during their ugliest and prettiest moments, clients are enabled to be more self-accepting and self-recognizing. Anchored to a real self, in the words of the prominent humanistic psychologist Maureen O'Hara, clients learn to "base their actions and life choices on their own particular authentic experience. Moreover, they discover that it is only by making such choices for oneself that one becomes a fully emancipated member of society."[13]

This is not to say that therapy favoring client authenticity simply breeds boorish expressions of honesty. To paraphrase the political philosopher Charles Taylor, who reminds us that the self is always a self-in-relation, to commit to being true to ourselves also requires us to be true to our relationships. The psychoanalyst Claudio Neri arrives at the same insight in his aptly titled article "Authenticity as an Aim of Psychoanalysis": "Being authentic involves giving up the luxury of naivety and taking on the responsibility for one's relationships and becoming aware of the effects of our words and actions on the other. It does not simply mean being sincere and direct and saying things that correspond to reality, but also saying things that correspond to the reality of relationships."[14] Therefore, to live more authentically is to assume the burden of social tact. In therapy, of course, there is a loosening of the need to be tactful. Clients are given license to regress, to get primal, to choose their words freely. But what makes talk therapy so liberating and relationally beneficial at the same time is that crude but honest iterations get expressed and then reexpressed in the never-ending struggle to communicate candidly yet sensitively.

Therapy that invites the honest expression of emotion does not lead, as those conservative pundits I quoted earlier would have it, to permissive and destructive actions. Rather, true self-control emerges with the expressive mastery of a variety of primal emotions. For instance, the ability to talk freely and confidentially in therapy about erotic and violent fantasies lessens the possibility that these will be

acted out in harmful ways. This outcome is good for one's close relationships and for society as a whole. Moreover, authentic selfhood
does not negate the need for supportive others. The American ideal of
rugged individualism centered on a lack of need for confirmation and
encouragement by others is a false ideal. Even the most psychologically evolved among us need others at key moments to acknowledge
our perspective, function as mentors, remind us of what we know to
be true, and push us beyond ourselves. Authenticity is an arduous pursuit. It's a perpetual work in progress. We are regularly tempted to
slip into safe habits, resist creative solutions, adopt conventional ideas,
and consume consumer values. But we must stay honest to ourselves
and our ideals. A caring psychotherapist can function as our existential
conscience. This is why many people who are on a journey of authenticity prize ongoing psychotherapy.

THE PURSUIT OF GENUINE HAPPINESS

Our founding fathers thought so highly of the pursuit of happiness,
they inserted it in the Declaration of Independence as an "inalien-
able right." In their pre-psychological era, they perceived the pursuit of happiness largely in terms of more equitable opportunities to
gain prosperity and freedom of religious expression. This was the new
democracy's counterposition to the fixed hierarchies of aristocratic
wealth and religious intolerance prevailing in Europe. In our own
time, we are more disposed to evaluate happiness in terms of endeav-
ors that are intrinsically, as distinct from extrinsically, satisfying.

Pursuits with intrinsic value are satisfying because they meet basic psychological needs. Experiences that provide inherent meaning
and enjoyment are considered intrinsically valuable. We count among
them spending time with loved ones and loving others, listening to
or creating music, observing or creating art, reading or being read to,
entertainment, leisure, physical activity, and being in nature.

Pursuits with extrinsic value are contingent on outside feedback to
make us feel satisfied. They include the pursuit of wealth, fame, status,
attractiveness, and popularity and the acquisition of possessions.

The available science corroborates our deepest human intuitions
regarding the folly of pursuing extrinsic sources of happiness centering

on materialism and consumerism. The more people self-identify as materialistic (focusing on acquiring wealth and possessions to convey status) the greater likelihood their overall well-being and personal satisfaction will suffer. Materialistic people report higher rates of anxiety and depression, more feelings of insecurity, and a greater incidence of health problems like headaches and stomachaches. They are less likely to perceive themselves as autonomous, competent, and appreciative of close personal relationships. These findings came from the country's leading researcher on materialism and well-being, Tim Kasser, professor of psychology at Knox College in Galesburg, Illinois. According to Kasser, a materialistic values orientation "is one way in which people attempt to compensate for worries and doubts about their self-worth, their ability to cope effectively with challenges, and their safety in a relatively unpredictable world."[15]

The pursuit of wealth and status can also constrict a person's emotional life, rendering the individual more self-involved and ill-disposed to keep others' concerns in mind. To that point, people on the higher end of the social ladder tend to show less empathy. A 2010 study in the journal *Psychological Science* reveals that compared with lower-income people, those with higher incomes perceive the feelings of others less accurately.[16]

And just as the mythic Greek hero Perseus bemoaned, "Oh what a void there is in things," the pleasure derived from acquiring possessions is short-lived.[17] A recent article in the *Journal of Consumer Research* on this subject concludes the same thing, but less poetically: "The state of anticipating and desiring a product may be inherently more pleasurable than product ownership itself." Science and ancient wisdom both attest that the urge to splurge does not purge the urge.[18] Social scientists, too, come down on the side of the so-called hedonic treadmill phenomenon, disconfirming the capitalist shibboleth that wealth brings happiness.

A specialist in this area, Carol Graham, who teachers in the School of Public Policy at the University of Maryland, draws on worldwide data to show how people's expectations and desires rise along with their income.[19] This relationship counteracts any progressive gain in happiness. Products and services once considered discretionary purchases quickly become mandatory ones. Wealthy people compare themselves with their wealthier counterparts and feel compelled to make and spend more to keep up. As Dartmouth College happiness historian Darrin McMahon writes, "Human beings' proclivity to grow accustomed to, and then dissatisfied with, the pleasures of this world is a phenomenon as old as humanity."[20]

To date, the most convincing evidence favoring intrinsic sources of happiness comes from the Harvard Study of Adult Development. This one-of-a-kind, seventy-five-year-old investigation has tracked the health and emotional well-being of 724 men from their teenage years, beginning in the late 1930s, into their old age. Participants spanned the socioeconomic spectrum from the Harvard-educated to those originating from some of Boston's poorest neighborhoods. The study happened to include four men who ran for US Senate seats and one president, John F. Kennedy. In a recent illuminating TED talk, the current project head, psychiatrist Robert Waldinger, summed up the study's conclusions: "Good relationships keep us happier and healthier, period." He added affirmatively, "People who were the most satisfied with their relationships at age fifty were the healthiest at age eighty." Waldinger's scientifically informed recommendation for living the good life is also an age-old Aristotelian one: "Lean into relationships."[21]

Should the reader question these findings because they are based exclusively on a sample of males, studies on females show similar results. Nobel Prize–winning psychologist Daniel Kahneman and several colleagues surveyed an ethnically diverse group of 909 working women in the United States. The top two activities listed as personally enjoyable were intimate relationships and socializing outside work. The bottom two were working for pay and commuting to work.[22]

Alongside the research affirming the role of healthy relationships in the fulfillment of genuine happiness are findings demonstrating our deficiency in this area. Take marriage. In his sobering text, *The Science of Happily Ever After: What Really Matters in the Quest for Enduring Love*, Ty Tashiro presents data indicating that, nowadays, the median length of a marriage in the United States is seven years. His conservative estimate of the divorce and permanent separation rate is

60 percent. When you add this percentage to the 7 percent of couples who remain married but report high levels of relationship dissatisfaction, Tashiro concludes that two-thirds of married couples do not live "happily ever after."[23]

Despite the mountain of evidence and age-old wisdom substantiating the need to accentuate intrinsic sources of happiness and resist materialistic ones in the pursuit of the good life, recent generations seem to be heading in the wrong direction. San Diego State University psychology professor Jean Twenge and several colleagues examined the generational differences between baby boomers (born 1946–1961), Gen Xers (born 1962–1981), and millennials (born after 1982) on their stated life goals. Nearly 75 percent of millennials and 71 percent of Gen Xers endorsed "being very well off financially" as a key life goal, compared with just over 44 percent of boomers. "Developing a meaningful life philosophy" was endorsed as important by 73 percent of boomers, as well as 47 percent and just under 45 percent of Gen Xers and millennials, respectively. Twenge and her colleagues sum up their findings pointedly: "The results generally support the 'Generation Me' view of generational differences."[24] Their conclusion squares with previous research by Twenge and W. Keith Campbell chronicling the rise in narcissism among millennials.[25]

Psychotherapy rooted in the psychoanalytic tradition is uniquely suited to treat the narcissistic vulnerabilities that often underlie a person's compulsive need for fame and fortune. People who strongly favor such factors as wealth, appearance, and popularity as a means to elicit admiration and praise from others frequently have self-esteem regulation problems. When they meet their grandiose standards—which they often do because of their charisma and drive for success—they have never felt better. However, minor failures and setbacks can leave them feeling deflated and worthless. Their emotional life is monopolized by desperate attempts to internally manage conflicting surges of pride and shame, as well as the external reactions of those around them to their prideful and shameful gestures.[26]

Psychotherapy that borrows from the existential-humanistic tradition has its own set of compelling ideas for understanding the psychological struggles of people lured by materialistic lifestyles. The avid pursuit of wealth, status, and attractiveness can be a way to avoid confronting the anxiety that emerges when we ponder our own mortality and that of those we love. Not knowing when or how death will occur builds unpredictability into our very existence. Stacking up possessions can be a desperate way to fend off the anxiety associated with such unpredictability. Overzealous exercise regimens and costly cosmetic procedures to make us feel young and fit only go so far to soothe the anxiety accompanying the aging process. Existential realizations can be dreadful. It can churn our insides acutely when we realize we are personally responsible for our own life course—balanced against our family and social obligations. The struggle to heed the call of our better selves; to stay true to our real talents, preferences, values, and ideals; and to do right by those we love can be daunting. The cumulative anxiety and proactive energy associated with living life authentically makes it easier than we want to believe to acquiesce to the juggernaut of consumerist messages circulating in dominant American culture.

Psychotherapy is a precious space for us to overcome our narcissistic vulnerabilities and existential anxieties that make us easily seduced by distorted notions of materialistic happiness. It serves the social good as a corrective against such corrosive cultural values and habits. Its principles and practices connect us to wellsprings of intrinsic happiness—self-acceptance, loving bonds with others, the cultivation of true talents and sources of personal enjoyment, living in the present. In this regard, psychotherapy serves the social good because it safeguards and perpetuates intrinsic sources of happiness. Along these lines, Rutgers University psychologist Nancy McWilliams notes: "Psychotherapy subcultures have flourished as a kind of alternative sensibility to the radically individualistic, consumeristic, technocratic culture we inhabit. . . . With every individual with whom they engage in a deeply therapeutic way, therapists quietly challenge many of the more facile and potentially destructive assumptions of the larger society."[27]

Since its inception, psychotherapy was considered a subversive cultural practice by leaders in authoritarian regimes, because of its ethic of emotional honesty, endorsement of sexual expression, and distrust of pretense. Freud's books were some of the Nazis' favorites to burn. But as we can see, psychotherapy is subversive in a regenerative fashion, because its clients tend to reprioritize intrinsic values in their lives. Alternatively, psychotherapy is an affirmative cultural practice. It's a purveyor of greater empathy and compassionate individualism, which, as I've outlined, are psychological prerequisites for people to become more democratically sensitized. Stronger democracies need citizens with well-developed democratic personalities.

The quintessential goals of therapy include freedom from the residual effects of trauma, greater awareness of and communicative flexibility with potentially destructive emotions, enhanced self-assuredness and the ability to live intentionally, better courage in showing and receiving love, and more empathy for self and others. The effort to realize these goals not only lessens the suffering of clients and fortifies their authentic selfhood, but also transforms them into more humane members of society.

We live in an age when the overreach of Big Pharma, extravagant expectations placed on medications, the underfunding of psychotherapy by health insurers, and the oversupply of brief, problem-solving therapies supported by slanted science all place traditional talk therapy in jeopardy. Now more than ever, there needs to be renewed focus among mental health educators, researchers, professionals, and other advocates to preserve humanistically informed and scientifically backed traditional talk therapy. We need it not only for its value in reducing emotional suffering and enhancing personal well-being, but also for the social good it provides.

ACKNOWLEDGMENTS

AS THE SAYING GOES, psychotherapy is a "talking cure." However, in reality it is a talking and listening cure; that is, something both ameliorative and affirming occurs when candid disclosure meets with careful and caring listening. In a more two-sided way, the same applies in friendships and in relationships with colleagues. I have been fortunate over the years to have had friends and colleagues intent upon engaging in true dialogue, reflecting a mutual desire to listen to, honor, and learn from one another's ideas. All too often, I talk more than I listen, which is a professional hazard for therapists when they themselves encounter an eager listener outside the consulting room. My dear friend Tom Peters, for whom I have the utmost respect as a therapist, has always been a rapt listener, indulging my need to unpack my latest clinical thinking, while offering inspirations of his own. The echoes of our umpteen late-night dinner discussions can be found in the pages of this book. Alan Karbelnig is one of those rare breed of psychotherapists whose intellectualism, nose for seeing through pretense, and suspicion of dogmatic ways of theorizing and practicing make him an invaluable friend and colleague. This is a book that he himself could have written. Art Hansen, a cultural historian and life-long mentor/friend, was the first person to whom I gave a rough draft of the book for an honest read. His prodigious interdisciplinary mind left its imprint on me when I was a young scholar, and he made it unmistakably alluring to trace the historical roots of psychotherapy and analyze its cultural value in this book. A special thank-you goes to Sam Alibrando and Janette Davis, treasured friends and fellow therapists, who frequently inquired with enthusiasm and true interest about how the book was progressing and shared numerous anecdotes from their own clinical work, confirming that the direction I was taking in the book was spot-on.

My first introduction to psychotherapy and encounter groups in the 1980s occurred in the Human Services Department at California State University, Fullerton, under the guidance of luminaries such as Patrick Callanan, Gerald Corey, and Michael Russell. This experience fed on itself, eventuating in graduate work in the Existential-Humanistic Psychology program at Seattle University, whose faculty—Steen Halling, Lane Gerber, Jan Rowe, and George Kunz—practiced what they preached regarding such existential-humanistic tenets as genuineness, inclusiveness, and real concern. The voice of Steen Halling—as dedicated a professor and mentor as one will find—continues to inhabit my mind and anchor me to existential-humanistic ways of conceptualizing and attending to client problems. In the clinical psychology department at Teachers College, Columbia University, there was precious immersion in psychoanalytic psychology, which Barry Farber and Rosalea Schonbar were determined to preserve as the pendulum in the field was swinging in the direction of eliminating such doctoral programs. John Broughton, another cherished mentor and friend, dazzled me at Columbia with the sheer breadth of his knowledge (able to quote Karl Marx, Eminem, Freud, and Noam Chomsky to drive home a point) and is largely responsible for me becoming the writer I am today.

The personal benefits of the devotion, attentiveness, and quiet wisdom manifested by my own therapists dating back over the years—Martin, Carol, and Helen—engendered the motivation to provide in kind for my own clients.

In my maturation as a psychotherapist, I have relied as much on relationships with texts as professional contact with flesh-and-blood colleagues. Authors who have appealed to me over the years have been those with a pragmatic bent, willing to set aside theoretical allegiances in the pursuit of a more honest and resolute understanding of human problems and more effective ways of reducing human suffering. Those whose writings have offered me thankful rewards are Lewis Aron, Jessica Benjamin, Michael Eigen, Erich Fromm, Irwin Hirsch, Irwin Hoffman, Stephen Mitchell, Adam Phillips, Martha Stark, Robert Stolorow, Paul Wachtel, and D. W. Winnicott (within the psychoanalytic tradition); Emmy van Deurzen, R. D. Laing, Peter Lomas, Rollo May, and Irvin Yalom (existentially oriented theorists); and philosophers Mari Ruti and Richard Rorty.

Amy Caldwell, my editor at Beacon Press, is worthy of special recognition due to the zeal with which she quickly informed herself about the world of psychotherapy, as well as her uncanny ability to detect and correct points I was making in the book in ways that, without exception, strengthened my arguments. She also had a knack for knowing when and how to give me a shot in the arm to embolden my acceptance of how valuable an undertaking this book was. For more than five years, she and the staff at Beacon Press have been stalwart supporters of my research and literary efforts to call attention to questionable national trends in mental health practice.

The loyal and consistent support of my in-laws, Steve and Donna Wickersham, has been important, as has that of my father-in-law, Donald Chunn, who, as a therapist himself, sowed the seed that I might follow in his footsteps. My parents, Rodolfo and Carmen Gnaulati, modeled the sort of work ethic necessary for this author to put in the grueling hours to see a book through to completion.

Most of all, I am indebted to my wife, and closest friend, Janet, for allowing me ample solitude to enter the writer's trance and engaging in discussion after discussion about client issues, drawing from the wide-ranging clinical knowledge and wholeheartedness she embodies in her work as a therapist. My son, Marcello, also deserves special mention for indirectly motivating me through the fantasy that one day he might read this book and for the first time have a tangible sense of the noble professional calling that his father earns a living at. Lastly, I am grateful to all the clients I have seen over the past thirty years whose subtle, and not-so-subtle, cues have taught me how, when, and why to be a better listener and more sensitive speaker.

NOTES

INTRODUCTION

1. Scott D. Miller et al., "The Outcome of Psychotherapy: Yesterday, Today, and Tomorrow," *Psychotherapy* 50, no. 1 (2013): 88–97.
2. Mark Olfson and Steven C. Marcus, "National Trends in Outpatient Psychotherapy," *American Journal of Psychiatry* 167, no. 2 (2010): 1456–63.
3. Ibid.
4. Jesse Pines et al., "Kaiser Permanente—California: A Model for Integrated Care for the Ill and Injured," Brookings Institution, May 4, 2015, https://www.brookings.edu/wp-content/uploads/2016/07/KaiserFormatted _150504RH-with-image.pdf.

CHAPTER ONE: IN THE BEGINNING, THERE WAS FREUD

1. Sigmund Freud and Josef Breuer, *Studies in Hysteria* (1895; New York: Penguin Books, 2004).
2. Robert Kaplan, "O Anna: Being Bertha Pappenheim: History and Biography," *Australian Psychiatry* 12, no. 1 (2004): 62–68.
3. Freud and Breuer, *Studies in Hysteria*, 25.
4. Ibid.
5. Mikkel Borch-Jacobsen and Sonu Shamdasani, *The Freud Files: An Inquiry into the History of Psychoanalysis* (New York: Cambridge University Press, 2012).
6. Kaplan, "O Anna: Being Bertha Pappenheim," 62–68.
7. Abram Kardiner, "Freud: The Man I Knew, the Scientist, and His Influence," in *Freud and the Twentieth Century*, ed. Benjamin Nelson (New York: Meridian, 1957), 89.

8. Smiley Blanton, *Diary of My Analysis with Sigmund Freud* (New York: Hawthorn Books, 1971), 47.

9. Freud and Breuer, *Studies in Hysteria*, 113.

10. Sigmund Freud, *Therapy and Technique* (New York: Collier, 1963), 57.

11. Freud and Breuer, *Studies in Hysteria*, 151.

12. Freud, *Therapy and Technique*, 146. Italics in original.

13. Freud and Breuer, *Studies in Hysteria*.

14. Ibid., 161.

15. Anthony Storr, *Freud* (New York: Oxford University Press, 1989).

16. Freud, *Therapy and Technique*, 141.

17. Peter D. Kramer, *Freud: Inventor of the Modern Mind* (New York: Atlas Books, 2006).

18. Peter Gay, ed., *The Freud Reader* (New York: W. W. Norton, 1989).

19. Quoted in ibid.

20. Joseph Wortis, *Fragments of an Analysis with Freud* (New York: Simon and Schuster, 1954).

21. Paul Roazen, *How Freud Worked: First-Hand Accounts of Patients* (Northvale, NJ: Aronson, 1995).

22. Freud and Breuer, *Studies in Hysteria*, 281.

23. Louis Breger, *Freud: Darkness in the Midst of Vision* (New York: Wiley, 2000), 178.

24. Roazen, *How Freud Worked*, 5.

25. Ibid., 27.

26. Quoted in Storr, *Freud*, 105.

27. Breger, *Freud*, 283.

28. Quoted in Roazen, *How Freud Worked*, 63.

29. Quoted in Storr, *Freud*, 105.

30. Quoted in Breger, *Freud*, 185.

31. Quoted in Roazen, *How Freud Worked*, 22.

32. Quoted in ibid., 12.

33. Borch-Jacobsen and Shamdasani, *The Freud Files*.

34. Peter L. Rudnytsky, Antal Bokay, and Patrizia Giampieri-Deutsch, *Ferenczi's Turn in Psychoanalysis* (New York: New York University Press, 1996).

35. Quoted in Phyllis Grosskurth, *The Secret Ring: Freud's Inner Circle and the Politics of Psychoanalysis* (New York: Addison-Wesley, 1991), 54.

36. Breger, *Freud*.

37. Quoted in Rudnytsky et al., *Ferenczi's Turn in Psychoanalysis*, 23.

38. Grosskurth, *The Secret Ring*.

39. Sándor Ferenczi and Otto Rank, *The Development of Psychoanalysis* (1924; Eastford, CT: Martino Books, 2012), 2.

40. Quoted in Edward Dolnick, *Madness on the Couch: Blaming the Victim in the Heyday of Psychoanalysis* (New York: Simon and Schuster, 1998), 36.
41. Quoted in ibid., 19.
42. Quoted in Judith Dupont, ed., *The Clinical Diary of Sándor Ferenczi* (Cambridge, MA: Harvard University Press, 1995), 93.
43. Quoted in Kramer, *Freud*, 186.
44. Wortis, *Fragments of an Analysis with Freud*, 18.
45. Quoted in Grosskurth, *The Secret Ring*, 206.
46. Dupont, *Clinical Diary of Sándor Ferenczi*.
47. Quoted in Breger, *Freud*, 348.
48. Dupont, *Clinical Diary of Sándor Ferenczi*.
49. Rudnytsky et al., *Ferenczi's Turn in Psychoanalysis*.
50. Ibid.
51. Martin Stanton, *Sándor Ferenczi: Reconsidering Active Intervention* (Northvale, NJ: Aronson, 1991).
52. Dupont, *Clinical Diary of Sándor Ferenczi*, 93.
53. Sándor Ferenczi, "The Confusion of Tongues Between Adults and the Child," *International Journal of Psychoanalysis* 30 (1949): 225–30.
54. Ibid.
55. Dupont, *Clinical Diary of Sándor Ferenczi*, 24.
56. Ferenczi, "Confusion of Tongues," 225–30.
57. Grosskurth, *The Secret Ring*.
58. Quoted in Bruno Bettelheim, *Freud and Man's Soul: An Important Re-Interpretation of Freudian Theory* (New York: Vintage Books, 1983).
59. Quoted in Freud, *Therapy and Technique*, 266.
60. Quoted in Dupont, *Clinical Diary of Sándor Ferenczi*, 130.
61. Ibid., 65.
62. Lewis Aron and Adrienne Harris, *The Legacy of Sándor Ferenczi* (Hillsdale, NJ: Analytic Press, 1993).
63. David Cohen, *The Escape of Sigmund Freud* (New York: Overlook Press, 2012).
64. Quoted in ibid.

CHAPTER TWO: BEFORE PROZAC
1. Quoted in Nathan G. Hale Jr., *The Rise and Crisis of Psychoanalysis in the United States: Freud and the Americans, 1917–1985* (New York: Oxford University Press, 1995), 191.
2. Jonathan Engel, *American Therapy: The Rise of Psychotherapy in the United States* (New York: Gotham Books, 2008), 45.
3. Lawrence J. Friedman, *Menninger: The Family and the Clinic* (New York: Alfred Knopf, 1990), 171.

4. Quoted in Ellen Herman, *The Romance of American Psychology: Political Culture in the Age of Experts* (Berkeley: University of California Press, 1996), 96.

5. Ibid., 115.

6. *Shades of Gray*, documentary about combat stress among World War II military members, 1947, available at https://www.youtube.com/watch?v =DuxuCGre2tA.

7. Hale, *Rise and Crisis of Psychoanalysis*, 282.

8. Ibid., 280.

9. Karl Menninger, *The Vital Balance: The Life Process in Mental Health and Illness* (New York: Viking Penguin, 1963).

10. Engel, *American Therapy*, 44.

11. Herman, *Romance of American Psychology*, 89.

12. Quoted in ibid., 247.

13. Harry S. Truman, "Special Message to the Congress Recommending a Comprehensive Health Program," November 19, 1945, Public Papers of the Presidents: Harry S. Truman, 1945–1953, Harry S. Truman Library & Museum, http://www.trumanlibrary.org/publicpapers/index.php?pid=483.

14. Hale, *Rise and Crisis of Psychoanalysis*, 209.

15. Ibid., 246.

16. Engel, *American Therapy*, 53.

17. James H. Capshew, *Psychologists on the March: Science, Practice, and Professional Identity in America, 1929–1969* (Cambridge, UK: Cambridge University Press, 1999), 172.

18. Michael S. Roth, ed., *Freud: Conflict and Culture* (New York: Alfred A. Knopf, 1998), 132.

19. Friedman, *Menninger*, 172.

20. Ibid., 198.

21. Quoted in "Medicine: Are You Always Worrying?," *Time*, October 25, 1948, http://content.time.com/time/subscriber/printout/0,8816,799409,00.html.

22. Quoted in Lawrence R. Samuel, *Shrink: A Cultural History of Psychoanalysis in America* (Lincoln: University of Nebraska Press, 2013), 78.

23. Hale, *Rise and Crisis of Psychoanalysis*, 246.

24. Ibid.

25. William C. Menninger, "An Analysis of Psychoanalysis," *New York Times Magazine*, May 18, 1947, 49–50.

26. Hale, *Rise and Crisis of Psychoanalysis*, 246.

27. "There's a Serious Shortage of Psychiatrists in the US," *Huffington Post*, September 8, 2015, http://www.huffingtonpost.com/entry/theres-a-serious -shortage-of-psychiatrists-in-the-us_us_55eef13ce4b093be51bc128f; Gardiner Harris, "Talk Doesn't Pay, So Psychiatry Turns Instead to Drug

Therapy," *New York Times*, March 5, 2011, http://www.nytimes.com/2011
/03/06/health/policy/06doctors.html.

28. Capshew, *Psychologists on the March*, 173.

29. Ibid.

30. Tom McCarthy, "Great Aspirations: The Postwar American College
Counseling Center," *History of Psychology* 17, no. 1 (2014): 1–18.

31. Ibid., 7.

32. Ibid., 13.

33. John C. Norcross, Gary R. Vandenbos, and Donald K. Freedheim, eds.,
History of Psychology: Continuity and Change (Washington, DC: American
Psychological Association, 2011), 40–42.

34. Nicholas A. Cummings and William T. O'Donohue, *Eleven Blunders That
Cripple Psychotherapy in America* (New York: Routledge, 2008).

35. Ibid.

36. Norcross et al., *History of Psychology*, 46–48.

37. Ibid., 51–56.

38. American Psychological Association, *2005–13: Demographics of the U.S.*
(APA Center for Workforce Studies, July 2015), http://www.apa.org/work
force/publications/13-dem-acs/index.aspx.

39. Engel, *American Therapy*.

40. Quoted in ibid., 161.

41. Herman, *Romance of American Psychology*, 3.

42. Ibid.

43. Paul Saxton, "Comments on Social Work and the Psychotherapies," *Social
Service Review* 65 (1991): 315–16.

44. Linda Plitt Donaldson et al., "Contemporary Social Work Licensure: Implications for Macro Social Work Practice and Education," *Social Work* 59,
no. 1 (2014): 52–61.

45. American Association for Marriage and Family Therapy, "Find MFT Li-
censing Boards," http://www.aamft.org/iMIS15/AAMFT/Content
/directories/MFT_licensing_boards.aspx.

46. Norcross et al., *History of Psychology*, 57.

47. Ibid., 58.

48. *Spellbound*, DVD, dir. Alfred Hitchcock (1945; Beverly Hills, CA: MGM, 2012).

49. Roazen, *How Freud Worked*, 21.

50. Lucy Freeman, *Fight Against Fears: A Very Personal Account of a Woman's
Psychoanalysis* (New York: Crown Publishers, 1951), xiv.

51. Ibid., 40.

52. Ibid., 118.

53. *Bob & Carol & Ted & Alice*, DVD, dir. Paul Mazursky (1969; Chatsworth,
CA: Image Entertainment, 2010).

54. *An Unmarried Woman*, DVD, dir. Paul Mazursky (1978; Los Angeles: 20th Century Fox, 2006).

55. *Ordinary People*, DVD, dir. Robert Redford (1980; Burbank, CA: Warner Bros., 2001).

56. Engel, *American Therapy*, 138.

57. Bernard J. Paris, ed., *Karen Horney: The Therapeutic Process* (New Haven, CT: Yale University Press, 1999).

58. Ibid., 138.

59. Quoted in ibid., 232.

60. Karen Horney, "Interpretations," *American Journal of Psychoanalysis* 16 (1956): 118.

61. Karen Horney, "The Quality of the Analyst's Attention," *American Journal of Psychoanalysis* 19 (1959): 28.

62. Karen Horney, "The Analyst's Personal Equation," *American Journal of Psychoanalysis* 17 (1957): 34.

63. Rainer Funk, ed., *The Clinical Erich Fromm: Personal Accounts and Papers on Therapeutic Technique* (New York: Rodopi, 2009).

64. Lawrence J. Friedman, *The Lives of Erich Fromm: Love's Prophet* (New York: Columbia University Press, 2013).

65. Quoted in ibid., 83.

66. Quoted in ibid., 124.

67. Erich Fromm, "Being Centrally Related to the Patient," in Funk, *Clinical Erich Fromm*, 27.

68. Ibid., 23.

69. Quoted in Funk, *Clinical Erich Fromm*, 95.

70. Quoted in ibid., 98.

71. Quoted in ibid., 97.

72. Fromm, "Being Centrally Related to the Patient," 27.

73. Jessica Grogan, *Encountering America: Humanistic Psychology, Sixties Culture and the Shaping of the Modern Self* (New York: Harper Perennial, 2013).

74. David Dempsey, "Love and Will and Rollo May," *New York Times*, March 28, 1971.

75. "Medicine: Psychiatry & Being," *Time*, December 29, 1958, http://content.time.com/time/magazine/article/0,9171,894046,00.html.

76. Jeffrey Mishlove, "Rollo May: The Human Dilemma (Part One Complete): Thinking Allowed," YouTube video, March 19, 2013, https://www.youtube.com/watch?v=HH-9XkjqYHY.

77. Rollo May, *The Meaning of Anxiety* (1950; New York: Norton, 1977).

78. Rollo May, *The Art of Counseling* (1939; New York: Gardner Press, 1989), 74.

79. Mishlove, "Rollo May: The Human Dilemma."

80. Stephen A. Mitchell, *Hope and Dread in Psychoanalysis* (New York: Basic Books, 1993).

81. Heinz Kohut, *The Analysis of the Self: A Systematic Approach to the Psychoanalytic Treatment of Narcissistic Personality Disorders* (New York: International Universities Press, 1971).

82. Darrell Smith, "Trends in Counseling and Psychotherapy," *American Psychologist* 37, no. 7 (1982): 802–9.

83. James O. Prochaska and John C. Norcross, "The Future of Psychotherapy: A Delphi Poll," *Professional Psychology* 13, no. 5 (1982): 620–27.

84. Engel, *American Therapy*, 231.

85. Peter D. Kramer, *Listening to Prozac* (New York: Penguin Books, 1993), xvii.

86. Adam Gopnik, "Man Goes to See a Doctor," *New Yorker*, August 24, 1998, 114–21.

CHAPTER THREE: PILLS FOR ALL ILLS

1. Lauren Slater, *Prozac Diary* (New York: Penguin Books, 1998), 25.

2. Kramer, *Listening to Prozac*, xv.

3. "More Seek Out Depression Treatment, but Not Psychotherapy," *Psych Central*, December 6, 2010, http://psychcentral.com/news/2010/12/06/more-people-seek-out-depression-treatment-but-not-psychotherapy/21547.html.

4. Robert Whitaker, *Anatomy of an Epidemic: Magic Bullets, Psychiatric Drugs, and the Astonishing Rise of Mental Illness in America* (New York: Crown, 2010), 290.

5. Mary Sykes Wylie, "Falling in Love Again: A Brief History of Our Infatuation with Psychiatric Drugs," *Psychotherapy Networker*, July–August 2014.

6. Ibid.

7. Janice Wood, "Antidepressant Use Up by 400 Percent in the US," *Psych Central*, October 25, 2011, http://psychcentral.com/news/2011/10/25/antidepressant-use-up-400-percent-in-us/30677.html.

8. Wylie, "Falling in Love Again," 27.

9. Kristen Fawcett, "Benzodiazepines: Helpful or Harmful?" *U.S. News & World Report*, February 19, 2015, http://health.usnews.com/health-news/patient-advice/articles/2015/02/19/benzodiazepines-helpful-or-harmful.

10. "Attention-Deficit/Hyperactivity Disorder Among Adults," National Institute of Mental Health, http://www.nimh.nih.gov/health/statistics/prevalence/attention-deficit-hyperactivity-disorder-among-adults.shtml.

11. Luke Whelan, "Sales of ADHD Meds are Skyrocketing; Here's Why," *Mother Jones*, February 24, 2015, http://www.motherjones.com/environment/2015/02/hyperactive-growth-adhd-medication-sales.

12. Ibid.

13. "America's State of Mind," Medco, http://apps.who.int/medicinedocs /documents/s19032en/s19032en.pdf.

14. Ibid.

15. Rhona Finkel, "The Atypical History of Atypical Antipsychotics," Drugsdb.com, September 9, 2012, http://www.drugsdb.com/blog/history -of-atypical-antipsychotics.html.

16. Megan Brooks, "Top 10 Most Prescribed, Top-Selling Drugs," *WebMD*, August 5, 2014, http://www.webmd.com/news/20140805/top-10-drugs.

17. Stuart Pfeifer, "Prescription Drug Spending up 13% in 2014," *Los Angeles Times*, April 14, 2015.

18. "Should You Take an Antidepressant Drug to Treat your Depression?" *Consumer Reports*, November 2011, http://www.consumerreports.org/cro /2011/11/should-you-take-an-antipsychotic-drug-to-treat-depression /index.htm.

19. Ibid., 2.

20. Joseph Glenmullen, *Prozac Backlash: Overcoming the Dangers of Prozac, Zoloft, Paxil, and Other Antidepressants with Safe, Effective Alternatives* (New York: Simon & Schuster, 2001), 256.

21. Ronald Pies, "Doctor, Is My Mood Disorder Due to a Chemical Imbalance?" *Psychiatric Times*, August 11, 2011, http://www.psychiatrictimes .com/blogs/doctor-my-mood-disorder-due-chemical-imbalance.

22. Chad Terhune, Noam N. Levey, and Sandra Poindexter, "Drug Firms' Ties to Doctors Detailed," *Los Angeles Times*, October 1, 2014.

23. Ibid.

24. Christine Chen and Tim Carvell, "Products of the Century in 1900: Our Homes Were Dusty, Our Children Were Bored, and Our Paperwork Was Dangerous," *Fortune*, November 11, 1999, http://archive.fortune.com /magazines/fortune/fortune_archive/1999/11/22/269110/index.htm.

25. Eli Lilly and Company, "Prozac (Fluoxetine Hydrochloride) on 'Products of Century' List," PRNewswire, November 22, 1999, http://www .prnewswire.com/news-releases/prozac-fluoxetine-hydrochloride-on -products-of-century-list-77287087.html.

26. "The Culture of Prozac," *Newsweek*, February 6, 1994, http://www .newsweek.com/culture-prozac-190328.

27. "Eli Lilly: Life After Prozac," *Bloomberg*, July 22, 2001, http://www .bloomberg.com/news/articles/2001-07-22/eli-lilly-life-after-prozac.

28. Margaret Eaton and Mark Xu, "Developing and Marketing a Blockbuster Drug: Lessons from Eli Lilly's Experience with Prozac," Stanford Graduate School of Education, February 25, 2005, http://www.gsb.stanford .edu/faculty-research/case-studies/developing-marketing-blockbuster -drug-lessons-eli-lillys-experience.

29. Ibid., 7.

30. G. Cowley et al., "The Promise of Prozac," *Newsweek*, March 26, 1990, 38.

31. Eaton and Xu, "Developing and Marketing a Blockbuster Drug," 9.

32. Ibid.

33. Ibid.

34. Ibid.

35. Jay Pomerantz, "Working with Primary Care Physicians in Treating Depression," *Carlat Psychiatry Report* 9, no. 4 (2011): 22–25.

36. Allen Frances, *Saving Normal: An Insider's Revolt Against Out-of-Control Psychiatric Diagnosis, DSM-5, Big Pharma, and the Medicalization of Ordinary Life* (New York: HarperCollins, 2013), 102.

37. Ibid.

38. Richard L. Kravitz et al., "What Drives Referrals from Primary Care Physicians to Mental Health Professionals," *Journal of General Internal Medicine* 21, no. 6 (2006): 584–89.

39. Carl Elliott, "The Drug Pushers," *Atlantic*, April 2006, http://www.theatlantic.com/magazine/archive/2006/04/the-drug-pushers/4714/.

40. Kevin B. O'Reilly, "Doctors Increasingly Close Doors to Drug Reps, While Pharma Cuts Ranks," *AmedNews*, March 23, 2009, http://www.ama-assn.org/amednews2009/03/23/prl10323.htm.

41. Elliott, "The Drug Pushers."

42. Gwen Olsen, *Confessions of an Rx Drug Pusher* (New York: iUniverse Star, 2005).

43. Gwen Olsen, "Confessions of an Rx Drug Pusher," YouTube video, July 24, 2015, https://www.youtube.com/watch?v=777ftSH_FQY.

44. Findings reported by Carolyn Thomas, "Fewer Physicians Are Now Agreeing to See Drug Reps," *The Ethical Nag*, May 28, 2010, https://ethicalnag.org/2010/05/28/fewer-physicians-see-reps.

45. Olsen, "Confessions of an Rx Drug Pusher."

46. Ibid.

47. Tracy Weber and Charles Ornstein, "Dollars for Docs Mints a Millionaire," *ProPublica*, March 11, 2013, https://www.propublica.org/article/dollars-for-docs-mints-a-millionaire.

48. Whitaker, *Anatomy of an Epidemic*.

49. David Healy, *Let Them Eat Prozac: The Unhealthy Relationship Between the Pharmaceutical Industry and Depression* (New York: New York University Press, 2004).

50. Dominick L. Frosch et al., "Creating Demand for Prescription Drugs: A Content Analysis of Television Direct-to-Consumer Advertising," *Annals of Family Medicine* 5 (2007): 6–13.

51. Findings listed in "Should Prescription Drugs Be Advertised Directly to Consumers?," ProCon.org, last updated September 7, 2016, http:// prescriptiondrugs.procon.org.

52. Ibid.

53. Regulations.gov, "Agency Information Collection Activities; Proposed Collection; Comment Request; Disclosure Regarding Additional Risks in Direct-to-Consumer Prescription Drug Television Advertisements," www .regulations.gov, February 18, 2014.

54. Findings reported in Ann Blake Tracy, *Prozac: Panacea or Pandora?* (West Jordan, UT: Cassia Publications, 1994).

55. Full report on the Wesbecker case available in Healy, *Let Them Eat Prozac.*

56. Tracy, *Prozac: Panacea or Pandora?*

57. Peter R. Breggin, "How GlaxoSmithKline Suppressed Data on Paxil-Induced Akathisia: Implications for Suicidality and Violence," *Ethical Human Psychology and Psychiatry* 8, no. 2 (2006): 91–100.

58. Andrew Solomon, "Personal History: Anatomy of Melancholy," *New Yorker*, January 12, 1998, 47–61.

59. Peter R. Breggin, "Suicidality, Violence and Mania Caused by Selective Serotonin Reuptake Inhibitors (SSRIs): A Review and Analysis," *International Journal of Risk and Safety in Medicine* 16 (2003–2004): 31–49.

60. Peter R. Breggin, "Recent Regulatory Changes in Antidepressant Labels," *Primary Psychiatry* 13, no. 1 (2006): 57–60.

61. "FDA Proposes New Warnings About Suicidal Thinking, Behavior in Young Adults Who Take Antidepressant Medications," US Food and Drug Administration, May 2, 2007, http://www.fda.gov/NewsEvents/Newsroom /PressAnnouncements/2007/ucm108905.htm.

62. Healy, *Let Them Eat Prozac*, 243.

63. Physicians' Desk Reference, *2010 Physicians' Desk Reference*, 64th ed. (Montvale, NJ: PDR Network, 2010).

64. Alessandro Serretti and Alberto Chiesa, "Treatment-Emergent Sexual Dysfunction Related to Anti-Depressants," *Journal of Clinical Psychopharmacology* 29 (2009): 259–66.

65. Winston W. Shen and Jeffrey H. Hsu, "Female Sexual Side Effects Associated with Selective Serotonin Reuptake Inhibitors: A Descriptive Clinical Study of 33 Patients," *International Journal of Psychiatry in Medicine* 25 (1995): 239–48; Angel L. Montejo-Gonzalez et al., "SSRI-Induced Sexual Dysfunction: Fluoxetine, Paroxetine, Setraline, and Fluvoxamine in a Prospective, Multicenter, and Descriptive Clinical Study of 344 Patients," *Journal of Sex and Marital Therapy* 23 (1997): 176–94.

66. Rebecca D. Stinson, "The Impact of Persistent Sexual Side Effects of Selective Serotonin Reuptake Inhibitors After Discontinuing Treatment:

A Qualitative Study," PhD diss., (University of Iowa, 2013, http://ir.uiowa
.edu/etd/5061.

67. Anna Moore, "Eternal Sunshine," *Guardian*, May 13, 2007, http://www
.theguardian.com/society/2007/may/13/socialcare.medicineandhealth.

68. For information on Thomson and Fisher's theories, see Susan Brink,
"Are Antidepressants Taking the Edge Off Love?" *Los Angeles Times*,
July 30, 2007, http://articles.latimes.com/2007/jul/30/health/he
-antidepressants30.

69. Adam Opbroek et al., "Emotional Blunting Associated with SSRI-
Induced Sexual Dysfunction: Do SSRIs Inhibit Emotional Responses?,"
International Journal of Neuropsychopharmacology 5, no. 2 (2002): 147–51.

70. Lew Holguin, Carlos Jorge, and Vaughan Bell, "'When I Want to Cry I
Can't': Inability to Cry Following SSRI Treatment," *Revista Colombiana de
Psiquiatria* 42, no. 4 (2013): 304–10.

71. Quoted in Charles Barber, *Comfortably Numb: How Psychiatry Is Medi-
cating a Nation* (New York: Pantheon Books, 2008), 6.

72. Slater, *Prozac Diary*.

73. Brink, "Are Antidepressants Taking the Edge Off Love?"

74. Carl Sherman, "Long-Term Side Effects Surface with SSRIs," *Clinical Psychiatry News* 26, no. 5 (1998). 1.

75. Jesse H. Wright, "Do SSRIs Cause Osteoporosis?" *Carlat Psychiatry Report*
5, no. 8 (2007): 3–4.

76. "Antidepressants Linked to Thicker Arteries," *Science Daily*, April 2, 2011,
http://www.sciencedaily.com/releases/2011/04/110402163856.htm.

77. "Study Links Pregnancy Risk, Antidepressants," Harvard Medical School,
October 31, 2012, https://hms.harvard.edu/news/study-links-pregnancy
-risks-antidepressants-10-31-12.

78. Elizabeth Lewis et al., "Data-Points: Patients' Early Discontinuation of
Antidepressant Prescriptions," *Psychiatric Services* 55 (2004): 494.

79. Irving Kirsch, *The Emperor's New Drugs: Exploding the Antidepressant Myth*
(New York: Basic Books, 2010).

80. Irving Kirsch et al., "Initial Severity and Antidepressant Benefits: A Meta-
Analysis of Data Submitted to the Food and Drug Administration," *PLOS
Medicine* 5, no. 2 (2008): e45, doi:10.1371/journal.pmed.0050045.

81. For comprehensive review of STAR*D results, see Robert Whitaker, "The
STAR*D Scandal: A New Paper Sums It All Up," *Psychology Today*, August
27, 2010, https://www.psychologytoday.com/blog/mad-in-america/201008
/the-stard-scandal-new-paper-sums-it-all.

82. H. Edmund Pigott et al., "Efficacy and Effectiveness of Antidepressants:
Current Status of Research," *Psychotherapy and Psychosomatics* 79 (2010):
267–79.

83. Melissa Leonhauser, "Antipsychotics: Multiple Indications Help Drive Growth," *pm360*, January 2012, https://www.pm360online.com/market -watch-antipsychotics-multiple-indications-help-drive-growth.

84. Katherine Sharpe, "A Happy Pill in Every Purse," *New York Daily News*, March 21, 2013, http://www.nydailynews.com/opinion/happy-pill-purse -article-1.1294381.

85. Glen I. Spielmans et al., "Adjunctive Atypical Antipsychotic Treatment for Major Depressive Disorder: A Meta-Analysis of Depression, Quality of Life, and Safety Outcomes," *PLOS Medicine*, March 12, 2013, http:// dx.doi.org/10.1371/journal.pmed.1001403.

86. Consumer Reports, "Using Antidepressants to Treat Depression: Comparing Effectiveness, Safety, and Price," *Consumer Reports Best Buy Drugs*, September 2013, https://www.consumerreports.org/health/resources/pdf /best-buy-drugs/Antidepressants_update.pdf.

87. Mark Olfson et al., "National Trends in the Office-Based Treatment of Children, Adolescents, and Adults with Antipsychotics," *Archives of General Psychiatry* 69, no. 2 (2012): 1247–56.

88. Ed Silverman, "Feds Do Little to Halt Antipsychotic Use Among Elderly Not in Nursing Homes," *Wall Street Journal*, March 2, 2015, http://blogs .wsj.com/pharmalot/2015/03/02/feds-do-little-to-halt-antipsychotic-use -among-elderly-not-in-nursing-homes.

89. Leigh Sales, "Concerns Grow over Top-Selling Drug's Side-Effects," ABC.net.au, November 27, 2013, http://www.abc.net.au/7.30/content /2013/s3900419.htm.

90. "AZ's Seroquel Legal Bill is $1.1 Billion and Getting Bigger," *CBS News*, October 30, 2009, http://www.cbsnews.com/news/azs-seroquel-legal-bill -is-11b-and-getting-bigger.

91. Randy A. Sansone and Lori A. Sansone, "Is Seroquel Developing an Illicit Reputation for Misuse/Abuse?," *Psychiatry* 7, no. 1 (2010): 13–16.

92. Caroline Fisher, "Management of Antipsychotic Induced Weight Gain," *Carlat Report*, December 2010.

93. "Monitoring the High-Risk Antipsychotic Drugs Unchanged Despite FDA Warnings," *Science Daily*, January 12, 2010, http://www.sciencedaily.com /releases/2010/01/100104161750.htm.

94. Findings reported in Michael Posternak, "Antipsychotics Roundup 2009," *Carlat Psychiatry Report* 7, no. 3 (2009): 6–7.

95. Michael J. Peluso, "Extrapyramidal Motor Side-Effects of First- and Second-Generation Antipsychotic Drugs," *British Journal of Psychiatry* 200, no. 5 (2102): 387–92.

96. Quoted in Arline Kaplan, "Benzodiazepines vs Antidepressants for Anxiety Disorders," *Psychiatric Times*, December 18, 2013.

97. Allen Frances, "The Globalization of ADHD," *Psychiatric Times*, December 23, 2014.

98. Richard Feloni, "These Are the Ridiculous Ads Big Pharma Used to Convince Everyone They Had ADHD," *Business Insider*, December 16, 2013, http://www.businessinsider.com/adhd-medication-marketing-techniques-2013-12.

99. Cynthia M. Hartung et al., "Stimulant Medication Use in College Students: Comparison of Appropriate Users, Misusers, and Nonusers," *Psychology of Addictive Behavior* 27, no. 3 (2013): 832–40.

CHAPTER FOUR: MANAGED CARE-LESSNESS

1. Cummings and O'Donohue, *Eleven Blunders That Cripple Psychotherapy in America*, viii.

2. Charles A. Kiesler, "The Next Wave of Change for Psychology and Mental Health Services in the Health Care Revolution," *American Psychologist* 55 (2000): 481–87.

3. Julie Cohen, Jeanne Marecek, and Jane Gillham, "Is Three a Crowd? Clients, Clinicians, and Managed Care," *American Journal of Orthopsychiatry* 76, no. 2 (2006): 251–59.

4. Richard G. Frank, Howard H. Goldman, and Thomas G. McGuire, "Trends in Mental Health Cost Growth: An Expanded Role for Management," *Health Affairs* 28, no. 3 (2009): 649–59.

5. Tami L. Mark et al., "Changes in US Spending on Mental Health and Substance Abuse Treatment, 1986–2005, and Implications for Policy," *Health Affairs* 30, no. 2 (2011): 284–92.

6. Frank et al., "Trends in Mental Health Cost Growth."

7. Kaiser Family Foundation, "Average Annual Workplace Family Health Premiums Rise Modest 3% to $18,142 in 2016; More Workers Enroll in High-Deductible Plans With Savings Option Over Past Two Years," *Kaiser Family Foundation Newsroom*, September 14, 2016, http://kff.org/health-costs/press-release/average-annual-workplace-family-health-premiums-rise-modest-3-to-18142-in-2016-more-workers-enroll-in-high-deductible-plans-with-savings-option-over-past-two-years.

8. "Aetna Raises 2014 Forecast," *Los Angeles Times*, October 29, 2014.

9. Amy Martyn, "Health Insurance Industry Rakes in Billions While Blaming Obamacare for Losses," *Consumer Affairs*, November 1, 2016, https://www.consumeraffairs.com/news/health-insurance-industry-rakes-in-billions-while-blaming-obamacare-for-losses-110116.html.

10. Elisabeth Rosenthal, "Doctor's Salaries Are Not the Big Cost," *New York Times*, May 18, 2014.

11. Steven Brill, *America's Bitter Pill: Money, Politics, Backroom Deals, and the Fight to Fix Our Broken Healthcare System* (New York: Random House, 2015), 5.

12. Dan Mangan, "Health Insurance Paperwork Wastes $375 Billion," CNBC.com, January 13, 2015, http://www.cnbc.com/2015/01/13/health -insurance-paperwork-wastes-375-billion.html.
13. "Health Insurance CEO Pay Skyrockets in 2013," PRNewswire, May 5, 2014, http://www.prnewswire.com/news-releases/health-insurance-ceo -pay-sky-rockets-in-2013-257974651.html.
14. Mara Lee, "Aetna CEO Mark Bertolini's Compensation Surged in 2016," *Hartford Courant*, April 11, 2017, http://www.courant.com/business /connecticut-insurance/hc-aetna-ceo-pay-20170411-story.html.
15. Ivan J. Miller, "Underfunding Mental Health Services—Disparity 2.0: Isn't It Time for Reform?," December 8, 2010, http://ivanjmiller.com /Mental_Health_Disparity_2.0,_II,_R9,R.pdf.
16. "Congress Should Halt Medicare's Plummeting Psychologist Payments," *American Psychological Association Practice Central*, March 2014, http://www .apapracticecentral.org/advocacy/state/leadership/slc-fact-medicare.aspx.
17. Miller, "Underfunding Mental Health Services."
18. Ibid.
19. Ivan J. Miller, "Mental Health Disparity, Version 2.0: An Open Letter About Financial Discrimination Against Mental Health Services," May 6, 2009, http://ivanjmiller.com/disparity_article.html.
20. Stephen Hayes, "A Conversation with Nicholas Cummings," *Scientist Practitioner*, November 1996, http://www.fenichel.com/Managed2.html.
21. Cummings and Donohue, *Eleven Blunders That Cripple Psychotherapy*.
22. Philip G. Gasquoine, "Comparison of Public/Private Health Care Insurance Parameters for Independent Psychological Practice," *Professional Psychology: Research and Practice* 41, no. 4 (2010): 319–24.
23. "Psychology Mounts Further Parity Challenges to Rate Cuts," *American Psychological Association Practice Central*, April 12, 2012, http://www.apa practicecentral.org/update/2012/04-12/rate-cuts.aspx.
24. Bob Herman, "Humana Aims for Medicare Advantage and Exchange Gains in 2015," *Modern Health Care*, December 4, 2014, http://www .modernhealthcare.com/article/20141204/NEWS/312049936.
25. "Psychologists Receive $2.2 Million Payout in Cigna Settlement; VACP Case Appeal Concludes," *Monitor* 35, no. 10 (2005), http://www.apa.org /monitor/nov05/cigna.aspx.
26. Jared Council, "ValueOptions Prepares for Reform, Growth," *Inside Business*, February 7, 2013, http://pilotonline.com/inside-business/news/health -care/valueoptions-prepares-for-reform-growth/article_f2a9c3f9-1fdd -505e-8081-a5424c0b62e1.html.
27. See review of Magellan Health Insurance Company by Health Insurance Providers, http://www.healthinsuranceproviders.com/magellan-health -insurance-company-review/.

28. Quoted in Jennifer Daw, "Fighting the Phantoms of Managed Care," *Monitor* 33, no. 2 (2002), http://www.apa.org/monitor/feb02/phantoms .aspx.

29. Milo Geyelin, "Magellan Health Services Receives Stream of Complaints for Its Care," *Wall Street Journal*, March 26, 2010, http://wjs.com/articles /SB98926776913298095 6.

30. Chad Terhune, "Anthem Is Again Sued Over Narrow Doctor Networks," *Los Angeles Times*, August 20, 2014.

31. Lisa M. Sanchez and Samuel M. Turner, "Practicing Psychology in the Era of Managed Care," *American Psychologist* 58, no. 2 (2003): 121.

32. Olfson and Marcus, "National Trends in Outpatient Psychotherapy."

33. Ronald W. Dworkin, "Psychotherapy and the Pursuit of Happiness," *New Atlantis* 35 (spring 2012): 69–83.

34. For the fall in psychotherapy referrals, see Nicholas A. Cummings, William T. O'Donohue, and Janet L. Cummings, "The Financial Dimension of Integrated Behavioral/Primary Care," *Journal of Clinical Psychology in Medical Settings* (January 11, 2009), doi 10.1007/s10880-008-9139-2. For the increase in mental health concerns, see Jean Twenge, "Are Mental Health Issues on the Rise?" *Psychology Today*, October 12, 2015.

35. "Bringing Behavioral Health into the Care Continuum: Opportunities to Improve Quality, Costs and Outcomes," *Trendwatch*, January 2012.

36. Thomas G. Kremer and Ellis L. Gesten, "Managed Mental Health Care: The Client's Perspective," *Professional Psychology: Research and Practice* 34, no. 2 (2003): 190.

37. Dorothy W. Cantor and Milton A. Fuentes, "Psychology's Response to Managed Care," *Professional Psychology: Research and Practice* 39, no. 6 (2008): 638–45.

38. "The OPTUM by United Behavioral Health, Coverage Determination Guideline for Outpatient Treatment of Generalized Anxiety Disorder," http://www.ubhonline.com/html/pdf/coverageDetermGuidelines/gen AnxietyDisorderOutpatient.pdf.

39. At the interviewee's request, I am using a pseudonym, because the individual did not wish to jeopardize any ongoing personal relationships with former professional colleagues within the Kaiser system.

40. Quoted in Russell M. Holstein, "Triage As Treatment: Phantom Mental Health Services at Kaiser-Permanente," *Kaiser Papers*, September 11, 2000, http://www.division42.org/MembersArea/IPfiles/IPSpring04/prof_practice /holstein.php.

41. National Union of Healthcare Workers, *Care Delayed, Care Denied: Kaiser Permanente's Failure to Provide Timely and Appropriate Mental Health Services*, November 2011, www.NUHW.org.

42. Ibid., 10. Italics in original.

43. John M. Grohol, "Kaiser Permanente's Sad Mental Health Care in California," *Psych Central*, March 24, 2013, http://psychcentral.com/blog/archives /2013/03/24/kaiser-permanentes-sad-mental-health-care-in-california.

44. Cynthia H. Craft, "Kaiser Mental Health Care Lacking, State Says; HMO Hit with a $4 Million Fine," *Sacramento Bee*, June 26, 2013.

45. "Care Delayed, Care Denied: NUHW's Effort to Improve Kaiser Permanente's Mental Health Services," National Union of Healthcare Workers brief mental health advocacy groups on Kaiser mental health care crisis, National Press Club, Washington, DC, December 10, 2014, video, YouTube, https://www.youtube.com/watch?v=IsJbdOpexFc.

46. "Kaiser's Mental Health Workers to Strike Jan.12," *Salon*, January 2, 2015, http://www.salon.com/2015/01/03/kaisers_mental_health_workers_to _strike_jan_12/.

47. For "time-limited, solution-focused" treatment, see Beacon Health Options, "Integrating Behavioral Health into Medi-Cal," July 15, 2015, 14, http://www.sfhp.org/files/Community/GGHI%202015/Integrating% 20Behavioral%20Health%20into%20Medi-Cal%20Slides.pdf. For reimbursement of shorter sessions, see Health Assets Management, Inc., http:// www.healthassets.com/mental_health_news/7/90834_vs_90837.html.

48. Stuart Pfeifer, "Kaiser Ordered to Pay Woman More Than $28 Million," *Los Angeles Times*, March 27, 2015.

49. Stuart Pfeifer, "Kaiser Mental Health Services Faulted," *Los Angeles Times*, November 28, 2014.

50. Martin E. P. Seligman, "The Effectiveness of Psychotherapy: The Consumer Reports Study," *American Psychologist* 50, no. 2 (1995): 965–74.

51. T. M. Luhrmann, "Redefining Mental Illness," *New York Times*, January 18, 2015.

52. J. Christopher Perry and Michael Bond, "Change in Defense Mechanisms During Long-Term Dynamic Psychotherapy and Five-Year Outcome," *American Journal of Psychiatry* 169, no. 9 (2012): 916–25.

53. Michael G. Newman, "Recommendations for a Cost-Offset Model of Psychotherapy Allocation Using Generalized Anxiety Disorder as an Example," *Journal of Consulting and Clinical Psychology* 68, no. 4 (2000): 549–55.

54. Karin Lee, "National Survey Tracks Prevalence of Personality Disorders in U.S. Population," *National Institute of Mental Health Science Update*, October 18, 2007, http://www.nimh.nih.gov/news/science-news/2007 /national-survey-tracks-prevalence-of-personality-disorders-in-us -population.shtml.

55. "1 in 5 Young Americans Has a Personality Disorder," Associated Press, December 1, 2008, http://www.nbcnews.com/id/28002991/ns/health -mental_health/t/young-americans-has-personality-disorder.

56. Falk Leichsenring and Sven Rabung, "Long-Term Psychodynamic Psychotherapy in Complex Disorders," *British Journal of Psychiatry* 199 (2011): 15–22.

57. Kate Morrison, Rebekah Bradley, and Drew Westen, "The External Validity of Controlled Clinical Trials of Psychotherapy for Depression and Anxiety: A Naturalistic Study," *Psychology and Psychotherapy: Theory, Research and Practice* 76, no. 2 (2003): 109–32.

58. Michael J. Lambert, Nathan B. Hansen, and Arthur E. Finch, "Patient-Focused Research: Using Patient Outcome Data to Enhance Treatment Effects," *Journal of Consulting and Clinical Psychology* 69, no. 2 (2001): 159–72.

59. John M. Grohol, "Howard Stern's Endless Psychotherapy," *Psych Central*, October 2010, http://psychcentral.com/blog/archives/2010/09/30/howard-sterns-endless-psychotherapy; Paola Palmiotto, "Frank Gehry: An Example of Transformation," *Immagini Della Psiche*, 2015, http://www.immaginipsiche.it/2015/01/18/frank-gehry-an-example-of-transformation.

60. Marty Nemko, "The Case Against Long-Term Therapy," http://www.martynemko.com/articles/case-against-long-term-therapy_id1427, accessed October 5, 2017.

61. Joel Paris, "How the History of Psychotherapy Interferes with Integration," *Journal of Psychotherapy Integration* 23, no. 2 (2013): 99–106.

62. Gregory E. Simons et al., "Early Dropout from Psychotherapy for Depression with Group- and Network-Model Therapists," *Administration and Policy in Mental Health and Mental Health Services Research* 39, no. 6 (2012): 440–47.

63. Olfson and Marcus, "National Trends in Outpatient Psychotherapy."

64. Alexander Blount et al., "The Economics of Behavioral Health Services in Medical Settings: A Summary of the Evidence," *Professional Psychology: Research and Practice* 38, no. 3 (2007): 290–97.

65. Ibid.

66. Gary R. VandenBos and Patrick H. DeLeon, "The Use of Psychotherapy to Improve Physical Health," *Psychotherapy* 25 (1988): 335–43.

67. Robert Lechnyr, "Cost Savings and Effectiveness in Mental Health Services," *Journal of the Oregon Psychological Association* 38 (1992): 8–12.

68. Cummings, O'Donohue, and Cummings, "The Financial Dimension of Integrated Behavioral/Primary Care."

69. Ibid.

CHAPTER FIVE: THE MISEDUCATION OF PSYCHOTHERAPISTS

1. Mary Sykes Wylie, "How Aaron Beck and Albert Ellis Started a Psychotherapy Revolution," *Psychotherapy Networker*, December 26, 2014.

2. Quoted in Brandon A. Gaudiano, "Cognitive-Behavioral Therapies: Achievements and Challenges," *Evidenced Based Mental Health* 11, no. 1 (2008): 5–7.

3. Aaron T. Beck, *Cognitive Therapy and the Emotional Disorders* (New York: Plume, 1979).

4. Ibid., 100–101.

5. Ibid., 253.

6. "Who Influenced Dr. Aaron Beck's Work? (Students Ask Dr. Beck—Part Two)," Beck Institute for Cognitive Behavior Therapy, August 15–17, 2011, YouTube video, https://www.youtube.com/watch?v=Iot IM3w4yXs.

7. "Seeking Safety 002," YouTube video, February 20, 2011, https://www.youtube.com/watch?v=wkL7v_x3t8U.

8. Aaron T. Beck, "Cognitive Therapy: Past, Present, and Future," *Journal of Consulting and Clinical Psychology* 61 (1993): 194–98.

9. Gaudiano, "Cognitive-Behavioral Therapies."

10. Joan M. Cook, "What Do Psychotherapists Really Do in Practice? An Internet Study of Over 2,000 Practitioners," *Psychotherapy: Theory, Research, Practice, Training* 47, no. 2 (2010): 260–67.

11. Laurie Heatherington et al., "The Narrowing of Theoretical Orientations in Clinical Psychology Doctoral Training," *Clinical Psychology: Science and Practice* 19, no. 4 (2012): 364–74.

12. Psychological Clinical Science Accreditation System website, http://www.pcsas.org.

13. Bruce E. Wampold, *The Great Psychotherapy Debate: The Evidence for What Makes Psychotherapy Work* (Mahwah, NJ: Routledge, 2001).

14. John C. Norcross, ed., *Psychotherapy Relationships That Work: Evidence-Based Responsiveness*, 2nd ed. (New York: Oxford University Press, 2011).

15. Barry L. Duncan et al., eds., *The Heart and Soul of Change: Delivering What Works in Therapy*, 2nd ed. (Washington, DC: American Psychological Association, 2010).

16. Kevin M. Laska, Alan S. Gurman, and Bruce E. Wampold, "Expanding the Lens of Evidenced-Based Practice in Psychotherapy: A Common Factors Perspective," *Psychotherapy* 51, no. 4 (2014): 467–81.

17. Jonathan Shedler, "Where Is the Evidence for 'Evidence-Based' Therapy?" Limbus Critical Psychotherapy Conference, Totnes, Devon, Dartington Hall, 2014, YouTube video, https://www.youtube.com/watch?v=3UpHl9kuccc.

18. Findings reported by Shedler, ibid.

19. Reported in David N. Elkins, *Humanistic Psychology: A Clinical Manifesto* (Colorado Springs, CO: University of the Rockies Press, 2009).

20. David Taylor, "Psychoanalytic and Psychodynamic Therapies for Depression: The Evidence Base," *Advances in Psychiatric Treatment* 14 (2008): 401–13.

21. David E. Orlinsky and Michael Helge Ronnestad, *How Psychotherapists Develop: A Study of Therapeutic Work and Professional Growth* (Washington, DC: American Psychological Association, 2009).

22. Jonathan Shedler, "The Efficacy of Psychodynamic Psychotherapy," *American Psychologist* 65, no. 2 (2010): 98–109.

23. For Health Net Clinical Practice Guidelines, see https://www.healthnet .com/portal/provider/content/iwc/provider/unprotected/working_with _HN/content/medical_policies.action.

24. Todd Dufresne, "Psychoanalysis Is Dead . . . So How Does That Make you Feel?," *Los Angeles Times*, February 18, 2004, http://articles.latimes.com /2004/feb/18/opinion/oe-dufresne18.

25. Shedler, "The Efficacy of Psychodynamic Psychotherapy."

26. Leichsenring and Rabung, "Effectiveness of Long-Term Psychodynamic Psychotherapy."

27. National Registry of Evidenced-Based Programs and Practices (NREPP) on the Substance Abuse and Mental Health Services Administration (SAMHSA) website, http://www.samhsa.gov/nrepp.

28. "VA to Increase Mental Health Staff by 1,900," Office of Public and Intergovernmental Affairs, US Department of Veterans Affairs, press release, April 19, 2012, http://www.va.gov/opa/pressrel/pressrelease.cfm?id=2302.

29. Brian A. Sharpless and Jacques P. Barber, "A Clinician's Guide to PTSD Treatments for Returning Veterans," *Professional Psychology: Research and Practice* 42, no. 1 (2011): 8–15.

30. Ibid.

31. Patricia A. Resick, Candice M. Monson, and Kathleen M. Chard, *Cognitive Processing Therapy: Veteran/Military Version*, October 2006, http://alrest.org /pdf/CPT_Manual_-_Modified_for_PRRP(2).pdf.

32. Kathleen M. Chard, "Cognitive Processing Therapy," continuing education course, National Center for PTSD, US department of veterans affairs, created November 3, 2011, http://www.ptsd.va.gov/professional /continuing_ed/cpt.asp.

33. Valerie D. Scott et al., "Addressing Deficits in the Utilization of Empirically Supported Treatments for Posttraumatic Stress Disorder: Training the Future of Army Psychologists," *Training and Education in Professional Psychology* 9, no. 2 (2015): 85–91.

34. Hector A. Garcia et al., "Evidence-Based Treatments for PTSD and VHA Provider Burnout: The Impact of Cognitive Processing and Prolonged Exposure Therapies," *Traumatology* 21, no. 1 (2015): 7–13.

35. Les R. Greene, "Dissemination or Dialogue?," *American Psychologist* 69, no. 7 (2014): 708.

36. Christopher Bollas, *Catch Them Before They Fall: The Psychoanalysis of Breakdown* (New York: Routledge, 2012), 2–3.

37. Shannon M. Kehle-Forbes et al., "Treatment Initiation and Dropout from Prolonged Exposure and Cognitive Processing Therapy in a VA Outpatient Clinic," *Psychological Trauma: Theory, Research, Practice, and Policy* 8, no. 1 (2016): 107–14.

38. Ibid.

39. Zac E. Imel et al., "Meta-Analysis of Dropout in Treatments for Posttraumatic Stress Disorder," *Journal of Consulting and Clinical Psychology* 81, no. 3 (2013): 394–404.

40. Jason C. DeViva, "Treatment Utilization Among OEF/OIF Veterans Referred for Psychotherapy for PTSD," *Psychological Services* 11, no. 2 (2014): 179–84.

41. Natalie E. Hundt et al., "Predisposing, Enabling and Need Factors as Predictors of Low and High Psychotherapy Utilization in Veterans," *Psychological Services* 11, no. 3 (2014): 281–89.

42. Judith Herman, *Trauma and Recovery: The Aftermath of Violence—from Domestic Abuse to Political Terror* (New York, Basic Books, 2015), 175.

43. John N. Briere and Catherine Scott, *Principles of Trauma Therapy: A Guide to Symptoms, Evaluation, and Treatment* (Thousand Oaks, CA: Sage Publications, 2014).

44. Patricia A. Resick, Candice M. Monson, and Kathleen M. Chard, *Cognitive Processing Therapy: Veteran/Military Version: Therapist's Manual* (Washington, DC: Department of Veterans Affairs, 2014), 4; http://psych.ryerson.ca/cptcanadastudy/CPT_Canada_Study/Study_Materials_files/Basic%20Therapist%20Manual%20Text_title%20page%20updated.pdf, 4.

45. Peter Lomas, *True and False Experience* (New York: Taplinger Publications, 1974), 19.

46. Brian A. Feinstein, "Doctoral Training in Clinical Psychology," *Clinical Science* 16, no. 1 (2013): 23–25.

47. LaVerne Bell-Tolliver, "Evidence-Based Social Work Practice in Adult Mental Health," course syllabus for SOWK 8230, University of Arkansas, Little Rock.

48. Brochure for David D. Burns, "Treating Patients with Trauma," continuing education course through Institute for Better Health, September 24–25, 2015, San Diego.

49. Scott D. Miller, "Becoming a Top Clinician," *Carlat Report* 13, no. 4 (2015): 4.

50. Quoted on Scott D. Miller blog, http://www.scottdmiller.com. Italics in original.

51. Quoted in Robert M. Centor, "To Be a Great Physician, You Must Understand the Whole Story," *Medscape General Medicine* 9, no. 1 (2007): 59.

52. Danielle Knafo et al., *Becoming a Clinical Psychologist: Personal Stories of Doctoral Training* (Lanham, MD: Rowman & Littlefield, 2015), 46.

53. "Therapy in America 2004 Poll Shows: Mental Health Treatment Goes Mainstream," *PRNewswire*, May 5, 2004, http://www.prnewswire.com /news-releases/therapy-in-america-2004-poll-shows-mental-health -treatment-goes-mainstream-73817497.html.

54. Jesse D. Geller, John C. Norcross, and David E. Orlinsky, eds., *The Psychotherapist's Own Psychotherapy: Patient and Clinician Perspectives* (New York: Oxford University Press, 2005), 3.

55. Suzanne Phillips, "Has Your Therapist Ever Been in Therapy?," *Psych Central*, May 18, 2011, http://blogs.psychcentral.com/healing-together/2011 /05/has-your-therapist-ever-been-in-therapy.

56. Ibid.

57. Jennifer L. Bearse, Mark R. McMinn, Winston Seegobin, and Kurt Free, "Healing Thyself: What Barriers Do Psychologists Face When Considering Personal Psychotherapy and How Can They Be Overcome?," *Monitor on Psychology* 45, no. 4 (April 2014): 62, http://www.apa.org/monitor/2014 /04/ce-corner.aspx.

58. John C. Norcross, Denise H. Bike, and Krystel L. Evans, "The Therapist's Therapist: A Replication and Extension 20 Years Later," *Psychotherapy Theory, Research, Practice, Training* 46, no. 1 (2009): 32–41.

59. Anton-Rupert Laireiter, ed., *Self-Exploration in Psychotherapy and CBT: Empirical Results* (Tubingen, Germany: dgvt-Verlag, 2000).

60. Quoted in Jonathan Shedler, "Why the Scientist-Practitioner Schism Won't Go Away," *General Psychologist* 41, no. 2 (2006): 9.

61. Orlinsky and Ronnestad, *How Psychotherapists Develop.*

62. Timothy B. Baker, Richard M. McFall, and Varda Shoham, "Current Status and Future of Clinical Psychology," *Psychological Science and Public Interest* 9, no. 2 (2009): 67–103.

63. David B. Stein, *The Psychology Industry Under a Microscope!* (New York: University Press of America, 2012), 15.

64. 2014 American Psychological Association Directory and 2010 Employment Update compiled by Center for Workforce Studies (Table 4 Employment Characteristics of APA Members by Membership Status, 2014), http:// www.apa.org/workforce/publications/14-member/table-4.pdf.

65. Peter D. Kramer, "Why Doctors Need Stories," *New York Times*, October 19, 2014.

CHAPTER SIX: THE HEALING RELATIONSHIP

1. Heinz Kohut, *How Does Analysis Cure?* (Chicago: University of Chicago Press, 1984), 182.
2. Carl R. Rogers, *A Way of Being: The Founder of the Human Potential Movement Looks Back on a Distinguished Career* (Boston: Houghton Mifflin Company, 1980), 137–38.
3. Sheldon Roth, *Psychotherapy: The Art of Wooing Nature* (Northvale, NJ: Jason Aronson, 1987), 229.
4. Walt Whitman, *Leaves of Grass* (1855; New York: Book-of-the-Month Club, 1992), 37.
5. Martha Stark, *Modes of Therapeutic Action* (Northvale, NJ: Jason Aronson, 1999), 155.
6. Jesse D. Geller, "Style and Its Contribution to a Patient-Specific Model of Therapeutic Technique," *Psychotherapy: Theory, Research, Practice, Training* 42, no. 4 (2005): 479.
7. Quoted in Anthony Molino, ed., *Freely Associated: Encounters in Psychoanalysis* (London: Free Association Books, 1997), 138.
8. Emmy van Deurzen, *Paradox and Passion in Psychotherapy: An Existential Approach* (New York: John Wiley & Sons, 2001), 108.
9. Allan N. Schore, *Affect Regulation and the Repair of the Self* (New York: W. W. Norton, 2003), 48.
10. Leslie S. Greenberg, "Emotions, the Great Captains of Our Lives: Their Role in the Process of Change in Psychotherapy," *American Psychologist* 67, no. 8 (2012): 700.
11. Sheldon A. Appelbaum, "Psychological-Mindedness: Word, Concept and Essence," *International Journal of Psychoanalysis* 54, no. 1 (1973): 35–46.
12. Bettelheim, *Freud and Man's Soul.*
13. Quoted in Roger Frie, ed., *Psychological Agency: Theory, Practice, and Culture* (Cambridge, MA: MIT Press, 2008), 41.
14. Daniel C. Russell, *Happiness for Humans* (Oxford, UK: Oxford University Press, 2012), 5.
15. Ibid., 19.
16. Irvin Yalom, *When Nietzsche Wept* (New York: Harper Perennial, 2011), 272.
17. Albert Camus, *The Myth of Sisyphus* (New York: Alfred A. Knopf, 1955), 54.
18. Quoted in Robin Wright, *Dreams and Shadows: The Future of the Middle East* (New York: Penguin Books, 2009).
19. See "The Samuel Beckett On-Line Resources and Links Pages," accessed March 24, 2017, http://www.samuel-beckett.net.

CHAPTER SEVEN: PRACTICING WITH PERSONALITY

1. Quoted in Joseph J. Shay and Joan Wheelis, eds., *Odysseys in Psychotherapy* (New York: Ardent Media, 2000), 115.

2. Freud and Breuer, *Studies in Hysteria*, 284.

3. Rogers, *A Way of Being*, 42.

4. James F. T. Bugental, *The Art of the Psychotherapist* (New York: Norton, 1987).

5. Jerome Frank, *Persuasion and Healing: Comparative Study of Psychotherapy* (Baltimore: Johns Hopkins University Press, 1991), 40.

6. Lewis Aron, *A Meeting of Minds* (Hillsdale, NJ: Analytic Press, 1996), 170.

7. David N. Elkins, *Beyond Religion: A Personal Program for Building a Spiritual Life Outside the Walls of Traditional Religion* (Wheaton, IL: Quest Books, 1998), 185.

8. A. C. Grayling, *The Heart of Things: Applying Philosophy to the 21st Century* (London: Orion Books, 2005), 134.

9. Maurice Friedman, *The Healing Dialogue in Psychotherapy* (New York: Jason Aronson, 1985), 137. Italics in original.

10. Irwin Z. Hoffman, *Ritual and Spontaneity in the Psychoanalytic Process: A Dialectical-Constructivist View* (Hillsdale, NJ: Analytic Press, 2001), 74.

11. Camus, *Myth of Sisyphus*, 73.

12. Jean-Paul Sartre, *Being and Nothingness*, 1943; ibid.

13. Max Roser, "Life Expectancy," OurWorldInData.org, 2017, http://our worldindata.org/data/population-growth-vital-statistics/life-expectancy.

14. Phil Mason, *Napoleon's Hemorrhoids and Other Small Events That Changed History* (New York: Skyhorse Publishing, 2010).

15. American Psychological Association, Presidential Task Force on Preventing Discrimination and Promoting Diversity, *Dual Pathways to a Better America: Preventing Discrimination and Promoting Diversity* (Washington, DC: American Psychological Association, 2012), http://www.apa.org/pubs /info/reports/dual-pathways-report.pdf.

16. Kwong-Liem Karl Kwan, "Counseling Chinese Peoples: Perspectives of Filial Piety," *Asian Journal of Counseling* 7, no. 1 (2000): 23–41.

17. Adrian van Kaam, *The Art of Existential Counseling* (Denville, NJ: Dimension Books, 1966), 29.

18. Marna S. Barrett et al., "Early Withdrawal from Mental Health Treatment: Implications for Psychotherapy Practice," *Psychotherapy: Theory, Research, Practice, Training* 45, no. 2 (2008): 247–67.

CHAPTER EIGHT: PSYCHOTHERAPY AND THE SOCIAL GOOD

1. Christina Hoff Sommers and Sally Satel, *One Nation Under Therapy: How the Helping Culture Is Eroding Self-Reliance* (New York: St. Martin's Press, 2005), 218.

2. Frank Furedi, *Therapy Culture: Cultivating Vulnerability in an Uncertain Age* (New York: Routledge, 2004), 34.

3. Joel Paris, *Psychotherapy in an Age of Narcissism: Modernity, Science, and Society* (New York: Palgrave MacMillan, 2013), 8.

4. Christopher Lasch, *The Culture of Narcissism: American Life in an Age of Diminishing Expectations* (New York: Norton, 1979).

5. Robert Woolfolk, *The Value of Psychotherapy: The Talking Cure in an Age of Clinical Science* (New York: Guilford Press, 2015), 145.

6. Barack Obama, "Obama to Graduates: Cultivate Empathy: The World Doesn't Just Revolve Around You," commencement address, Northwestern University, June 19, 2006, http://www.northwestern.edu/newscenter /stories/2006/06/barack.html.

7. Barack Obama, *The Audacity of Hope: Thoughts on Reclaiming the American Dream* (New York: Random House, 2006), 66–69.

8. Jamil Zaki, "What, Me Care? Young Are Less Empathic," *Scientific American*, January 1, 2011, http://www.scientificamerican.com.

9. Martha C. Nussbaum, *Not for Profit: Why Democracy Needs the Humanities* (Princeton, NJ: Princeton University Press, 2010), x.

10. Michael E. Morrell, *Empathy and Democracy: Feeling, Thinking, and Deliberation* (University Park: Pennsylvania State University Press, 2010), 114.

11. D. W. Winnicott, "Thoughts on the Meaning of Democracy," *Human Relations* 4 (1950): 171–85.

12. Erich Fromm, *Escape from Freedom* (New York: Rinehart & Company, 1941), 252.

13. Maureen O'Hara, "Relational Humanism: A Psychology for a Pluralistic World," *Humanistic Psychologist* 20, no. 2 (1992): 439–46.

14. Claudio Neri, "Authenticity as an Aim of Psychoanalysis," *American Journal of Psychoanalysis* 68 (2008): 325–49.

15. Tim Kasser et al., *Psychology and Consumer Culture: The Struggle for a Good Life in a Materialistic World* (Washington, DC: American Psychological Association, 2004), 14.

16. Michael W. Kraus, Stephane Cote, and Dacher Keltyner, "Social Class, Contextualism, and Empathic Accuracy," *Psychological Science* 21, no. 11 (2010): 1716–23.

17. Quoted in Helga Dittmar et al., "The Relationship Between Materialism and Personal Well-Being: A Meta-Analysis," *Journal of Personality and Social Psychology* 107, no. 5 (2014): 879–924.

18. Marsha L. Richins, "When Wanting Is Better Than Having: Materialism, Transformation Expectations, and Product-Evoked Emotions in the Purchase Process," *Journal of Consumer Research* 40, no. 1 (2013): 1–18.

19. Carol Graham, *Happiness Around the World: The Paradox of Happy Peasants and Miserable Millionaires* (New York: Oxford University Press, 2009).

20. Darrin M. McMahon, *Happiness: A History* (New York: Grove Press, 2006), 460.

21. Robert Waldinger, "What Makes a Good Life? Lessons from the Longest Study on Happiness," TED Talk, November 2015, https://www.ted.com /talks/robert_waldinger_what_makes_a_good_life_lessons_from_the _longest_study_on_happiness.

22. Daniel Kahneman, "A Survey Method for Characterizing Daily Life Experience: The Day Reconstruction Method," *Science* 306 (2004): 1776–80.

23. Ty Tashiro, *The Science of Happily Ever After: What Really Matters in the Quest for Enduring Love* (Ontario, Canada: Harlequin, 2014).

24. Jean M. Twenge, W. Keith Campbell, and Elise C. Freeman, "Generational Differences in Young Adults' Life Goals, Concern for Others, and Civic Orientation, 1966–2009," *Journal of Personality and Social Psychology* 102, no. 5 (2012): 1045–62.

25. Jean M. Twenge and W. Keith Campbell, *The Narcissism Epidemic: Living in the Age of Entitlement* (New York: Free Press, 2009).

26. William G. Herron, *Narcissism and the Relational World* (New York: University Press of America, 1999).

27. Nancy McWilliams, "Preserving Our Humanity as Therapists," *Psychotherapy: Theory, Research, Practice, Training* 42, no. 2 (2005): 139–51.

INDEX